TRUCKING NORTH

on

CANADA'S MACKENZIE HIGHWAY

Roberta L. Hursey

Detselig Enterprises Ltd.

Calgary, Alberta, Canada

Trucking North on Canada's Mackenzie Highway

© 2000 Roberta L. Hursey

Canadian Cataloguing in Publication Data

Hursey, Roberta

Trucking north

Includes bibliographic references.
ISBN 1-55059-204-1

1. Mackenzie Highway (N.W.T.)--History. 2. Trucking--Alberta, Northern--History.
3. Trucking--Northwest Territories--History. I. Title.

HE5635.A8H87   2000   388.3'24'097193   C00-910701-0

Detselig Enterprises Ltd.

210-1220 Kensington Rd. N.W.

Calgary, AB T2N 3P5

Telephone: (403) 283-0900/Fax: (403) 283-6947

e-mail: temeron@telusplanet.net

www.temerondetselig.com

We acknowledge the financial support of the Government of Canada through the Book Publishing Industry Development Program (BPIDP) for our publishing activities.

ISBN 1-55059-204-1

SAN 115-0324

Printed in Canada

Cover design by Dean Macdonald and Alvin Choong

Front Cover Photo: One of the early truck convoys over the Grimshaw-Hay River winter road, c. 1941. Hank Thompson collection.

Dedication

To the heroes of the Mackenzie Highway: the trail blazers, catskinners, surveyors, and construction crews; pioneer truckers and trucking companies; families who ran stopping places; bus drivers; and the people living along the highway who depended upon its existence. Thank you for sharing your stories.

Contents

Acknowledgements

Many individuals have helped me along a journey of discovery about the importance of trucking and the Mackenzie Highway. I wish to thank Fred and Bernice Lorenzen, who encouraged me in the beginning to write this book. Four years ago, my husband Bob and I met Fred and Bernice when they still lived in Manning. During our conversation that day, and in subsequent visits and phone calls since then, you lit a fire under me to do a project that would have daunted me otherwise. And when I got too busy with other projects, you gave me a gentle prod. Thank you.

To John King and Les Stranaghan, I owe you both a debt of gratitude for your help in collecting information, stories, and photographs of pioneer truckers who no longer live in the North, or who no longer are with us except in spirit. Thanks, John and Les.

To Stella Friedel and Paul Rubak, for your careful critiques of the manuscript. Stella, your knowledge of northern peoples has been invaluable to me. Paul, your insights on the trucking industry are much appreciated.

It was a pleasure working with Detselig Enterprises on the publication of this book. To Linda Berry, managing editor and publicist, thanks for your guidance and attention to details.

I am indebted to the Alberta Historical Resources Foundation for partly funding the travel to do the research and for publication of this book.

To my husband, Bob, thank you for your constant encouragement and for being a companion on many trips, an advisor through all the stages of researching and writing this book, and for keeping my computer running. To my daughters Alex, Barb, and Cathi – thanks for your moral support.

RLH

🚚 Preface 🚛

Many Canadians have a special love-hate relationship with trucks. Trucks are big, noisy, and smelly. The presence of trucks on highways is a constant pain to car drivers when we are in a hurry and try to pass them. When truckers are in more of a hurry, we may even feel threatened by them as they pass us. Perhaps because trucks are always around and often in our way, we tend to take them for granted and overlook the fact that Canadians are utterly dependent upon trucks arriving on time and delivering foods, drugs, dry goods, and raw and manufactured materials that are essential to our way of life.

This book is primarily about truckers and truck transportation on the Mackenzie Highway and its tributaries. It is also about other forms of northern transportation that are linked to trucking, and about northern peoples, communities, and industries that depend upon truck transportation for survival.

From September 1995 to July 1996, I had a contract with the Spirit of the Peace Museums Network to write an overview of the history of the Peace River Country. During the many trips I took into the Peace to do my research, I did a lot winter driving north of Edmonton on Highways 43, 2, and 35. It was a long, hard winter. It seemed that every time I went into or out of the Peace River Country, I was driving through a snow storm. Few cars were on the roads, mostly trucks: 18-wheelers, tanker trucks, tractor units pulling lowboys loaded with pipe and machinery for oil rigs, logging and chip trucks, single-axle delivery trucks, and many, many four-wheel-drive pickups.

At first I felt as intimidated by the trucks as I was about driving in winter conditions in the North. I spent a lot of time pulling over and letting the big guys pass me by. But after the first few trips, I began to think of truckers as my neighbors. I took comfort in knowing that the truckers' "Code of the Road" was still very much alive and well in northern Alberta. If I were to have an accident or breakdown, a trucker would come by eventually to give a helping hand or to call in to the RCMP on his cell phone or CB radio.

During these long, lonely trips into the Peace Country, I began doing a lot of thinking about the importance of trucks and highways in this part of the world – and how little has been written about them. Much has been published about the history of other forms of transportation in the Peace, and about the building of the Alaska Highway, which begins in the Peace River Country at Dawson Creek, B.C. But very few, other than community histories in the North Peace area, even mention the history of the Mackenzie Highway (Alberta 35, Northwest Territories 1), which was (and still is) far more important to Canadians.

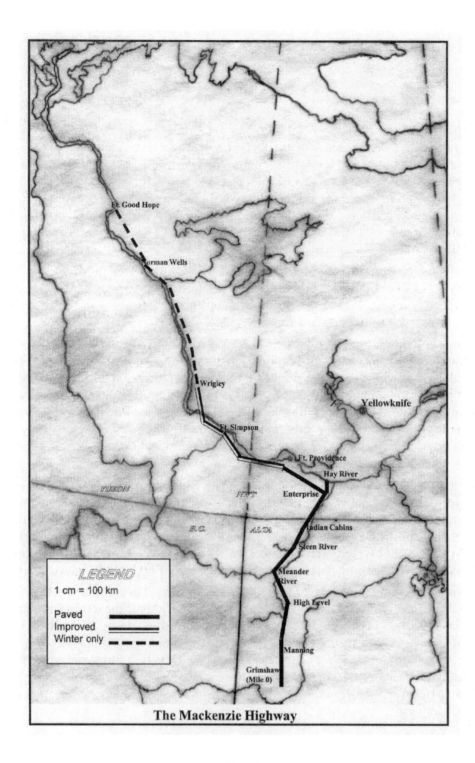

The Mackenzie Highway

In discussions with my husband Bob, we talked about truck transportation as a type of communication. Because truckers are constantly on the road, they carry news to and from their destinations. They report on road conditions, accidents, weather, traffic, where the RCMP usually hang out, and which weigh station attendants are the real sticklers. Truckers often run errands for people, bringing goods that are not ordinarily available locally and news from the "Outside." In the early days, truckers even delivered the mail. The freight they haul is part of the complex two-way communication between those who order goods and the companies that supply the goods. A department store in Hay River, Northwest Territories, does not order bikinis and suntan oil for the winter. But motor oil, antifreeze, mukluks, and parkas that will protect you or your car to -60° C [-50°F] would definitely be on the order. Bills of lading can provide as much information to the researcher about the wants and needs of people as the meticulous records fur traders kept 200 years ago for the Hudson's Bay Company and North West Company.

For over 50 years the Mackenzie Highway was, and still is, the only direct overland route into the Northwest Territories. The highway was built *for* trucks, *by* trucks. In a sense, truck transportation and the Mackenzie Highway are so interrelated and intertwined that a person cannot tell the story of one without the other. This realization has led me on a three-year journey to discover the story of trucking on the Mackenzie Highway. I learned that there are many stories that would fill many books. My research has taken me from Edmonton to Grimshaw, Alberta (Mile 0), and "down north" to Hay River, NWT, meeting with and interviewing truckers, their families and employees, people who ran stopping places, farmers, business and professional people, politicians, Metis and First Nations people, and other folk who depend upon the trucks getting the goods there on time.

I have spent many pleasant hours on the phone interviewing people all over North America, who no longer live in the North but had trucked up and down the Mackenzie Highway many times. There are inevitably people who should have been included in this book but who have been overlooked. History does not stop at 1950 or 1980 or 2000, and that is true of trucking on the Mackenzie Highway. This is only the beginning, so keep gathering stories and preserving photographs. Who knows? Maybe the highway will be finished all the way to the Arctic someday. If so, there will be many new stories to tell.

Roberta Hursey
March 1, 2000

A note or two about the terminology used in this book. "North" refers to the North Peace area and the Northwest Territories collectively. "Far North" designates the region north of the Arctic Circle. I have used "Dominion Government" in relation to events taking place before 1950, and the more common spelling, "Mackenzie," to denote the highway and the river. I have used the masculine pronoun in reference to early truckers on the highway. Although many women drove trucks, almost all who made a living at trucking were men until recent times.

🚗 Chapter 1 – Introduction 🚚

The Mackenzie Highway – An Imaginary Journey

Every highway has a history. In Western Canada, most highways are built in, or adjacent to, the roads that preceded them. These older roads were built upon earlier wagon roads, horse trails, or footpaths. Early aboriginal and fur traders' pack trails followed seasonal game trails made by large mammals. A network of trails covered the northern bush, which has been inhabited by Athapaskan-speaking aboriginal people for thousands of years. These trails, first packed by dog teams and later horses, skirted around muskegs, taking the high ground. They crossed creeks and rivers at the shallowest spots, or zigzagged up and down steep banks. They paralleled boulder-strewn mountain valleys and ravines. First peoples, Métis, trappers, fur traders, and, later, missionaries and settlers all travelled these trails that would form, in part, the root of the Mackenzie Highway (Alberta's No. 35 and the Northwest Territories' No. 1). But the people who built the Mackenzie Highway were in more of a hurry. Unlike the bush trails, the highway more or less runs due north in a straight line.

Fasten your seatbelts, folks! We're heading north on an imaginary journey, from Grimshaw, Mile 0 of the Mackenzie Highway, to the end of the road in the Northwest Territories. From Grimshaw, we drive due north, where the highway cuts a swath through prairie farmland. We pass by the communities of Chinook Valley, Dixonville, and North Star. At Manning, 84 km [52 mi.] north of Grimshaw, the highway dips down into the first of three deep river valleys, which locals still call the First, Second, and Third Battles. You won't find these names on your highway map; the rivers appear as the Notikewin, the Hotchkiss, and the Meikle, respectively. Once we cross the Notikewin River and top the hill, we pass Notikewin, now almost a ghost town but once the original Battle River Prairie hamlet. Now we enter the boreal forest and begin to drive through land more rolling and heavily forested with spruce, jack pine, larch, aspen, and birch. The farms are few and far between until we arrive at Keg River Cabins, which is really a stopping place. The more populated settlement is Keg River, 22 km [14 mi.] further west.

North of Keg River Cabins we come to Paddle Prairie, the largest Métis settlement in Alberta. The long, lonely stretch north of Paddle Prairie is heavily dotted with muskeg, with islands of black spruce and birch. It is good moose country, so watch out for them crossing the highway, especially if you are driving at night.

We stop at the bustling town of High Level to gas up, because from here to Enterprise, NWT, there are no service stations and the only communities you'll pass through are Meander River, a Dene (Slavy) reserve; Steen River, where the Alberta

Forest Service maintains an emergency air strip; and Indian Cabins, a former café and stopping place for truckers. At the Alberta/NWT boundary there is a large visitor's centre, where we stop to pick up a good map of the Northwest Territories. North of the boundary, the highway follows along the edge of the beautiful Hay River escarpment, where the river cuts through sedimentary layers of Devonian limestone and tumbles over two spectacular waterfalls – the Alexandra and Louise falls.

Arriving at Enterprise, we have completed the first leg of the Mackenzie Highway and have been pampered with 556 km [345 mi.] of paved highway all the way. From Enterprise we can turn east to the town of Hay River, along the old Mackenzie Highway, which is now NWT No. 2.

Originally, the Mackenzie Highway went to Old Town, the original town of Hay River before the spring flood of 1963, and terminated at the barge landing on the west channel of Great Slave Lake. Today the town is located on higher ground, but you can still see some of the old buildings, like the Hay River Hotel and the HBC Post, in the original waterfront town.

To travel today's Mackenzie Highway, we have to backtrack to Enterprise and head west to where the mostly paved Providence Highway (No. 3), branches off into Fort Providence and on to Yellowknife, the capital of the Northwest Territories. It is tempting to follow that route, but we really want to continue on the Mackenzie Highway. From the turnoff, the highway continues in a northwesterly direction, becoming an improved all-weather gravel road, mostly paralleling the Mackenzie River for some 511 km [317 mi.]. Before you reach Fort Simpson, the Liard Trail (NWT No. 7) branches off to Fort Liard and Fort Nelson, B.C. We'll have to save that trip for another day as well.

The all-weather gravel section of the Mackenzie Highway continues on until it terminates at the town of Wrigley. Beyond Wrigley, the next 480 km [298 mi.] of road is passable only in the winter, to Tulita (Fort Norman), Norman Wells, and Fort Good Hope, the end of the road.

We have covered a distance of 1500 km [930 mi.]. To go any further, we would have to go by boat on the Mackenzie River to Inuvik and Tuktoyaktuk on the Arctic Ocean.

A Vital Link to the North

The Mackenzie Highway and its vast network of tributaries provide a vital transportation link between the Northwest Territories and the rest of Canada. To the people who make their home in the North, it is more than a highway. It is a lifeline.

The construction of the Mackenzie Highway began during the spring of 1946 and was completed in late summer of 1948. The highway was a post-war project of the Dominion and Alberta governments, and its purpose was to provide an all-weather overland route to the North's rich mining and fishing resources. The highway brought in a new era of truck transportation, which provided an alternative to the long-established and seasonal water transportation route via the Peace, Athabasca, and Slave rivers, through Fort Smith and Fort Resolution, across Great Slave Lake and down the Mackenzie River to the Arctic. Although tug boats and barges still carry freight across Great Slave Lake and down the Mackenzie River, river transportation on the Peace and Athabasca rivers all but disappeared by 1952. It was far more economical and reliable to ship goods by truck over the Mackenzie Highway.

To better understand the reasons for the Mackenzie Highway, and why the highway has become so important to the North and the rest of Canada, we need to go back prior to 1946 to look at earlier forms of transportation, and how these paved the way for truck transportation and construction of the Mackenzie Highway.

Early River Transportation

The Peace River Country has always been difficult to get to, in both time and distance. Surrounded by the Rocky Mountains to the west, the Swan Hills in the south, and boreal forest to the east and the north, a traveller, even today, gets the feeling of "going into" and "out of" the Peace Country. Perhaps the first travellers felt the same way. Occupation of the Peace River Country by First Peoples goes back some 10 500 years.[1] Early aboriginal people travelled on foot, as did their descendents, the ancestors of today's Athapaskan peoples, the Dunne-za (Beaver), and the Dene peoples (Slavy, Yellowknife, Chipewyan, and Dogrib). In the summer, dugout and birch bark canoes were used on rivers and lakes; in winter, dog teams pulled sleds and carrioles across the ice and snow.

European settlement of the North has been a fairly recent event, a little over 200 years. The first highways used by the fur traders of the North West Company (NWC) and Hudson's Bay Company (HBC) were rivers: the Athabasca, Peace, and Slave rivers all fed into the Mackenzie, the one big river highway that continues "down north" all the way to the Arctic Ocean. Fur traders from Montreal arrived in northern Alberta as early as 1776. Peter Pond crossed the Methy Portage (near Frobisher Lake, in western Saskatchewan) and travelled down the Clearwater and Athabasca rivers, where he established the first "white man's residence" on the Athabasca River, some 64 km [40 mi.] upstream from where it joins Lake Athabasca.

In 1788 Alexander Mackenzie sent his cousin, Roderick Mackenzie, to establish a NWC trading post on the south shore of Lake Athabasca. This became the first Fort Chipewyan. That same year Alexander Mackenzie sent Charles Boyer up the Peace River to build a post just downstream of today's Fort Vermilion. Fort Chipewyan and Fort Vermilion are the oldest continuously settled European communities in Alberta.

In 1789 Alexander Mackenzie and his companions left Fort Chipewyan in three canoes to make the historic journey down the Mackenzie River to its mouth at the Arctic Ocean. After covering a total of 4812 km [2990 mi.] in 102 days, they returned to Fort Chipewyan, disappointed that they had not found the legendary Northwest Passage to the Pacific Ocean. In fact, Mackenzie called it "the River of Disappointment."[2]

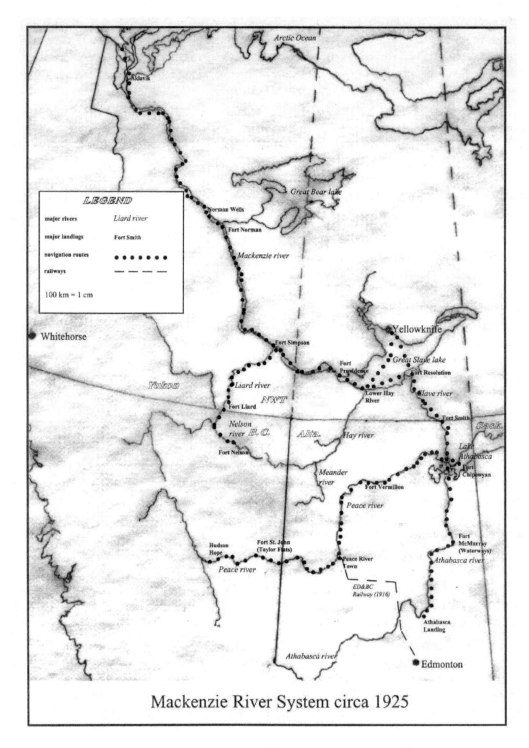

Mackenzie River System circa 1925

The North West Company, and later the Hudson's Bay Company (HBC), had established a complex river transportation system for trading with local Native tribes for furs and pemmican. The main transportation route to and from the Peace River and Athabasca districts was east and west via the Methy Portage. Following the amalgamation of the NWC and HBC in 1821, Fort Chipewyan continued as the entrepôt for the Peace-Athabasca district until 1824, when the HBC cut the Fort Assiniboine Trail from Fort Edmonton through to the Athabasca River and shifted travel on a north-south axis into the Peace and northern districts. Fort Edmonton became the entrepôt and Fort Chipewyan was downgraded to a minor outpost.

The HBC eventually established several access routes from Fort Edmonton into the Peace Country and further North. By the end of the 19th century – about the time when the Klondikers invaded the Peace Country – there were two main access routes into the North: (1) north from Edmonton, along the Athabasca Landing Trail to the Athabasca River, down river to Fort McMurray and Fort Chipewyan, then north on the Slave River to Great Slave Lake and on to other points north, or upstream on the Peace River. The other way was an overland route from Edmonton to Fort Assiniboine, over the Swan Hills to the settlement of Lesser Slave Lake (later Grouard) and along the Grouard-Peace River Trail, which was originally the old Cree War Road that warriors used. An alternate route was to travel upstream by boat from Athabasca Landing up the Athabasca River to the mouth of the Lesser Slave River, upriver to the east end of Lesser Slave Lake and across the lake to Grouard, or overland around the south side of the lake to connect up with the Grouard-Peace River Trail. This route became known as "the Long Trail" and was the way by which the first wave of settlers reached the Peace River Country, in wagons pulled by horses or oxen. "The Long Trail" was the forerunner of portions of today's Highway 2. Prior to 1911, travellers destined for the Grande Prairie area had to

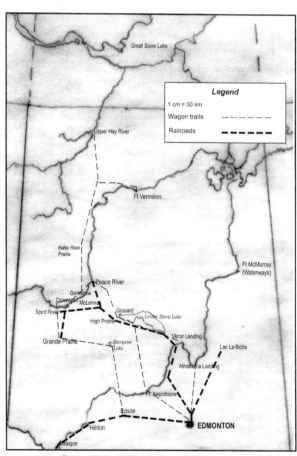

Routes into the Peace River Country 1916

A Journey into the Peace River Country, 1886

In the spring of 1886, 16-year-old Sheridan Lawrence began a long, arduous journey into the Peace Country, from Winnipeg to Fort Vermilion. Sheridan travelled with his mother Maggie, six brothers and sisters, and his Uncle Isaac Lawrence. The family was joining Henry Lawrence, who worked as a farm instructor at the Anglican mission at Fort Vermilion. They left Winnipeg in early May, taking the CPR train to Calgary. From Calgary they travelled north along the Edmonton Trail in ox-drawn wagons that averaged about 15 miles [24 km] a day. Sheridan and his brother Jim herded several cattle and pigs. One of the wagons had a bulky 12-horsepower stationary steam engine with a big upright boiler, for use to power a flour mill and sawmill they were also transporting.

At Edmonton the Lawrences crossed the North Saskatchewan on the ferry and continued north along the HBC trail to Athabasca Landing, where Maggie and the younger children joined a boat brigade of York boats, manned by robust Metis boatmen, who poled and tracked up the Athabasca and Lesser Slave rivers to Lesser Slave Lake. When they reached the eastern end of the lake, the boatmen put up a sail and sailed west along the length of the lake to the HBC post at Lesser Slave Lake on Buffalo Bay. Meanwhile Sheridan and Jim herded the livestock overland through the bush and eventually met up with the rest of the family at Lesser Slave Lake. From there they journeyed another 90 miles [144 km] along the old Cree War Road (Grouard-Peace River Trail) to Peace River Crossing.

To get down the steep hill overlooking the Peace River, they had to rough-lock the wheels of the steam engine and hitch one team of oxen in the front to get it going and the other two teams in the back to slow its descent. When they arrived at the shores of the Peace River, it was the first week of August. Another uncle, Erastus Lawrence, had arrived from Fort Vermilion to help them build a raft 30 feet wide and 60 feet long [9 x 18m]. For the next six days Erastus guided the raft down the Peace River. Fifteen miles [24 km] upstream of Fort Vermilion, the boys fired up the steam engine and blew the shrill whistle to announce their arrival. It was August 18, 1886, four months from the time they left Winnipeg. The sound of that steam whistle heralded in a new era of steam power on the Peace River.[3]

continue from Peace River Crossing to Dunvegan, then cross the Peace River again and travel south along another trail between Dunvegan and Grande Prairie. From 1911 to 1916, settlers could enter the Grande Prairie area by the shorter route along the Edson Trail.

Stern-wheelers on the Mackenzie River System

For many years, steamships provided a vital link in the transportation system to remote areas of the Peace River Country and the Northwest Territories. There was ample wood for fuel, and steamships, with their shallow draft, could navigate most of the larger rivers from break-up to freeze-up. There was always the risk, however, that the boats would get stranded on a sandbar or swept over rapids.

The HBC built and operated the first steamship in northern Alberta. The *S.S. Graham* was built at Fort Chipewyan in the winter of 1882-83. It plied the Athabasca and Great Slave rivers and negotiated 322 km [200 mi.] of the lower Peace River, as far as the Vermilion Chutes. At the chutes, all passengers and freight had to go by portage around the rapids and into canoes and scows for the rest of the way upriver. In 1886, the HBC built another stern-wheeler at Fort Smith, the *S.S. Wrigley*. The *Wrigley* plied the Mackenzie River and was the first to cross the Arctic Circle. In 1902, the company built another, the *Mackenzie River*, which became the first stern-wheeler to operate on the lower Mackenzie River. The largest stern-wheeler on Great Slave Lake and the Mackenzie River was Lamson-Hubbard's *S.S. Distributor II*, built in 1920. It plied the river system from Fort Smith until 1946. In the North, steamships were gradually replaced by gasoline-powered tugs and aircraft, as air transportation gave passengers a quicker way to traplines, missions, trading posts, and mines.

The first steamship on the upper Peace was built at St. Augustine's Mission in Shaftesbury, with parts purchased by Bishop Grouard during a trip to Ontario. These parts had to be portaged over the Grouard Trail and across the Peace to the mission. The steamer, christened the *St. Charles*, was 60 feet long and had a 12-foot beam [18 x 4m]. On its maiden voyage, May 18, 1903, Bishop Grouard was on board, with Father LeTreste at the helm. The Oblate missionaries operated this steamer until 1911, when it was sold to Fred Lawrence.[4]

Observing the success of the Oblate's *St. Charles*, the HBC began building a larger steamship at Fort Vermilion in 1904 and launched it in 1905. The *Peace River* was a stern-wheeler 110 feet long [33.5m], with accommodations for 25 passengers and a freight capacity of around 80 tons.

Soon other companies began to build steamships to meet the increasing needs of settlers pouring into the Peace Country to homestead. Fred Lawrence, cousin of Sheridan Lawrence, went into a partnership and formed the Peace River Trading and Land Company, which built and launched the *S.S. Grenfell* in 1912. The *Northland Call* was built across the river from Peace Crossing in 1915 by J.K. "Peace River Jim" Cornwall and his partners of the Peace River Navigation Company. They later refurbished the steamer in 1920, giving her the new name of *Hudson's Hope*. But the grandest steamship of them all was the *D.A. Thomas*, built by Lord Rhonda, David Alfred Thomas.

The *D.A. Thomas* was launched in June of 1916 and headlined by the Peace River *Record* as the "Largest Steamboat to Ply the Canadian Inland Waters." It was unquestionably the largest boat on the Peace River, 161.9 feet [49m] in length, 37 feet [11m] breadth and a depth of 6.3 feet [2m], powered by a 21.6 horsepower engine. She had a gross tonnage of 1114 and accommodations for 160 passengers.[5] In 1924 the HBC purchased the *D.A. Thomas*. The following year the steamship suffered some damage to her hull when the captain tried to navigate Peace River Canyon. The HBC continued operating the *D.A. Thomas* until 1929, when she grounded in a sandbar. Then in 1930 she came to the end of her service when she was washed over the Vermilion Chutes, suffering extensive damage. After receiving minor repairs, she was taken down river as far as Fort Fitzgerald, where her engines were dismantled and sold for scrap. All that remains of the *D.A. Thomas* is the wheel shaft, salvaged and brought to the Peace River Centennial Museum, where it is on display.

The D.A. Thomas, *the largest, grandest steam ship on the Peace River. 1920s. Glenbow Archives, Calgary, Canada, NA 2898-7.*

The ignominious end of the *D.A. Thomas* also marked the beginning of the end for the great steamships on the Peace. The last of the stern-wheelers arrived during the Second World War, when the *Alcan* was built to transport materials for the bridge over the Peace at Taylor Flats, near Fort St. John. In 1946 the *Alcan* was taken over the Vermilion Chutes and purchased by Imperial Oil, which had plans to operate the boat farther north.

Motor boats, which had long shared the waters of the Peace with steamships, came into their own. They were smaller but cheaper to run and they could venture where steamships would founder. At first they were used to shuttle goods and passengers from the larger boats. In 1915 the HBC launched the *Beaver*, with Captain John Gullion as skipper, to navigate the upper Peace to Hudson's Hope, B.C., and up the Smoky River as far as Bezanson. It was Gullion's last boat, as he died of a heart attack on the boat in

Tompkins Landing, Buffalo Head Prairie, 1940s. Ben Peters Collection.

September 1915. The *Beaver* continued to operate for five more years until it caught fire and burned. The Peace River Development Corporation also operated a gasoline launch, the *Lady Mackworth*. The HBC launched the *Weenusk*, a tug with two barges, in May of 1921.

During the Great Depression another wave of settlers, whose lands had dried out in the prairies, began moving into the Peace River Country to start over again. Michael Raychyba saw an opportunity and built a scow, which he powered with an engine from a Cletrac tractor and propelled with two homemade side-wheels. Dubbed in jest *The Russian Navy*, the unique craft could go to Fort Vermilion and return for a fraction of the cost of fuel to operate a steamship. The HBC launched the *Weenusk II* in 1940 to replace the *Weenusk*. The *Weenusk II*, captained by Douglas Cadenhead, operated until 1951, when it too was replaced by the *Watson Lake*, with Captain Jack O'Sullivan at the helm.

The *Watson Lake* was the last commercial boat to operate on the Peace. Captain O'Sullivan took the boat on its last voyage on September 21, 1952. The boat was then loaded onto a flat car and shipped to Waterways (Fort McMurray) to operate on the Athabasca River and farther north.

Truck transportation on the newly-built Mackenzie Highway, and the building of another gravel road, Highway 58, into Fort Vermilion, marked the end of commercial navigation on the Peace. River navigation on the Athabasca, Slave, and Mackenzie rivers continued a little longer, but Hay River, NWT, became the launching point down the Mackenzie, rather than Fort Smith, once the Mackenzie Highway was opened. Barges still ply the water transportation system each summer, as it is still cheaper to ship bulk items by water than by any other form of transportation in the North.

Railways in the North

From the 1880s to the First World War, the southern parts of the prairie provinces saw expansions of railway lines to attract new settlers and to ensure that there was a steady source of revenues from freight and passengers. The CPR had crossed Alberta by 1885 and had built a branch line between Calgary and Edmonton in 1891. By the end of the first decade of the 20th century, the Grand Trunk Pacific (GTP) and the Canadian Northern Railway (CNoR) had also built lines, almost side by side in some places, through Edmonton, Edson, and Jasper.

The Peace River Country had to wait until 1915 before it had a railway. There were plenty of "paper railways." Grouard by 1910 had become the largest metropolis and the gateway to the Peace. It had a Dominion lands office and was the regional headquarters of the HBC and the North West Mounted Police, as well as having a meteorological and telegraph station. On paper, it had no less than three railway lines converging at the town. The CPR, GTP, and CNoR all had charters approved by the Alberta government to run lines north. But it took the visionary John Duncan McArthur of Winnipeg to put it all together.[6]

McArthur's brainchild was the Edmonton, Dunvegan & British Columbia railway (ED&BC). In March of 1912, McArthur began to acquire land for town sites and the right-of-way. Survey crews were hired to begin surveying the right-of-way, which ran north from Edmonton to Dunvegan and continued on to the Parsnip River in B.C. In actual fact, the railway never reached either Dunvegan or B.C. And it never went through Grouard. The founding of High Prairie as a railway town, and McLennan as a division point, sounded the death knell of Grouard as the hub of the Peace. At McLennan the lines split off into two branches, one heading north to Peace River Crossing, and the end of steel was at the top of Judah Hill overlooking the Peace River by mid-October, 1915.

By the following year, the ED&BC arrived at Peace River Crossing. The other branch headed west from McLennan, crossing the Smoky River at Watino and reaching Spirit River by December 1916. Although the road bed was in place west from Spirit River almost to the B.C. border, the rails were never laid down. (For many years, farmers in the area used the old road bed to haul their grain in wagons to Spirit River, the end of steel.) Instead of continuing on to the B.C. border, McArthur decided to build a branch line from Rycroft to Grande Prairie instead, where settlement was booming.

Canada's entry into the First World War had a disastrous effect upon the ED&BC in the Peace Country and the Alberta and Great Waterways (AG&W), another railway that McArthur built from Edmonton to Waterways, to access the river transportation system via the Athabasca, Slave, and Mackenzie rivers. The railway had many outgoing passengers, men abandoning their homesteads and heading to Edmonton to enlist in the Canadian or British army. Steel rails were also needed for the war effort. With a shortage of workforce and capital, McArthur was in deep financial trouble by the end of the war. In July of 1920, the Alberta government and the CPR took over the management of the ED&BC, giving McArthur a seven-year option to regain possession of his railway. But his death in 1925 put an end to his dream. By 1930 McArthur's ED&BC and AG&W were operated jointly by the CPR and CN under the name of Northern Alberta Railways. This agreement lasted until 1980, when CN took over operation under its own name.

Despite the many problems of the ED&BC (nicknamed "Extremely Dangerous and Badly Constructed"), the railway had opened the Peace Country in a way that no previous transportation could have. It provided a much faster route to the outside world and allowed farmers close to the railhead to ship their grain. When the rail line was extended to Grimshaw in 1922, farmers in northern Alberta could now ship their wheat to distant markets instead of feeding it all to hogs and cattle. Access roads suddenly became a necessity to haul wheat to the railway.

Northern Alberta Railways' last mail train into Grimshaw, 1958. Peter and Doris Loras collection.

Early Roads in the Peace

Motorized transportation was delayed in the Peace River Country, especially in the northern districts where the deplorable condition of the roads (if you could call them that) made motorized transportation almost impossible most of the year. Despite continual lobbying from people in northern Alberta, the provincial governments of both Alberta and British Columbia turned a deaf ear when it came to spending money on

George Levine, North Star, hauling two seed drills. 1937. Ed Dillman collection.

decent roads. The provincial governments also had a vested interest in seeing that the railways got the lion's share of moving freight and passengers.[7]

Roads that existed prior to 1930 were hardly more than wagon trails or tote roads, ungravelled muddy bogs in the spring and summer and deep, frozen ruts, as hard as concrete, in winter. Native people and early settlers in the North put in wagon trails, without any aid from the government. The Lawrence family of Fort Vermilion cut a primitive wagon road as early as the teens to drive cattle to the railhead at Grimshaw.[8] The Battle River Trail was still the main overland link between Notikewin and Peace River by the time Dr. Mary Percy arrived in 1929. When the telegraph line was extended between Notikewin and Fort Vermilion, the right of way became an overland trail for horse-drawn teams.

At first only cars and small trucks, such as converted Model T Fords with their high clearance, could negotiate the deep ruts that formed in the spring after breakup, and froze solid after freeze-up along these early wagon trails. However, the first car into the Peace River Country over the Edson Trail was not a Ford but a 1912 Cadillac driven by A.M. Bezanson and A.J. Davison, in 1913. By 1915, a couple of young entrepreneurs were operating the Red Line Motor Service with a converted Model T Ford truck on the Grouard-Peace River Trail.

In the 1920s and 1930s, farmers around Dicksonville, North Star, and Deadwood began to haul grain to the grain elevators at Grimshaw. It took them five or six days by wagon on the Battle River Trail, from Battle River Prairie to Grimshaw, until the road was improved in 1926 so that it was possible to take one-ton trucks over it. But north of

Battle River Prairie, there were only bush trails, accessible only by horse drawn wagons or dog sleds.

Fred Mercredi of Fort Vermilion recalls a trip he made in 1925 from Paddle Prairie to Grimshaw. He was 16 years old at the time and helping a rancher herd some polled Angus cattle to Grimshaw. The trip took a total of 21 days.

"It snowed, eight inches [20 cm] *of snow. We had cattle mixed up with [Frank] Jackson's – 30 head. Four-year-old steers, three-year-old steers, and one cow. That cow, she wouldn't stay back. At Keg River we rented a horse there from a guy. One of these – well, you know the song about the strawberry roan? Only it was a black horse. The first day it kicked the grub box and threw out all the food. We had to eat bannock and peanut butter. We got to Battle River, right where Manning is today. They had a store there, run by a Frenchman – Joe Bissett was his name. There were no farms, no fences, nothing.*

"They left me at Lac Cardinal. When they came back with a buyer, he bought the 30 head for $430. We got $30 for the cow, that was separate. Then we got a big electrical storm. The cow was laying on the street and some of the steers were killed by lightning."[9]

In 1929, the Alberta government started to build a telegraph line from Peace River to Fort Vermilion. Frank Jackson of Keg River Post put in part of the right of way. By 1930 it had arrived at Notikewin, on the First Battle. The telegraph right-of-way between Notikewin north was used for many years by locals as an access road for wagons and early cars and trucks.

The Battle River Prairie was a long way from the railhead, and farmers found out the hard way that transporting wheat by horse team on the Grimshaw Road was expensive. Orville Guttau of Manning recalled such a trip:

"It was in 1932 or 1933, and we had just finished an early winter threshing. Some of the threshers wanted to be paid so I decided to sell some wheat to raise some money. I therefore loaded two sleigh boxes with wheat and started for Grimshaw....Travelling in this manner it took me two days to reach Grimshaw. In Grimshaw I sold the wheat and bought two barrels of distillate and five barrels of oil, which the threshers had ordered. I stayed in Grimshaw that night and ate supper in the restaurant....I returned home after four days and took stock of my finances. I had sold the wheat at 31 cents a bushel. Balanced against the earnings on the wheat, I had bought distillate at one dollar a barrel and oil at less than one dollar a gallon. My expenses for the trip were five dollars. After these amounts were subtracted, I was left with 65 cents and the threshers had to take their pay in distillate and oil."[10]

It is little wonder that many farmers, from Battle River Prairie to Fort Vermilion, fed their grain to cattle or pigs, rather than sell wheat at such a loss. A better road would mean that larger trucks could replace wagons and sleighs and lessen the time and expense of hauling grain to the elevators at Grimshaw.

Air Transportation

In 1920, oil was discovered near Fort Norman and Imperial Oil was impatient to get passengers and freight to the new well-site. It would take several weeks to travel by dogsled from the railroad at Peace River or cope with the vagaries of river transportation after spring breakup. The company decided to try air transportation into the remote outpost on the Mackenzie River. Imperial purchased two Junkers and had Wop May and George Gorman fly them from New York to Edmonton. May landed his Junkers at Blatchford Field on January 5, 1921, and Gorman arrived two weeks later with the other Junkers. At the end of February, George Gorman and Elmer Fullerton took off for the North, with seven passengers and 450 kg [992 lbs.] of equipment.[13] The pilots flew first to Peace River, where Imperial had already set up a base. The route they decided on was to follow the Hudson's Bay posts, which kept a supply of fuel for motor boats. They also established a fuel cache at the HBC post at Upper Hay River (Meander River).

The flight began to have its problems, beginning March 24 when the pilots took off for Fort Norman. Poor visibility forced them to land at Fort Vermilion instead of Upper Hay River. Then after taking off again, they were forced to land at Fort Simpson; the propellers on both aircraft had suffered damage. A local woodworker was enlisted to help the mechanic to make a new propeller "fashioned from boards and a glue made from moose hide and hooves." Arrival of breakup in late April meant that there wouldn't be enough snow for their skis, so they decided to fly back to Peace River. Finally in late May, one of the Junkers, equipped with a new propeller and a set of pontoons, took off and was successful in landing at Fort Norman.

Although it was three months since the Junkers had left Edmonton for Fort Norman, Gorman and Fullerton had paved the way for future flights into the North. In 1922, the first plane landed at Fort Smith, and in 1926, another landed at Fort Chipewyan. But it would take several more years before commercial air transportation became established in the North, and Edmonton would once more become the Gateway of the North.

Two events in January 1929 brought the dream of commercial air transportation out of mothballs. Diphtheria had broken out at Little Red River, 50 miles [80 km] downstream of Fort Vermilion, and a wire message was sent by Dr. H.A. Hamman that antitoxin serum was urgently needed. The fastest way to get it there was by airplane. On January 1, in -33°F [-36°C], Wop May and Vic Horner took off in an open cockpit Avro Avian, equipped with charcoal burners to keep the antitoxin, and their feet, from freezing. Radio station CJCA had broadcast the route the pilots would fly. They landed the first night at McLennan, as visibility became too poor to land at Peace River. The next morning they landed at Peace River, fueled up, and took off for Fort Vermilion, where they delivered the serum to Dr. Hammon. The pilots returned to Blatchford Field in Edmonton to a hero's welcome.[14]

The other event marked the beginning of aerial surveying and scheduled air mail service into the North. Western Canada Airways (WCA) of Winnipeg was already establishing a base at Fort McMurray and began advertising in the Edmonton *Journal* for customers to fly north. In the same month as May's and Horner's mercy flight to Fort Vermilion, C.H. "Punch" Dickins of WCA flew from Waterways on an unofficial mail flight down the Mackenzie River, in a Fokker Super Universal G-CASB. Accompanied by T.J. Reilly, a postal inspector, Dickins took off on January 23, and made 10 stops between Waterways and Aklavik. Thus he became the first pilot to fly along the coast of the Arctic Ocean. That same year, he flew Gilbert Labine, manager of the Eldorado Mines, over Great Bear Lake, where Labine spotted a cobalt bloom that looked promising.[15] The next year Labine returned to Great Bear Lake to stake the claims that were rich in uranium oxide, the source of elements that would later be used in the Manhattan Project to make the atomic bomb. Despite Dickins's highly publicized and successful flight, Commercial Airways, WCA's chief competition, landed the contract for regular air mail service and Commercial Airways moved its operations from Edmonton to Fort McMurray. In December 1929, the first official air mail flight took off from Fort McMurray. There were weekly flights to Fort Resolution, monthly flights to Fort Simpson, and a flight every two months to Aklavik.[16]

By the 1930s the North had become a mecca for prospectors, mining engineers, and trappers, all seeking to extract its rich resources. Winter fishing became an important industry, and some pilots, like Grant McConachie, got started in commercial aviation hauling fish to the railhead.[17] Mining development around Great Bear Lake and Lake Athabasca provided more opportunities for aviation entrepreneurs. Leigh Brintnell, who started Mackenzie Air Services out of Edmonton in 1931, hired pilots Matt Berry and Stan McMillan to fly into the North. Brintnell landed a lucrative contract in the winter of 1932-33 to carry 500 pounds [226 kg] of fresh vegetables to the Eldorado Mines on Great Bear Lake.[18]

Locally, the Town of Peace River formed its own aviation company, Peace River Airways, in 1930, with the purchase of a biplane, an American Eagle. More and more flights took off from Edmonton, Fort McMurray, Fort Smith, and Yellowknife. Anglican ministers, Catholic priests, trappers, RCMP officers, prospectors, geologists, biologists, doctors and nurses, and government bureaucrats were flying regularly into the North. While the rest of Canada foundered during the Depression, the North held the hope of much-needed jobs. Air transportation, though expensive, provided the fastest access, and Edmonton, with its well-equipped airport and link to rail connections, once more became the Gateway to the North.

Air transportation provided a much-needed service in the North, where it could take weeks, and sometimes months, to reach your destination by any other mode of transport. However, it was very costly and could not possibly supply all the demands of delivering goods, especially heavy equipment and bulk cargo. River transportation, for all its slowness and unreliability, continued to carry most of the freight for the North.

By the end of the 30s, events happening outside the Peace River Country brought about a significant change in the transportation system and, ultimately, the lifestyles of the people living in the North Peace and Northwest Territories. In 1938, the Alberta government began surveying a route for a winter road for cat trains, from the Third Battle to Hay River, NWT. Called the Grimshaw-Hay River winter road, it was a forerunner of today's Mackenzie Highway. The winter road, with a few minor exceptions, followed the same route as today's highway.

Notes

[1] Archaeological excavations in the 1970s at Charlie Lake Cave, a few miles north of Fort St. John, B.C., uncovered artifacts and bones carbon-dated to 10 500 B.P.

[2] James G. MacGregor, *A History of Alberta*, Edmonton: Hurtig Publishers, 1972, pp. 36-37. Another excellent source on the explorations of NWC on the Mackenzie River system is James Parker's *Emporium of the North: Fort Chipewyan and the Fur Trade to 1835*, Edmonton: Alberta Culture/Canadian Plains Research Centre, 1987.

[3] From Eugenie Louise Myles, *The Emperor of Peace River*, Saskatoon: Western Producer Prairie Books, 1978.

[4] Evelyn Hansen, *Where Go the Boats: Navigation on the Peace 1792 - 1952*, a pamphlet published by the Peace River Centennial Museum, Peace River, no date, p. 9.

[5] Hansen, p. 13.

6 The main source used for the story of the ED&BC and Northern Alberta Railways is Ena Schneider's *Ribbons of Steel: The Story of the Northern Alberta Railways*, Calgary: Detselig Enterprises Ltd., 1989.

7 Alberta's Liberal government had heavily subsidized the building of railway lines, including MacArthur's ED&BC and the A&GW. The fiscal collapse of several railway syndicates, including McArthur's, forced the government into taking over these lines in the 1920s. The UFA government approached the CPR and CNR to take over the failed railways. In 1929, the government negotiated an agreement that formed Northern Alberta Railways, which was jointly owned by CPR and CNR.

8 Kevin Richard, "A Road Leading 'Nowhere,'" an unpublished term paper about the history of the Mackenzie Highway.

9 Interview with Fred Mercredi, at High Level, August 19, 1998.

10 *Saga of Battle River – We Came, We Stayed*, Manning: Battle River Historical Society, 1986, pp. 719-20.

11 Cornelia Lehn, *The Handmade Brass Plate: The Story of Mary Percy Jackson*, Keg River: Anne Vos, publisher, 1994, pp 49-56.

12 *The Handmade Brass Plate*, pp. 102-3.

13 Patricia A. Myers, *Sky Riders: An Illustrated History of Aviation in Alberta 1906-1945*, Saskatoon: Fifth House Ltd., 1995, pp. 56-58.

14 Eugenie Louise Myles, *Airborne from Edmonton*, Toronto: The Ryerson Press, 1959, pp. 112-115.

15 A bloom is a stain from minerals leaching out of rocks and is an important indicator to geologists of certain ores. A blue or green stain may indicate the presence of copper, which in turn may contain cobalt, silver, and other valuable ores; a red stain indicates the presence of iron oxides.

16 Myles, *Airborne from Edmonton*, p. 78.

17 Myers, *Sky Riders*, p. 128.

18 Myles, *Airborne from Edmonton*, p. 205.

🚗 Chapter 2 – A Winter Road for Cat Trains 🚚

On March 9, 1939, three tractor trains belonging to the Yellowknife Transportation Company (YTCL), left the town of Grimshaw to begin an historic 500-mile [800 km] journey over a new winter road to Lower Hay River, NWT, and across the Great Slave Lake to Yellowknife. Owner and general manager Earle Harcourt and his partners, L.J. "Bert" Nieland and Stuart McLeod, travelled with a crew of 15. Carrying 120 tons of heavy freight that was destined for the mines at Yellowknife, the cat trains took a little over a month to complete the journey, arriving at Yellowknife on April 12th. This unprecedented overland journey by tractor trains through northern Alberta and the Northwest Territories would revolutionize northern transportation.

Any new transportation system comes about for a good reason, usually because the existing mode is inadequate or fails altogether. In the late 1930s, Canada's North needed a faster way to haul goods and equipment into the mines at Yellowknife on Great Slave Lake and Port Radium at Echo Bay on Great Bear Lake. River transportation, which operated four months of the year, started after break-up when the ice went out of Great Slave Lake, usually by mid-June. Freeze-up usually came anytime after September 15. An early freeze-up could also delay some freight until the next year. Passengers and some of the lighter freight could go by air transport, of course, but not the heavier freight. What was needed was a winter overland route that would connect with the railways to the south.

The situation came to a head in 1938, when low water on the Athabasca River prevented the river boats from moving some vital equipment from the railhead at Waterways. A new winter road was born.

Earle Harcourt – Pioneer in Northern Transportation

In 1932, 20-year-old Robert Earle Harcourt of Edmonton followed the news of the mining activities in the North. The country was deeply into the Depression and there were few jobs around for young men. He and Bill Graham decided to go North to get in on the action.

"I went north in 1932. At that time uranium had just been discovered on the east shore of Great Bear Lake. A friend of mine, Bill Graham, and myself decided we'd go up there and stake some mines and become wealthy. So we put together an outfit. Bill, my partner, went in with a sleigh from Fort St. John to the headwaters of the Sikanni Chief River system, and I came in a month later and walked in with a dog pack and met him on the upper river."[1]

They had portaged a 16-foot canoe to the headwaters of the Sikanni Chief River. After break-up they travelled downstream to the Liard River, then to the Mackenzie River, making their way north to Fort Norman and, from there, up the Bear River to Great Bear Lake. They blithely paddled their small canoe for another 200 miles [322 km] along the shores of this vast, turbulent inland sea to Port Radium at Echo Bay.

"I spent the summer there staking a bunch of claims, a couple of them right next to the El Dorado Mines. I had left Edmonton in late May and we didn't get back till August. We came straight south overland from Great Bear Lake to Great Slave Lake and up the Slave River, through the system to Waterways."

Although the trip did not bring riches, it was an exciting adventure. The following year Harcourt decided to go north again. At that time a laborer in the northern mines could earn $5 a day, and a shaft worker, even more. Harcourt got a job at the White Eagle silver mines on the Camsell River for awhile, until he was gassed by dynamite fumes and fell down a mine shaft, 45 feet [14m] head first. He was flown out to the University Hospital in Edmonton, where he recuperated for the rest of the summer.

This experience didn't diminish Harcourt's enthusiasm for the North, but it did end his mining career. He turned to transportation instead. He had met his future partner, Bert Nieland, in northern B.C. in 1932. "Nieland was building a scow at the time and was going down to Aklavik to see what he could do to open up the country. Later we teamed up together when we were working at the Bear mines. He was a carpenter timbering mining shafts."

Harcourt and Nieland decided to quit working at the mine and go into their own transportation business in 1934. Harcourt remarked, "There are three things that the North actually requires: It has to have transportation; it has to have food, and it has to have fuel or energy of some kind. We decided we'd do all of those."

Nieland was an experienced carpenter and boat builder, and together they built a 38-foot [11m] boat out of the boards they had used earlier to build a scow in Fort McMurray. "We would run from mine to mine, taking things here, there, and everywhere. We got a contract with El Dorado Mines to cut and haul cordwood and timber."

They also had a contract to haul fish to the mines. By this time they had taken on a third partner, Stuart McLeod, also from Edmonton. They set up their headquarters about 50 miles [80 km] south on the Camsell River, and took advantage of the fall run of whitefish. "We put out a couple of nets and there was so many fish that they were twisting that net up into a rope. As fast as we could set the nets, they'd fill them."

While Harcourt was returning alone from delivering the fish at El Dorado, he had a harrowing experience that tested his northern survival skills to the utmost.

"I was trying to beat the ice back to Camsell to our camp there in behind Richardson Island, and I ran into some fairly heavy ice. Tried to break through it with the boat, but all I did was cause the ice to cut sections of the bow out, and I sank the boat. I didn't have a canoe aboard or anything, so I had to swim ashore. I got ashore on

an island, and there was a broken down tree that had fallen into deep water. I had put some matches under my toque, so I got a fire going and dried out. I took my clothes off, my parka was freezing. It was nasty. The next morning the ice was frozen enough that I could cross it."

Later he and Nieland were able to salvage the boat and spent most of the following summer putting it back in service. By this time it was late fall, and they began looking for coal on Great Bear Mountain. Off McVicker Arms, a winter storm caught up with them and blew them ashore, where they were frozen in. They had to walk the 150 miles [240 km] back to Cameron Bay. "That was kinda nasty too, because we ran out of food and wound up with tea, a little sugar, and a bunch of butter to keep us going."

In 1937, they had a falling out with the management at El Dorado and decided to move their transportation business to Yellowknife. They began to operate under the name of Yellowknife Transportation Company. By this time they had a tug and a few barges they had built themselves. They ran these between Yellowknife and Waterways along the established water route. In 1938, Nature played a hand in adding overland transport to their already successful water transportation business.

"In the fall of 1938, there was low water and some of the heavy freight for the mines was too heavy for the barges on the Athabasca River. So it was left behind. We decided we would take it overland. It was not quite a war priority but close to it on the material that was going in there. So we decided we would put a [cat] train together and take it in. We didn't even question doing it. We lined up a bunch of contracts, then decided we'd better have a look and see what we were getting ourselves into. I went over to Fort Resolution and got George Roberts and a dog team and we went into Lower Hay River. We went south along the Hay River to find out what the behavior of the falls were and if we could get over them. It was no problem, so we came back and went out to Grimshaw and put a train together."

They bought the sleighs from Art Coursier in Wolf Creek, near Edson. Harcourt explained,

"They were far, far more than just the ordinary farm sleigh. The runners on those were solid oak and nine feet long [3m] and six inches wide [15cm]. Coursier had used them for hauling logs. He was also the agent for International Harvester. It was through Art that we bought International TD6s. They weren't Cats. We thought the Caterpillar D8s would be far too heavy for the ice."

While Harcourt and Nieland were putting the tractor train together, the Alberta government had sent surveyors and brush cutters a few months before, to begin clearing a winter tractor road.

The New North Road

In the fall of 1937, the Alberta government received funding from the Dominion government to begin building a road to Great Slave Lake. W.A. Fallow, Minister of

Public Works, had recognized the benefits that such a road would have to the people of northern Alberta. A fairly passable wagon road already existed from Grimshaw to Upper Hay (Meander) River, but further north there were several alternate trails that had been used by dog teams and pack horses. These trails went to Hay Lakes, Bistcho Lake, and Kakisa Lake, but were considered too hilly to use for the winter cat road and were rejected. A more direct route was needed.

In January 1939, an aerial survey was completed by A.M. Narraway, chief of aerial surveys for the Dominion government, and J.L. Grew. By February there were three survey teams at work marking the route.

Construction on the new winter road to Hay River began in December 1938. Costs would be shared by the Alberta and Dominion governments; $52 000 was allocated to complete the winter project. The costs for the NWT section of the road would be covered by the Dominion government, as well the cost of a section of the road south of the Alberta/NWT boundary. Alberta's Department of Public Works hired the workers, supervised the clearing, and provided the equipment, which included brush cutters and bulldozers. Clearing was done to a 30-foot width [9m]. By April 1939, 239 miles [385 km] were completed from Meikle River to the Alberta/NWT boundary. Work resumed in August 1939, and the stretch between the boundary and Lower Hay River Post was completed early in 1940.[2]

> *"Harry Camsell of Hay River acted as a guide on the northern section, driving dog teams and bringing supplies. Brush cutters soon followed, cutting a double swath through the bush. Three clearing crews, of about twenty axemen each, cleared the remaining ground by hand. They were paid about 40 cents an hour."*[3]

Many local people worked on the road helping to cut brush by axe and hand saw. Hans Eggli from Grimshaw was hired on for one of the crews that worked on the south-

Clearing crew corduroying across muskeg and creek crossing, 1938. Bourke Tackaberry collection.

ern section. His son Dolph Eggli, Bourke Tackaberry, and E.T. Blakley – all from Grimshaw – worked with the same clearing crew, with Hans Eggli as the foreman and E.T. Blakley the "straw boss" or second-in-command.[4] Other members of the crew were new homesteaders from the Deadwood, North Star, and Notikewin areas.

Several workers came from southern Alberta to work on the winter road; many of them had been unemployed. Dr. Mary Percy Jackson remembers vividly when 26 men came through Keg River. They had walked all the way from Notikewin.

"They were sent north by bureaucrats who knew nothing of the northern winter conditions. The men were in poor physical condition after living on one meal a day; they were inadequately clothed, had no mitts, and were wearing shoes. They had to walk from Notikewin to Keg River – 80 miles [128 km] *by the telegraph line - without anything to eat, because the food provided (bread, bologna, cans of pork and beans) was all frozen solid and impossible to thaw at a campfire.*

"A number of men played out on the trail and wanted to just lie down and rest, but others knew enough to keep them going, so nobody was frozen to death. When they reached Keg River, however, I saw more frostbitten faces and fingers and toes than I'd seen in all the previous six years."[5]

Dave Jenkins of Didsbury had worked for Public Works since 1933. He was one of the few experienced operators of Caterpillar tractors at the time, and the government had just purchased several. In December 1938, he was offered the job of lead catskinner for the new road, and he headed north to begin clearing brush with Caterpillar tractors specially equipped with brush cutters.[6]

The crews worked from dawn to dusk, clearing trees and brush, mostly by hand. Local Natives also helped with the clearing. Stan Smith of Fort Vermilion started out as a brush cutter in 1938. He travelled by dog team to Indian Cabins and was put in charge of three other men to begin clearing with axes the large trees that the brushcutter couldn't handle. "There were these big trees, you couldn't cut them down, you know, with that brush cutter. So, we had to cut them by hand, level with the ground."[7] Years later, in 1946, Stan Smith worked as a rodman on the survey crew that surveyed the route for the Mackenzie Highway, thus earning the distinction of having worked on survey crews for both the winter tractor trail and the Mackenzie Highway.

Dave Jenkins recalls that 1938-39 was a very cold winter, with snow up to their waists. He was behind one of the Cats equipped with brush cutters. The snow pack on the trees would cut loose when the trees were felled, and snow would fall down on top of the Cat, so that it was difficult to get one's bearings. The men, up to 20 and 30 at times, worked from dawn to dusk and slept in canvas tents. They ate in the cookhouse, a caboose that was pulled along behind by a Cat. "The worst part was the lack of communication," said Jenkins. Their only link with civilization was an airplane, which delivered supplies and messages. These were picked up by dog team and taken to the wherever the camp was set up.

Jenkins recalls that crossing creeks and rivers could be treacherous. Once a sled broke in half as it was being pulled across a stream. The Native workers built a wooden platform, placed the broken sleigh on it and continued on. Another time, crossing a river that was partly thawed caused concern to the crew. When they took the tractor train across, the water was running on top of the ice, but they managed to get across without breaking through or losing equipment.

After several months of living in the bush, the clearing crew finally reached Lower Hay River Post on Great Slave Lake. At that time, Hay River was a small community of mostly Dene (Slavey) people. There was the HBC post and Anglican and Catholic missions.

Hay River's history dates back to 1868, when John Hope of the HBC had built a temporary post on the east channel and the Oblates established a small mission. But due to lack of trade, both were closed within a year. In the 1880s a band of Slavey established a semi-permanent community and were visited periodically by the HBC's steamboats. In 1893, Thomas Marsh set up St Peter's Mission for the Anglican Church. At the time that the first tractor train arrived in the spring of 1939, about 150 people lived there. The construction of the winter road for cat trains, and later the all-weather Mackenzie Highway, would turn this sleepy little village into the southern terminus for the boat and barge traffic that flowed north to the Arctic.

The crew that Jenkins lived with for almost four months had developed a special camaraderie. They had little time and energy for petty squabbling. Most were young men, grateful to have the work. They had spent months together in the bush, put up with the fact that there was no way to take a bath; for private needs, one went behind the nearest tree. The lack of baths was a problem at first, as the men had to live in close quarters. Jenkins remarked, "After a few weeks, one stopped noticing."

When Jenkins got back to Grimshaw, the first thing he wanted was a bath. Although the Grimshaw Hotel had no hot running water, the manager told him to come back after dinner and he could have his bath. "Oh it was a lovely bath." That is, until he realized that the room he was in faced the centre of town with huge windows and had no window coverings. "I was practically in the middle of town." But by that point he didn't care. It was just nice to have a hot bath after a job well done.[8]

The First Cat Trains from Grimshaw to Hay River

The Yellowknife Transportation Company's three tractor trains left Grimshaw on March 9, 1939, starting out along the cleared trail between Grimshaw and the Third Battle. They had one tractor equipped with a brush cutter bolted to the tractor. It was like a big snowplow, and on the bottom was a flat cutter, shaped in a "V".

"The trail that was cut from Grimshaw to there was cut for horses and sleighs used by farmers. The depth of their rollers across the front of their sleigh was close to 10 to 12 inches [25-30 cm], which could go over the stumps," said Harcourt. "On our logging

The Alberta government brush cutter arrives at North Star to begin clearing the winter road north to Upper Hay River Post, 1938. When the brush cutter broke apart at Paddle Prairie, Ed Dillman of North Star welded it together, using his acetylene torch. Ed Dillman collection.

sleighs the rollers were down to 4 inches [10 cm]. Any stumps that were cut would just break our rollers as we went through. So, in quite a few places where there had been an established road, we weren't able to use it. We had to make our own way."[9]

Each of the three trains consisted of a tractor pulling five sleighs, with a sleeping caboose at the back of two trains and the cookshack at the end of the third. A sleigh on each of the trains carried enough diesel fuel in barrels to run from Grimshaw to Yellowknife. "That's what we had to have, because there was no refueling stop," Earle explained with a laugh. The empty barrels were carried along rather than discarded, as these could be sold back to Imperial Oil. "Barrels at that time in the Northwest Territories were legal tender. That's how all the oil had to be moved. I say it's legal tender because Imperial Oil accepted them. Each barrel was worth eight dollars." The rest of the sleighs hauled the mining machinery and other supplies.

All three partners – Earle Harcourt, Bert Nieland, and Stu McLeod – were along on the first trip. Harcourt rode on the third tractor most of the time. Several young men in the North Peace were part of the crew of that first cat train – Buck McFadden and Alex Morrison were among them.

"The men were all young, all single. At that time there was no work outside, and you had your pick of who you wanted. Our cook, for instance, was Russ Way. He just turned up one day and said, 'I'm going with you.' I said, 'The hell you are. We have a

Earle Harcourt, manager of the Yellowknife Transportation Company, on the first cat train over the winter road. Spring, 1939. Earle Harcourt collection.

crew.' Russ replied, 'Yeah, but I'm a better man than some of those. I'm going with you anyway.'"

So Russ Way hired himself on as the cook for the crew, and he became a real morale builder. As cook, he had to make meals on the go, as the men worked in shifts of six hours on and six hours off. There was no time to stop the trains and have the crew eat all together. The cookshack was equipped with a long table and benches on each side. At the front end was the cookstove. Harcourt recalls,

"I can remember that stove. We were going over some really rough stuff with it. The sleigh runners were down and back and forth. Russ was cooking a roast in the oven. The oven door flew open, the roast flew out and went the length of the caboose, skidding on the floor – and Russ hard after it. He grabbed it, threw it back into the pan and popped it back into the oven. It had a few splinters in it and a little snow and mud, but it tasted just fine."

Each individual tractor train was sometimes called a "swing." The operation and organization of tractor trains followed the standard pattern of the day. Like a ship at sea, they had to be completely self-contained and self-sufficient. And like the captain of a ship, the "swing boss" commanded the train and bore the responsibilities of anything that happened. There were also the catskinners and brakemen. The catskinners drove the tractors and the brakemen, sometimes called "brakies" or "swampers," did all the odd jobs like uncoupling the sleighs, or braking the swing. The brakeman was usually an apprentice position for those starting out with a cat train. Some companies operating cat trains had an engineer who accompanied the trains, and was responsible for all repairs to the tractor in case of breakdowns.

After the swing boss, the cook was probably the key person on any cat train. He was responsible for the men's morale and was hygiene officer, making sure the men kept the sleeping cabooses and cookhouse clean.[10]

Catskinners had the toughest, most dangerous job, and it required the most experience, not only with tractors but also with being able to read the conditions of the trail or the ice on lakes and rivers. It was also the coldest job, as these robust men were

"Going over humpy muskeg north of Upper Hay River Post." First cat train to Yellowknife. Note the empty oil barrels, which were kept and returned to Imperial Oil for $8.00 a barrel. Oil barrels were an important medium of exchange in the North in 1939. Earle Harcourt collection.

"Which way do we go?" Bert Nieland and Earle Harcourt on top of YTCL's brush cutter. First cat train to Yellowknife. Earle Harcourt collection.

anchored to the metal tractor seat for six hours. By the end of the shift they could hardly get off the tractor without help. They were also in imminent danger when crossing frozen rivers and lakes. If the ice broke through, they had a split second to abandon the tractor or risk going down with it. Several deaths from drowning occurred on the big northern lakes when the drivers weren't able to jump in time and were pulled down through the ice. During the three years that the YTCL ran tractor trains, no one drowned, and no tractor broke through the ice. Harcourt explained:

> *"We formed our own criteria as to how much ice you required for the operation of the train. It was quite a simple little recipe. You had to have 16 inches [40 cm] of solid ice and an inch per ton of the weight of your tractor. We never lost a unit. To the point where the insurance companies insured the cat trains coming after us, providing they followed our trails."*

Travelling 24 hours a day meant that one also had to sleep on the move. According to Harcourt, the winter road was "rougher than a cob. You had to get worn to a frazzle before you could sleep. The sleighs, with nine-foot [3m] runners on them, would run across a log and then drop. And you, of course, would drop with it." The sleighs were hooked together so there was slack between each sleigh.

> *"We used what we called bunting poles that held the sleighs apart so that they wouldn't run into each other. They were fastened with cables. We'd hook them all up, so that there was sufficient slack, so that the load in the next sleigh would have about a two-foot run before it would come – then wham!"*

Before the tractor trains reached Hay River, they caught up and passed the government crew clearing the bush. The government's brush cutter had broken down. Later, the YTCL's own brush cutter also fell apart, just as they reached the shore of Great Slave Lake, but it had done the job of getting them there.

From the south end of the lake they headed east along the lake ice to Fort Resolution, where YTCL's boats and barges were dry-docked. That, of course, was not the shortest route to Yellowknife, but the safest. The direct route was due north from Hay River straight across 128 miles [206 km] of ice. Great Slave Lake was really an inland sea, and subject to blizzards and white-outs. The safer but longer way was to cross the east arm. The three tractor trains arrived in Yellowknife on April 12, a little over a month after they left Grimshaw. The following day, the Edmonton *Journal* recorded the historic event:

> *"The tractor haul from Grimshaw to Yellowknife over the new road route is believed to be the longest of its kind in the Dominion....They are the first to complete a journey to Yellowknife from farther south than Fort Resolution, on the south shore of Great Slave....Successful completion of the trip signifies the beginning of a new phase in transportation between the outside and northern mining communities."*[11]

Yellowknife Transportation Company's tractor trains no sooner arrived in Yellowknife when the company got a job from Consolidated Mines and Smelting to haul out some big compressor engines that were required at a mine in B.C.

"This was getting to the point where it was a war effort. They told us they wanted them out, and they didn't give a damn how we got them out. So, we put a train together after this one got in, and sent it south. Bert Nieland went with it. They got as far as High Level and they just bogged right down. The country melted out from underneath them. And their runners were cutting right through the muskeg and piling up on the bunks. The single tractor hauling one sleigh, that's all they had.

"So Bert, being very ingenious, went into Fort Vermilion, and he hired 28 teams of horses. He took 'em out, hooked the whole bloody works up in front of the tractor and brought the sleigh into Fort Vermilion. By then it was open water on the Peace River, and they shipped the compressor out from there to the railway at Peace River town.[12]

On another trip, Bert Nieland had an ingenious idea for a backhaul. He was originally from Holland, where his father had been a butcher; so he knew quite a lot about cattle and butchering them. When they got to High Level, Nieland took one sleigh that they had emptied of fuel oil, and one tractor.

"He beetled into Fort Vermilion. At the time, Fort Vermilion had cattle in that area that were all grain-fed. It didn't pay the people to ship their grain out, because the only access they had was by Peace River in the summer. They fed their grain to the cattle and drove them on out.... But doing that cost them a lot of money. So Bert bought the cattle – a whole bloody sleigh-load of them – and butchered them. I don't know what it was, eight or nine tons. It was still freezing enough at night to look after that.

Bert Nieland, c. 1940s. Vern Estabrook collection.

"Then he took the meat into Yellowknife to sell it. At that time all the meat they had in Yellowknife was flown in. That was the only way they could get in there. It was a dollar a pound on air freight, and then the cost went up from there. So, we were able to sell our meat for over 85 cents a pound, and still double our money. The second year, though, we met with resistance. The RCMP came and told us that we couldn't do anything with this meat because it wasn't government inspected. So, we went and made application and agreed to fly a man from Edmonton into Fort Vermilion to inspect the meat for us. Then the government told us to go fly a hoop. If we wanted to buy meat, buy it from Fletchers or Burns [in Edmonton].

"We disregarded that. We bought the meat and took it into Yellowknife, and we sold as much as we could. We filled the market. Then the RCMP came down and said we had to do something about the meat because it would be seized by the next day if we still had it. What meat we had left we sold that night. The RCMP had warned us, they were friends. They didn't believe in it either, because the real losers were the people of Yellowknife. They still had to pay up to two dollars a pound for meat flown in."

First Truck on the Winter Road

The first recorded incidence of a truck over the winter road was a 2-ton Fargo driven by L.A. "Louie" Alexander and his helper "Babe" Feldman, of Flin Flon, Manitoba. On March 20, 1939, the Edmonton *Journal* published the following story:

"Expecting to reach Yellowknife by truck before spring breakup, L.A. Alexander of Flin Flon left here over the week-end for the northern mining centre. He drove a new 2-ton truck, with a load of about five tons, including a caboose on a sleigh and other equipment.[13] The truck is equipped with snow plows for each wheel. `Babe' Feldman, also of Flin Flon, is accompanying Alexander. They will follow the trail of the tractor train and when Yellowknife is reached the truck will be used for winter hauling."[14]

Babe's wife, Edith Feldman of Atlin, B.C., wrote the following story titled "Cat Train North":

"C.C. (Chummie) Plummer, Babe's uncle, was in the process of building a gambling casino on the rock in 'Old Town' and Louie agreed to try to take a truck from Edmonton to Yellowknife. They were to follow the Yellowknife Transportation Co.'s Cat Train from Grimshaw, Alberta, with freight for Mr. Plummer. It was decided that Babe would go along with Louie...to do his share of driving the truck and all the other odd jobs that were necessary to get the whole outfit to its destination before the ice went out of Great Slave Lake. ...[They] had help from the cat skinners to get them over the bad places and to let them down the steep river hills safely."[15]

The Edmonton *Journal* article, dated April 13th, followed the progress of the second truck, which was driven by Charles Hansen.

"Second haul over the new road, construction of which is nearing completion, now is in progress...It is being made by Charles Hansen, Fort Simpson trader, with a sin-

First truck over the Grimshaw-Hay River winter road. Louis Alexander and Babe Feldman followed YTCL's cat train in Alexander's 2-ton Fargo. This shows Louis Alexander and the Fargo near Great Slave Lake. Babe Feldman probably took the photograph. Edith (Feldman) Nelson collection.

gle, small train. He left Grimshaw southern terminus last weekend. His destination is Providence post in the west arm of Great Slave."

"Making the trip as assistant with Mr. Hansen is Lorne Binnie, America-wide hitchhiker, who recently returned to Edmonton after touring 7000 miles [11 200 km] through the U.S. in 17 days. Now he's going north to boost his travel total by tractor, instead of the usual car."

The Edmonton *Journal*, April 14th, relates that

"...The truck which left here some time later is also thought to be traversing the distance between the shores of the lake and Yellowknife. When last reported a week ago, it was at Indian Cabins, only about 30 miles [48 km] from the lake."[16]

The *Journal* did not follow the progress of this second truck after Indian Cabins, so there is no documentation of them having arrived at Fort Providence.

The above documentation appears to set the record straight, that the Fargo truck on the North Road was driven by Alexander and Feldman and the Hansen truck was the second.

Babe Feldman worked for the Yellowknife Transportation Company on subsequent trips by cat train. Edith recalls Babe telling her about life on the cat train. "I remember

Babe telling about when they were on the cat trains. The first one up in the morning got the best socks. Everybody took their socks off to dry them around the fire. Usually Earle was left with the worst pair."

Truck Convoy on the Winter Road

The North Road was maintained and upgraded the following winter season, allowing trucks as well as cat trains to haul over the road.

Vern Estabrook of Grimshaw started working for Bert Nieland in March of 1941; he was a pioneer in his own right, and would later form his own company, Estabrook Construction, which specialized in northern road construction. In *Tales of the Mackenzie Highway*, Estabrook describes the problems early truckers encountered trying to pull freight on the winter road, and the extraordinary know-how and self-sufficiency of the men who worked in the North.[17]

"One of my early ventures was being hired by Bert Nieland to assist freight trucks to follow the winter cat trail into Hay River. The small gas powered Cat [we had] was a 2-ton Caterpillar with no dozer blade that we used for farming, and hoped it would be useful to help trucks up the hills and through rough muskeg. This was in mid-March of 1941, and we slept in the open, with the help of a good Woods sleeping bag. Cooking was done over an open camp fire, it sure was no picnic. Many weeks later we finally reached Lower Hay River Post with the Cat and small sleigh, but the trucks were in such poor condition they abandoned their freight near the Louise Falls on the Hay River, and returned south.

"Bert Nieland brought a cat train back from Yellowknife, and left most of the sleigh camp on the ice at the mouth of the Hay River. He had a TS-40 International cat and freight sleighs, which he continued south with to pick up the abandoned truck freight. They ran out of luck, [and] ran the TS-40 in a swamp hole. They managed to get it out but it was no longer fit to run. Nieland made his way on foot back to Hay River. He had to swim the west channel of the Hay River to reach Jack Cameron's. Jack owned a freighter canoe and kicker, which Bert hired to go upriver to pick up the balance of the crew near Louise Falls. They were hungry, wet, and dog tired when we found them under a spruce tree, too far gone to stand up.[18]

"Our next problem was to get our small Cat off the island and onto the north side of the Hay River, where the sleigh camp was now sitting on the main ice of Great Slave Lake. They found another freighter canoe, and some ice bridging timbers to set on top of the two canoes, run the small Cat on top and ferry the entirety across the main channel of the Hay River.

"All this went well, and we proceeded across the lake ice to Fort Resolution, where the YTCL had a dry dock on the Wagle Channel, with a tug and barges there, stored for the winter. When the tug and barges were shipshape, we proceeded up the Slave

River to Fort Smith. The Cat was off-loaded at Fort Smith and I caught a float plane to Peace River and back to work.

"This was the first of several winters I spent on the Mackenzie Highway and further north, but the first trip was the most memorable, without doubt."[19]

Yellowknife Transportation Company ran cat trains on the winter road for three winters. Having enough fuel along on these trips posed a problem. Andy Ressler from North Star recalled being on the crew of the cat train during the winter of 1940.[20]

"In the winter of 1940 a cat train comprised of three small tractors and 10 sleighs went to Yellowknife. After it left Peace River [Grimshaw] the cat train stopped at North Star to pick up Art Simpson, Edward Wallisser, Dan Landry, John Reed, Sid Ressler, and me for part of the crew.

"It took 49 days and nights to reach Yellowknife. We travelled on Great Slave Lake for 14 days and nights with temperatures of -66° Fahrenheit [-54°C].

"When we reached High Level crossing (High Level) we left four sleighs behind because towing them we wouldn't have enough fuel to reach Hay River. When we arrived in Hay River we got more fuel and went back to get the sleighs. The round trip took 16 days and nights and when we arrived in Hay River we got more fuel and finally reached Yellowknife. On the trip we broke 14 sleigh runners and bunks which had to be replaced by those fashioned from spruce logs."

By the end of the Second World War, the days of using cat trains exclusively for hauling freight over the winter road came to an end, as trucks replaced them. The last cat train over the winter road was hauled by the Sheck Brothers the winter of 1946-47. The Mackenzie Highway was near completion and trucks could haul freight much cheaper and faster than cat trains.

Notes

[1] Interview with Earle Harcourt, Edmonton, July 15, 1998.

[2] Alberta Transportation, "Grimshaw-Slave Lake Highway," c1949. This report was written sometime after the completion of the Mackenzie Highway, but no date appears on the copy.

[3] David A. Harrison, "The First Winter Road Ever," *Up Here*, March/April 1990.

[4] Interview with Frank Blakley, Calgary, October 12, 1999.

[5] Cornelia Lehn, *The Homemade Brass Plate*, p. 188-89. This is a fascinating story told by Dr. Mary Percy Jackson to Ms. Lehn, and published in 1994 by Dr. Jackson's daughter, Anne Vos. As far as I know, the book is now out of print, and so are two books of Anne's father, Frank Jackson – *Candle in the Grub Box* and *Jam in the Bedroll*. The three books present a view of life in northern Alberta that are unique. Dr. Mary Percy Jackson came to northern Alberta from England to Notikewin in 1929 to provide medical services in Battle River Prairie. The following year she married Frank Jackson, a fur trader and rancher from Keg River.

[6] Interview with Dave Jenkins, Didsbury, October 28, 1998.

[7] Interview with Stan Smith, High Level, August 20, 1998.

[8] Ceilidh McClurg, "It was a tough job, but somebody had to do it," The Didsbury *Review*, July 15, 1998.

[9] Harcourt interview, July 15, 1998.

[10] Svein Sigfusson, *Sigfusson's Roads*, Winnipeg: Watson & Dwyer Publishing Ltd., 1992, pp. 4-5.

[11] "North Tractor Hauls Ended on New Road," Edmonton *Journal*, April 13, 1939.

[12] Bert Nieland was known and well respected by many people in the North. Harcourt and Nieland continued to work together for many years. Earle Harcourt remembers that they had a very fine working relationship. "Bert was just a bit more of a loner than I was. It got to the point where Bert loved to go down the river with a load of freight, stop off with the trappers, sit on the bank, gossip, and enjoy himself. Maybe lose a couple of days – so what? We never fought or got abrasive, or anything like that. It got to the point where he no longer was enjoying himself and wanted out. He asked me to buy him out and I did. This must have been about the 50s. He made a deal with a trapper, and they were going to open a place in Yellowknife. This again was with a tractor train. Bert brought a tractor train from Grimshaw and was crossing the ice straight from Hay River directly across (128 miles [206 km] of lake ice) to Yellowknife. He ran out of fuel. He must have thought he was just a few miles, just out of sight of shore. He didn't even hesitate. He just grabbed an axe and started to walk. Turns out he was over 30 miles [48 km] off shore. He disappeared." His body was never found. Even today, the mystery surrounding Bert Nieland's death on Great Slave Lake continues to haunt many of the oldtimers who knew and worked with him.

[13] Edith (Feldman) Nelson said, in a telephone conversation with her on January 18, 2000, that the truck was pulling a sleigh, but there was no caboose on it.

[14] Edmonton *Journal*, March 20, 1939. My thanks to Dr. David A. Harrison for providing me with newspaper articles and correspondence from Edith Feldman to *Up Here*, a magazine published in Yellowknife. Previously it was thought that the first truck that followed in the wake of the first cat train was driven by Charles Hansen of Flin Flon, accompanied by the first "hitchhiker," Lorne Binnie. That was actually the second truck.

[15] Edith Feldman, "Cat Train North," sent to *Up Here* with a cover letter dated May 4, 1990.

[16] In Dr. Harrison's letter to Edith Nelson, dated September 9, 1990, he wrote, "Whether the Charles Hansen party reached its destination I do not know. The journal of the St. Peter's Anglican Mission in Hay River for April 24, 1939, simply states 'Man on tractor on way to Fort Simpson walked into Fort today.'" So herein lies a mystery. Did the second truck ever reach Fort Providence?

[17] Bernice Lorenzen, editor, *Tales of the Mackenzie Highway*, 50th anniversary collector's edition, privately published in Grimshaw, Alberta, 1998.

[18] In *Land of Hope and Dreams*, p. 622, Vern Estabrook wrote further about the condition of these truckers: "…the food that some wolfed down was thrown up promptly. However, next day they were all back in shape again."

[19] *Tales of the Mackenzie Highway*, p. 10.

[20] From *Saga of Battle River – We Came, We Stayed*, p. 39.

🚙 Chapter 3 – Canol 6 Road 🚚

Three Wartime Construction Projects

The 10-foot-wide winter road for cat trains, brushed out in 1939, was one of two forerunners of the Mackenzie Highway. The other was a winter road built by the American Army during the Second World War. Referred to as Canol 6, this winter road followed much the same course as the cat train route between Grimshaw and Hay River. Of the three wartime projects – the Northwest Staging Route, the Alaska Highway, and the Canol Project – the Canol had the most profound effect upon the North Peace and the Northwest Territories. It had as much impact on this region as the Alaska Highway had on northern British Columbia and the Yukon. Had it not been for the Canol 6 spur road, the building of the Mackenzie Highway may have been delayed for many years. The argument could be made that it might have never been built at all.[1]

Following the bombing of Pearl Harbor by the Japanese on December 7, 1941, the United States feared that Alaska would be vulnerable to attack and a possible point through which the Japanese would invade North America. The fear was a legitimate one at the time, as the Japanese had invaded the western part of the Aleutian Islands. The United States and Canada signed the Ogdensburg Agreement, which opened the way for collaboration between the two countries for defense of the Northwest. A Permanent Joint Board of Defense (PJBD), made up of five members from each country, was set up to facilitate this wartime collaboration.

The Grimshaw winter road had been considered early in the Second World War as a possible route to build the Alaska Highway. Known as Route D, this was the route that Viljammar Stefansson, the famous Arctic explorer and writer, had recommended to the U.S. as the route for the highway to Alaska. Alberta's Minister of Highways, W.A. Fallow, had gone to Washington D.C. to lobby for the Grimshaw route as early as 1939. Eventually the Grimshaw road and the other routes were bypassed in favor of Route C, from Dawson Creek, B.C., through northern British Columbia, the Yukon, and interior Alaska, largely because this route linked up with the air bases that had been built for the Northwest Staging Route, and thus could provide overland support to the airbases.

The Canol Project

Of the three northern wartime construction projects, the Canol Project is the least known and it has been eclipsed, from the standpoint of historical documentation, by both the Northwest Staging Route and the Alaska Highway. The overall purpose of the Canol Project was to make northwestern North America self-sufficient in petroleum.

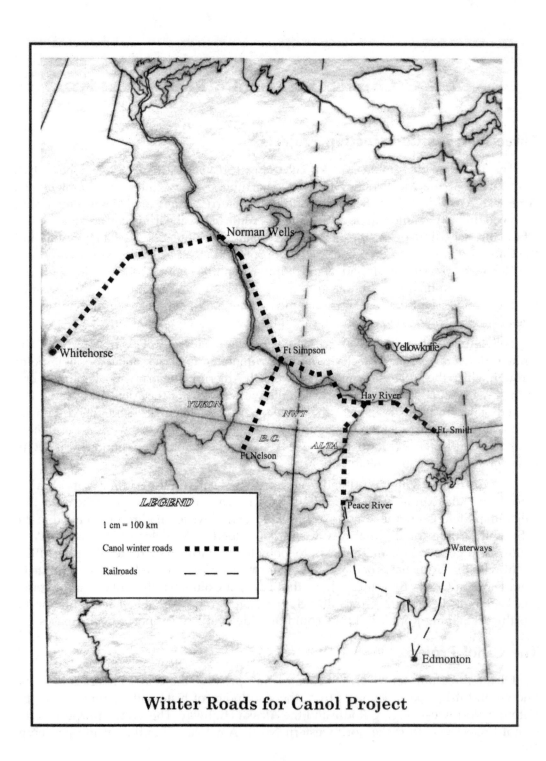

Winter Roads for Canol Project

Again, the fear by both the U.S. and Canadian governments was that ocean transport of petroleum in tankers along the northwest Pacific coast would be too vulnerable to attacks by the Japanese. The construction of a pipeline from Norman Wells, NWT, to a refinery in Whitehorse, Yukon, would provide a safe and continuous supply of fuel to Alaska.

The Canol Project was also the most complex and versatile of the three wartime construction projects. It involved not only building pipelines and a refinery, but also building access roads, airports, and landing strips to transport personnel and equipment. It also required an infrastructure that included warehouses, loading docks and facilities, housing and maintenance buildings, and barges to ship the thousands of tons of cargo from the end-of-steel at Waterways and down the Mackenzie River system to Norman Wells.

In 1942, the U.S. government entered into an agreement with Imperial Oil to drill new wells in addition to the nine wells that were already producing at Norman Wells. The Army Corps of Engineers contracted Bechtel, Price, and Callaghan (BPC), a consortium of nine American companies, known as the "Constructor," to manage the project. On May 28, 1942, an advance guard from the Corps of Engineers, officials from BPC, and the architect engineer arrived at Edmonton, which was to be the headquarters of the Canol Project. "2500 engineer troops, with hundreds of tons of equipment, were now pouring through Edmonton. They were sent over the Northern Alberta Railways 450 km [280 mi.] to Waterways, the end of steel and the starting point for the 1100-mile [1770 km] water trek to Norman Wells."2

The original plan was for the American army to do all the hauling of equipment, which was estimated at 50 000 tons. But, as time was critical, both the Hudson's Bay Company and Northern Transportation Company (a subsidiary of Eldorado Gold Mines) were enlisted to haul equipment on their boats and barges. A surplus refinery in Corpus Christi, Texas, was dismantled and shipped to Norman Wells. The Army and BPC also brought in diesel-powered tugs from the Mississippi River system and built wooden barges, and later steel barges, at Waterways.

In the meantime, BPC was hiring men and women civilians in the U.S. who would work as carpenters, welders, pipefitters, office workers, and innumerable other jobs. The "Constructor" put up a sign warning potential employees about working and living in the North:

The American Army and BPC constructed military and civilian camps at Waterways, Fort Smith, Fort Fitzgerald, the Slave River delta, Fort Resolution, Lower Hay River Post, Wrigley Harbor, Fort Providence, Fort Simpson, Fort Wrigley, and Norman Wells – and later, a base camp at Peace River, and auxiliary camps at Meikle River, Paddle Prairie, Upper Hay River (Meander River), and Alexandra Falls.[4] Across the Mackenzie River from Norman Wells, Camp Canol was constructed as the starting point for the Canol Road and the pipeline, which would run along the surface for hundreds of miles, over muskegs and steep, mountainous terrain that required 10 pumping stations to pump the oil through the four-inch [10 cm] pipes over a maximum elevation of 1384 meters [5860 ft] to Whitehorse. Other pipelines were built in 1942-43, from Whitehorse to Skagway, Whitehorse to Fairbanks, and from Carcross to Watson Lake. In total, almost 1000 miles [1600 km] of pipeline were constructed.[5]

Why the Canol 6 Road was Built

The Canol Project got off to a precarious start. At the end of the summer of 1942 there were many tons of equipment and supplies still waiting to be shipped, but freeze-up had put an end to river transportation out of Waterways. Some effort was made to transport freight by air, using commercial airlines and some of BPC's own planes. However, the ski and float planes could only carry mail express, personnel, and smaller freight. Another snag was that there were no airports or landing strips in the Northwest Territories, as the bush planes used the river and lakes as their runways. Wheeled aircraft were out of luck. Thus, the BPC had to build a string of airfields and landing strips. In all, 10 fields were built between Edmonton and Norman Wells.

Air transportation, however, could not handle the heavier freight. The only viable transportation method was to use cat trains and trucks over the winter road from Grimshaw. But the trail, as it existed, was unfit to accommodate the large 6 X 6 Army trucks and the volume of freight that would have to be hauled over the road. In the winter of 1942-43, the Army sent three companies of the 90th Engineers, assisted by a company from the all-black 388th Engineer Battalion, to improve the old winter cat trail.

Another group of civilians hired by BPC would blaze out a new winter trail from Hay River to Norman Wells, crossing the Mackenzie River at Mills Lake.

"Meanwhile, all cargo still at Waterways after freeze-up would be sent 600 miles [965 km] *by rail via Edmonton to Peace River. From there it would head north on trac-tor-drawn sledge trains close behind BPC's trailblazers. As is usual with simple con-cepts, the headaches came in the details, which in this case included building a new camp for 800 troops at Peace River and attempting to move 19 000 tons of cargo more than 1600 miles* [2574 km] *by rail and tractor train in subzero weather."*[6]

The Invasion of Peace River

In *Peace River Remembers*, Fred Fox described the sudden arrival of the U.S. Army troops to Peace River:

"Early in October, 1942, on a Sunday morning around 8:00 a.m., a long mysteri-ous looking train wound down the Judah Hill into the town of Peace River. It consist-ed of about 40 United States Pullman type cars and train load upon train load of mil-itary material, including tractors, trucks, caterpillars, etc. As was the tradition in small towns, many people turned out at the station to satisfy their curiosity. About 800 colored troops of the United States 388th Engineer Battalion were on board. On seeing so many children at the station, they invited them aboard the train for break-fast."[7]

Until December, some 5000 American soldiers and civilians had to live in tents, real-ly double tents, one inside the other for warmth. The black troops were from the Deep South and poorly equipped in clothing and experience to withstand the bitter cold. Their suffering must have been acute. A camp was built on the west bank of the river, across from Peace River town, on an area called Jackpine Flats. Fred Fox describes this make-shift camp as a small city in itself.

"The military cleaned out every sawmill for miles around gathering lumber. It was a great day for the lumbermen. The military hired anyone that wanted to work and many were put on payroll as carpenters. Some of these carpenters would bring their old dull saws and get these sharpened, then take them home and come back the next morning with their neighbor's saw. There never were so many sharp saws in this coun-try, thanks to the good saw files in the camp."

The town of Peace River had very little advance warning of the arrival of the U.S. army troops, which were racially segregated. Fox wrote:

"For the first few weeks the troops of only one color would be allowed out. For awhile the Negroes were only allowed to cross over to town when on duty, such as driving a truck and helping catskinners....Gradually they found they were able to let both white and colored troops out on the same night without any serious incidents occurring. The colored troops were surprised to find no discrimination in the cafés, the-atres, or beverage rooms."[8]

This relatively peaceful invasion had changed the town overnight. The army rented Athabasca Hall to use as a post office and administrative offices. It was also used as a dance hall. The army held dances and invited the local population. Fox stated that "As a result of this interaction between the local residents and the soldiers, about five per cent of the Battalion [50 of 1000 men] married girls from the area."

The beer parlors in town did a booming business as well. "Even though liquor was rationed, everyone over 21 had a permit and got their full quota each month, which consisted of two cases of beer, one bottle of wine, and one bottle of spirits. This became a major form of currency. For a 26 oz. [760 ml] bottle of whiskey one could secure a 100 pound [45 kg] sack of sugar."[9]

Truck Hauling in Wartime

In order to get trucks to Norman Wells, the winter road between the Third Battle and Lower Hay River Post was brushed out and widened. From Norman Wells another spur road was built on the east side of the Mackenzie River to the army camp at Mills Lake, to link up with the Canol 6 road. Tractor train convoys, and later trucks, began to roll steadily on this road to Norman Wells. American and Canadian civilians destined to work on the Canol pipeline and new oil wells at Norman Wells, were also drivers on the truck convoys in army trucks along Canol 6. Civilian trucks fell in line. Bergman's of Calgary was the first civilian trucking company to run two semi-trailers over the Canol 6 road in the winter of 1942-43. The trailers were pulled by DS-40 and DS-50 Internationals. One of the drivers was Jack Parnell, who made his home in Hay River for many years.[10]

Part of the equipment going to the Canol pipeline, by way of the Grimshaw-Hay River road, 1944. Left to right: Hilda Reinders, Wallace Bye, and Mickey Reinders, sitting on a "kitten" in front of Mac's Store, Dixonville. Hilda (Reinders) Ressler collection.

Hilda (née Reinders) Ressler, of Manning, was a teenager at the time the trucks started coming through in the winter of 1943-1944. "All this traffic was a great boost to the economy, and I would say it was the first time any great amount of work was done on the Mackenzie Highway."[11]

Vern Estabrook on the Canol Project

Vern Estabrook from Grimshaw was hired by Bechtel, Price, and Callahan in December 1942. He worked as a tractor operator on a number of winter roads out of Lower Hay River, NWT. His letters to his father, Ernest Estabrook, give many insights into the work that was going on in the North on the Canol Project. Vern was probably living at Camp No. 4 much of the time, as his father had posted a letter there on January 7, 1943. In a letter posted from Lower Hay River, NWT, and dated January, 9, 1943, he wrote his father:[12]

"We're camped about 12 miles [19 km] from the lake right now. This is supposed to be as far north as we go this time, going to work the road back as far as Upper Hay again and back to Lower Hay.

"They just brought up a new rooter; sort of a frost breaking tool and they figure they can cut down a lot of bad hills between here and Upper Hay with it. If we hadn't started working back on the road [we were] supposed to start cutting out a new road toward Fort Smith. We'll likely go on that when we get back to here...There don't seem much chance of me getting out for quite a while yet. It's about 400 miles [643 km] into Peace River from here, that makes it at least a 5 day round trip, and they don't want to be without a truck around camp for that long. There sure isn't much in the way of hard work to the job I've got – haul the men in from work at meal times, haul fuel oil and gas and ice for water...."

In the same letter he mentioned that his time was cut down to 12 hours a day and Vern figured that he would earn about $60 U.S. a week – good wages at that time. By January 23, from Upper Hay River, he wrote to his dad that the temperature was very cold, -60° F [-50° C]. "I suppose this cold snap hit down there too, wish it would let up a bit, truck gets so stiff it won't hardly steer and brakes sure get stiff."

By the next month Vern was working on the winter road between Mills Lake and Norman Wells. In a letter to his father, posted from Lower Hay River, NWT, on February 7, 1943, he wrote: "We got a wire yesterday to start north for Mills Lake and work north from there, will go about 175 miles [280 km] further north from here. We're supposed to get $1.25 [U.S. dollars] when we get north of Mills Lake..." By the next day, plans were changed, and he was working on a road east from Lower Hay River towards Fort Smith. In his letter dated January 8th he wrote:

"The superintendent came along and told us to work a road through to Smith, so we're about 10 miles [16 km] in, east of Lower Hay tonite. Don't figure on going all the way to Smith. It's supposed to be about 190 miles [305 km] but we only go 100 [160 km]

Vern Estabrook collection – photos from the Canol project, 1942-43.

Right: THIS IS NO PICNIC.

Directly below: Dozer foundered in muskeg.

Directly above: U.S. Army camp at Lower Hay River.

Left: A "Traxcavator" front end loader used on Canol project.

and come back and then start for Mills Lake again, as far as we know. We'll be close to 2 weeks before we get back to the lake again we figure. They just want the road put in passable shape to bring about 50 trucks through from Smith to haul freight."

On March 9, 1943, Vern posted a letter to his father from Norman Wells.[13]

"Dear Dad, Sorry about not being able to write for so long, was figuring on wiring but seems I can't do that either. Outfit got in late last night are at a company camp here on the west bank of the Mackenzie, pretty fair sized camp. Sure plenty of planes going through here, six of them stayed here last night. No trouble at all getting out at least to Edmonton so I'll be sure of getting out O.K. Pay is $1.20 an hour but I hear they want to cut a man down to 9½-10 hours at this camp; if they do, I'll try getting out with some road crew as quick as I can. This outfit is supposed to stay here for about 2 weeks repairing cats and equipment, then they don't know what.

"They've got quite a start on the pipeline road but I don't know how far, figure we'll go out on it. Think I'll go see if I can find some sort of post office and see if I got any mail of cheques....Sure a windy day out, camp is in a sandy place and wind sure moved it around, haven't much of an outfit here – about 15 cats and a few trucks, bunch of army boats and Hudson's Bay boats froze in here. Sure a big river when it gets down this far.

"Well, seems to be about all for now, will write soon, probably when mail gets in.

"Your loving son, Vernon"

During that winter on the Canol Project, Vern took a number of rolls of photographs that show vividly the difficult terrain he worked in, the construction equipment, trucks, camps, and the living conditions.

Canol Project – A Boon to Northern Truckers

The Canol 6 road was heavily travelled for two years and many a local trucker in the North got his start hauling for the American army. In the winter of 1942-43, John King was in his teens when he made his first trip north in a flat bed Dodge truck his father had bought. John and his brother Don were the drivers. "With neither one having any experience at all we had some mighty interesting experiences learning to drive on the longest, roughest, coldest bush road in Western Canada."[14] Fred Lorenzen also got his start in trucking, driving the same winter, for Bechtel, Price, and Callahan. He drove a 1939 2-ton Ford owned by John Myshyniuk of North Star. Hank Thompson and Henry Erickson, both seasoned truckers over the winter road, hauled almost steadily during the war years. Erickson had three trucks, a 1937 Ford, a 1939 Fargo, and a 1942 Fargo, when he hauled for the American Army in the winter of 1943-44.[15] Tony Tretick, the first commercial trucker in the Fort Vermilion area, also did a lot of hauling at this time.

Local people not working for BPC were discouraged from using the road. Anne Vos of Keg River remarks, "It was made clear to us locals that we were not welcome to use it, but we used it anyway."[16]

Effect of Canol Project on Native People

While the Canol Project may have been a boon to non-native people, it was particularly disruptive to aboriginal people living in northern Alberta and the Northwest Territories. Dr. Patricia McCormack described the impact of the Canol Project upon the lifestyle of the Natives living in Fort Chipewyan.[17] Her insights also apply to much of the North. She states that the spin-offs of the Canol Project to Fort Chipewyan had short-term benefits.

> *"The local transport industry could not handle the mass of material and generated a need for boats and personnel. Natives and non-natives were hired, with their boats to move the material....Women did laundry for the American troops station[ed] near Fort Chip. They could make as much as $25 per week."*

But in the long run, the Canol Project had a disruptive affect upon the traditional lifestyle of the Natives, whose means of making a living centered around trapping, fishing, and subsistence hunting. Amelia Gratix from Fort Smith described this sudden invasion:

> *"We were very shocked to find ourselves one day with a whole army descended on us. We were unprepared. Our way of life changed drastically. The disruption of people's lives lasts forever."*[18]

> *"Far from benefiting, Native peoples were usually hurt by post-war northern economic growth [in] the attempt to impose a southern-directed 'modern' way of life....While Natives sought employment...they were rarely if ever hired in a position that paid a 'living wage,' one that would have enabled them to abandon bush productive activities."*[19]

Totaling up the Bill

The Canol Project (including the pipeline, road, access roads, and telephone line) was started in October 1942 and completed by March 1943, an incredible feat that was accomplished in six months! The final bill for the Canol Project was $135 million, which the Dominion government kindly let the United States government pay for in exchange for allowing the Army to invade the North. Within a few months after the completion of construction, the danger to ocean transport had greatly lessened. The Japanese had been driven from the Aleutian Islands by July and August of 1943.

> *"In September 1943, the Joint Chiefs of Staff abandoned any plans for using Alaska as a major base for an assault on Japan in view of the successes of the naval and island hopping campaigns in the mid-Pacific sector. These developments greatly*

reduced the need for the Canol, airway, and highway enterprises. The Canol Project, which had barely got under way by 1943, was drastically curtailed. By the time oil from Norman Wells began arriving in Whitehorse in April 1944, supplies were far easier to procure by tanker from outside....At the end of 1945, when fewer than four tanker-loads of petroleum had been delivered from Norman Wells, the pumping stations and refinery units began to be closed down. From a military standpoint, the $135 million spent on Canol was almost an utter waste." [20]

The dismantling of the Canol Project went on for years following the war. The Dominion government had no interest in taking over the Canol infrastructure. Most of the tugs and other water facilities that had been brought in from the Mississippi system were removed by 1945 by Marine Operators, one of the subcontractors. Later, the same company purchased the Whitehorse refinery, and had it dismantled and shipped to Edmonton, where it was installed to service the oil from Leduc wells. Imperial Oil later purchased the refinery for $1 000 000. [21] Then there were all those miles and miles of pipeline. One section between Norman Wells and Johnson's Crossing was sold for scrap to a U.S. company, and the pipe was taken up and shipped to Skagway, or up the Mackenzie River system to Fort McMurray. The Canol roads quickly fell into disuse and decay. Today the Canol 1 Road between Camp Canol and Whitehorse is a heritage trail for hikers.

Morris Zaslow, in *The Northward Expansion of Canada*, reflected upon the legacy of the wartime projects in the North.

"By making large parts of the North far more accessible, the United States' wartime activities had brought the region's resources appreciably closer to the stage of profitable exploitation and had even gone a long way towards changing the character of the North. Post war inhabitants...could list such improvements as ...airports, landing strips, the telephone system that provided the whole region (including the Peace River district settlements) with its first telephonic connections with the outside world." [22]

The Canol Project was not a total loss militarily to the Allied Forces, however, when one considers that the transportation infrastructure in place in the North aided the shipments of uranium that ended up in Chicago for the Manhattan Project.

Eldorado Gold Mines at LaBine Point on Great Bear Lake had been closed during the early years of the war. In 1941, the Dominion government opened the silver-radium mine because of the importance to the research into the use of atomic energy by Allied powers. Before World War II, uranium was used primarily to cure some forms of cancer, and a Belgian company held practically a monopoly on the world's uranium source. At the request of C.D. Howe, Minister of Transport, Eldorado was reopened, and for two years the Dominion government financed the work of restoring the mine to operation. The mine was drained and cemented to permit the removal of ore from beneath Great Bear Lake.

Dismantling the Canol Pipeline – Harry Jones' Story

"May 10, 1949. We were hired on with Elmer Larson to go to Norman Wells and over to the Canol line to work at taking out the old pipeline that was put in to take crude oil from Imperial Oil at Norman Wells to Whitehorse. This pipeline was put in by the American Army in 1942....We were to go in and salvage this pipe and bring it to the river at the old Canol base camp across from Norman Wells. We used the equipment that was left there by the army after the project was finished.

"There were three of us that went from Hythe [Alberta], being myself, Harry Jones, [along with] Carl Lester and Leon Reauwyne, and some other men from elsewhere. We went into the old camp and found a 6 X 6 Studebaker truck that would run and had pole trailers that had been used to haul the pipe. Some of these trucks were unused, but by then they were seven years old. We used cats to pull out the pipe, about a half a mile at a time. We then cut it into 30- or 40-foot lengths [9-12m]. We loaded this onto the trailers, all by hand. We were paid $7.00 per day and our board and room, not knowing that the days were from daylight to dark. But it never got dark up there in the summer. As it turned out it was just an experience. We were never paid any wages, and board was Bully Beef and corn.

"About the middle of July we had enough of this, so the three of us walked about 35 miles [56 km] and we had to swim a couple of

This truck, with its load of pipes, jacknifed when it lost its brakes. Harry Jones collection.

the rivers. When we got to the base camp at the [Mackenzie] river, the tug boat with the barges was there, so we helped load the pipe and worked our trip back to Hay River. When we got there, the fellow that owned the tug boat asked me to stay and be the engineer on the tug, which I did. We made four complete trips to Norman Wells before freezeup in the latter part of October. By now we could only run the river [during] daylight hours, so when we would tie up to the river shore, we would leave the engine run in order to keep the tug from freezing into the ice. It would take us two days and three nights to run from Hay River to Norman Wells, downstream, but 15 days and nights to return with two 100-foot [30m] barges loaded with pipe (approx. 200 tons) we had salvaged from the Canol line.

"The tug boat that I worked on was called the *Thunder River*. Registered in Vancouver, it was powered by two 6-61 Detroit diesel engines. We would push the two barges, one in front of the other, on the river. But on the [Great Slave] lake we would have to tow them one behind the other, because of the waves on the lake. We had about 500 feet [152m] of tow line between them so they couldn't pile up on each other. These notes are being written 49 years later, so I have probably missed some things."[25]

Morris Zaslow explains the urgency of the government to expropriate Eldorado Gold Mines in 1944: "…in the midst of mysterious dealings with agents of the former Belgian monopoly and unedifying scandals that finally led the government to expropriate Eldorado Gold Mines and its properties (including Northern Transportation Company) under the War Measures Act….From Port Radium came much of the fissionable material that went into the making of the first atomic bombs and ushered in the nuclear age."[23] Thus, the Dominion government seized not only the Canadian North's supply of uranium but also controlled the shipping of uranium to the United States.

During the last years of the Second World War and during the post-war period, the Grimshaw winter road (Canol 6) became a conduit for many truckloads of pitchblende, an ore high in uranium and radium.

> "*Approximately 250 tons of uranium concentrate (pitchblende) was hauled over the winter trail to Grimshaw, Alberta, loaded in box cars and shipped to the University of Chicago Stadium, where top scientists and material were brought together to form the Manhattan Project, which would develop the first Atom Bomb. The A-bomb was sent with its horrendous message of destruction to Japan.*"[24]

Legacy of the Canol Project

The Canol Project may not have been a success as a military venture, but for many northern people it was the chief event that pulled them out of years of poverty and deprivation that started in the 1920s and continued through the Dirty Thirties. Rather than having a strong resentment toward the Americans for invading the North, many people in the North recognize that this interlude, after years of struggling to make ends meet, gave them much-needed employment.

The good wages they earned during the war years provided cash to pay off debts, a nest egg to buy more land, invest in a business, or acquire a larger truck or tractor. The main criticism of those who lived through that period concerned the waste following the war. There was entirely too much machinery, equipment, and material to ship all of it back to the United States. Rather than selling or giving these supplies to local people, most of it was destroyed or stockpiled and buried by bulldozers, including tractors and 6 X 6 trucks. Enterprising people knew the locations of these caches and later salvaged machinery and parts for their own use.

The war that few people know was the war after the war – on all the machinery, food, and supplies left behind. Larry Sheck was at Fort Smith for a good part of the time during and after the war:[26]

> "*When we were in Fort Smith in '42, there was 1500 Negro soldiers and 1500 white soldiers. They were all Americans and, boy, they had all kinds of trouble. Them poor Negroes, they brought them up and it was -40, -50 below [-40° to -45°C]. They burned more diesel fuel trying to keep warm. Oh, and the waste! I seen waste after waste after waste.*

"When the Americans moved out of Fort Smith, they couldn't give it away. It was the Canadian government's mistake. They couldn't sell it, they couldn't do anything with it. They couldn't even give it to the Indians. So, what did they do? They had to destroy it. All the buildings on the waterfront at Fort Smith, they just took a bull dozer and bull-dozed them into the river. All the grub, the groceries, truckload after truckload, they dug a great big hole and they backed up with these cases and dumped it in the hole and then tramped over it with a D-8 Cat and buried it. And they had soldiers there keeping people away. One fellow got close enough to take some pictures. I don't know who it was, it was all hush, hush. The machinery that come out, they took it all the way to Waterways and destroyed it.

"About 16 miles [25 km] *between Fort Fitzgerald and Fort Smith there wasn't a post where there wasn't trucks and tractors parked. And if one broke down, they just shoved it in the ditch and took another one. They just had so many, eh? When this stuff went out by boat, they shipped it all to Waterways. On the other end they took it all the way to Dawson Creek and destroyed it. And this one truck had a front end smashed up, brand new six-cylinder. They brought the six-cylinder Ford engine into this country. All brand new tires on it. It never run anywhere and never done anything. They hauled it down to the dump. There was air-tight stoves out there, not a thing wrong with them. Dozens of lamps for Caterpillar tractors. We got a whole washtub full of them out of there. We were allowed to go down to the dump and pick this stuff out as long as we didn't take it and sell it."*

Theft was not uncommon.

"People stole these machines from them [the army]. People were driving stolen machines and hauling fuel for them, from Grimshaw up to Hay River. One of the guys on that train there, he had a 1944 Chev stolen from the army; he took it home, took the cab off and put a 1938 cab on it."

The peaceful invasion of the Americans in the Peace River Country and the Northwest Territories had a lasting positive influence on northern transportation. In putting in the Canol 6 road, the American Army had widened the old winter cat road. This would become essentially the route of the Mackenzie Highway, completed in 1948. So finally after 30-some years of lobbying the provincial government, the North Peace was going to have an all-weather graded, gravel road!

Well, sort of. In some seasons, anyway.

Notes

1 Bob Irwin, "Edmonton, Peace River, and Roads North: The Canol Project in 1942," in Bob Hesketh, ed., *Three Northern Wartime Projects* [Edmonton: Canadian Circumpolar Institute and Edmonton & District Historical Society, 1996] p. 202. Irwin states that the Mackenzie Highway could be attributed to the Canol Project. He also quotes Pierre Gauvreau, long time resident of Peace River as saying, "…one of the black blots on Canadian history [is] that the

only real development handed out to the hardy pioneers fighting for existence, would have to come from a foreign power."

[2] Richard Finnie, *The Canol Project*, San Francisco, 1945, p. 5. This oversized book was published by Bechtel, Price, and Callaghan, and, for all its enthusiasm, it is perhaps the best source of information on the Canol Project. At the end of the book is a roll-call of names of men and women civilians, both U.S. and Canadian, who were on the payroll of BPC, on the Canol Project for nine months or more.

[3] Finnie, p. 6.

[4] Bernice Lorenzen, in *Tales of the Mackenzie Highway*, wrote about the Paddle Prairie camp, which had a hospital but had no doctor. Instead, the dentist in residence became very proficient in treating frostbite, and the locals all got their teeth fixed.

[5] Morris Zaslow, *The Northward Expansion of Canada, 1914-80*, Toronto: McClelland and Stewart, 1988, p. 219.

[6] Heath Twitchell, *Northwest Epic: The Building of the Alaska Highway*. New York: St. Martin's Press, 1992. p. 199.

[7] Sir Alexander Mackenzie Historical Society, *Peace River Remembers*. Peace River, 1984, p. 533.

[8] Ibid., p. 534.

[9] Ibid., p. 533.

[10] Interview with Fred Lorenzen, October 12, 1999.

[11] Correspondence from Hilda Ressler, Manning, Alberta, September 7, 1996.

[12] My thanks to Dennis Estabrook for permission to use his father's correspondence and photographs from the period he worked on the Canol Project as a tractor operator.

[13] In a letter dated March 18, 1943, Ernest Estabrook wrote to Vern: "Just received your two letters one from Norman Wells dated March 9th. Am sure glad to hear from you and that you are well. I thought that you were heading north. I have a letter written and will enclose in this envelope. I have sent photos and letters to Mills Lake some time ago. I will send Chet's letter you wrote to him. Haven't much time left before mail closes. Everything O.K. here about 6 inches snow in fields, not melting any so far. Still stays cool. Now Vernon as long as you get out by last of April it will be O.K. Good by for now. Dad."

[14] *Tales of the Mackenzie Highway*, p. 22.

[15] Ibid., p. 21.

[16] Ibid., p. 9.

[17] Patricia McCormack, "Canol Project at Fort Chipewyan," in *Three Northern Wartime Projects*, pp. 191-194.

[18] As quoted in *Denendeh: A Dene Celebration*, published by the Dene Nation, p. 18.

[19] Op. Cit., pp. 195-96.

[20] Zaslow, pp. 221-222.

[21] Ibid., p. 226.

[22] Ibid., p. 227.

[23] Ibid., p. 206.

[24] Bernice Lorenzen, in the foreword to *Tales of the Mackenzie Highway*, p. 2.

[25] Unpublished story by Harry Jones, Pouce Coupe, B.C., 1998.

[26] Interview with Larry Sheck, Grimshaw, August 17, 1997.

🚙 Chapter 4 – The Mackenzie Highway 🚚

A Tale of Two Governments

Toward the end of the Second World War the Dominion and Alberta governments were ready to return to peacetime projects. One of these was building an all-weather road between Grimshaw and Great Slave Lake to replace the winter cat trail. The two governments began preliminary negotiations before the war ended. Both the Dominion and Alberta governments had different reasons for wanting to see this road completed. Since the 1920s, the Peace River Country had lobbied the Alberta government for decent roads. But the Social Credit government's road improvement efforts were focused on central and southern Alberta, on the prairies where it was easier and cheaper to build and where a larger population base existed. Building roads over muskeg was another matter.

Edmonton's Chamber of Commerce supported the efforts of the North Peace Associated Chambers of Commerce and began to lobby W.A. Fallow, Minister of Public Works, for road improvement in the Peace Country.[1] A joint agreement with the Dominion government to construct an all-weather road from Grimshaw to Great Slave Lake would satisfy both the Peace River constituency and Edmonton's business interests as well.

The Dominion government's interest, of course, was in the development of northern resources, namely mining, fishing, and forestry. A better transportation link to these resources was of primary concern. An all-weather road between the railhead at Grimshaw and Lower Hay River Post would provide a faster, cheaper way of distributing freight by truck to the barges, which carried the freight the rest of the way across Great Slave Lake to Yellowknife or down the Mackenzie River to northern mines and communities. Cat trains were too slow, too expensive, and could only operate a few months during the winter and early spring. Although cat trains continued to cross Great Slave Lake into Yellowknife in winter, most of the goods destined for northern mines had to be stockpiled at Lower Hay River until the ice on the lake went out for another season. When freeze-up came in late September or early October, the tugs and barges were dry docked, and those goods that did not get shipped north had to wait for next season or be air-freighted.

By 1943 the Dominion government had taken over the operation of the El Dorado Gold Mines at Great Bear Lake. The Dominion government now owned the Northern Transportation Company Ltd. (NTCL), a crown corporation that operated both barges and air transportation. Airplanes satisfied El Dorado's light transportation needs, but they did not present a viable way to haul heavier goods and materials to the mines. The new gold mines at Yellowknife, discovered in the mid-30s by prospectors for Consolidated Mines, had triggered a boom, and the thriving community of miners and entrepreneurs demanded a cheaper way to have goods and supplies hauled in from the south.

Correspondence began in earnest between Fallow and T.A. Crearer, Minister of Mines and Resources, in early 1944. In a letter dated February 15, Fallow wrote:

"It is felt that action by the Dominion Government should be taken to place this road in such condition that trucks would have reasonable chance of operating on it during most of the seasons of the year. About 50 local trucks are at present employed hauling mixed freight....Any money now spent on this road that will place it in reasonable condition for the transport of freight by truck will not be wasted."[2]

Fallow's letter also mentioned that the trucks could provide backhauls of concentrates from El Dorado Mine (i.e., radium and uranium). When the Dominion government requested a complete profile of the Grimshaw-Hay River Road, Fallow wrote a letter dated December 29, 1944, to Richard Finnie, author of the book *Canada Moves North*, and a strong supporter of an all-weather road from Grimshaw to Hay River. In his letter, Fallow stated that the Dominion Government was prepared to pay a portion of the cost to construct the all-weather road. By January 12, 1945, Fallow's Deputy Minister, G.H.N. Monkman, had outlined in a memo an estimate of costs for the construction of the Grimshaw Road to the Northwest Territories boundary. Even by the standards of the time, these early estimates appear to be very low: Clearing, $45 450; Grubbing, $33 000; Grading, $856 180; Culverts, $69 420; Bridges (over the Meikle, Keg, Hay, and Steen rivers), $75 000 for a total of $1 079 050 plus 10% contingency and overhead.[3] The final cost of construction of the 247 miles [397 km] of road between the Third Battle (Meikle River) and the Northwest Territories boundary was $2 850 000, of which Alberta paid $1 476 000, about 52 %. The entire cost of construction the Mackenzie Highway was around $4 300 000.[4]

In a letter dated May 5, 1945, from Charles Camsell, the new Minister of Mines & Resources, to W.A. Fallow, Camsell states that "Now that it would appear that hostilities in Europe are about to cease, it is most desirable that no time should be lost in completing the necessary surveys that will be required before contracts can be let for construction of the road."

Through continual negotiations for almost a year, Fallow was able to get the Dominion Government to agree to pay 50% of the costs to the Fort Vermilion turnoff, which was classified as an agricultural road. From the Fort Vermilion turnoff (Mile 162) to the boundary, the road was classified as a mining road, and the Dominion Government would pay two-thirds of the costs in northern Alberta and 100% of the costs in the Northwest Territories. Further dickering between governments finally resulted in a draft of a Memorandum of Agreement by September 1945, which was officially signed by both governments on November 3, 1945.

The survey work, beginning at the Third Battle (Meikle River) to the boundary, was to be conducted by the Alberta Government and commenced before the end of the year. J.H. Johnston, District Engineer at Peace River, was put in charge of supplies and communication. Construction work on the Alberta side of the border began almost immediately. Commencement of construction on the Northwest Territories section of the road, however, was delayed until the fall of 1946 because barges carrying the equipment for Bond Construction Company sank in Great Slave Lake while enroute to Hay River.[5]

By January 1946, tenders were received for the Meikle Bridge and the Dominion Bridge Company received the contract to build the 175-foot [53m] bridge for $16 000. A letter dated July 12, 1946, from L.P. Davis, Supervisor of Publicity and Promotion, to E.S. Clarry, with Alberta's Trade Commission, outlined the terms of reference: The construction work was to start on May 1, 1946, and be completed by December 31, 1947. The route of the highway would follow the general route of the old winter road for cat trains, built eight years previously, but avoiding low areas as much as possible. It would have a grade surface 20 feet wide [6m] and a maximum grade would be 7%. Four steel bridges were to be constructed, one at Third Battle (Meikle), Keg River, Hay River, and Steen River. In addition, 35 timber bridges were erected. Government bridge crews built the bridges.

The general contract for construction of the 397 km [247 miles] of the Alberta section of the road was awarded to Standard Gravel & Surfacing Company and Dutton & Fred Mannix & Company of Calgary, with sub-contractors Jim Robertson, Bill Dutton, and Watson-McKinnon. In the Northwest Territories, Bond Construction Ltd., with headquarters in Edmonton, was awarded the tender to build 130 km [81 miles] of road from the boundary to Lower Hay River at Great Slave Lake. Today's contractors may be interested in the rental rates for road equipment at the time: TD 40 Cat & angle dozer, $3.05/$1.10 per hour; D7Cat and angle dozer, $2.75/$1.10 per hour; and for a 2 1/2-ton truck to service camps, $1.50 a day.

Surveying the Mackenzie Highway

The survey for the Mackenzie Highway, done in 1945-46, followed essentially the original winter road of 1939. The Alberta Department of Public Works had conducted this survey, all the way to Lower Hay River. J.P. "Jack" Church, who had been in charge of the survey of the Grimshaw-Hay River winter road, was now resident engineer on the 1945-46 survey for the Mackenzie Highway. Public Works was responsible for the survey to the Northwest Territories boundary, and the Dominion government carried out the survey in the Territories. The Grimshaw-Hay River road was in fairly good shape up to the Third Battle, but thereon north it was bush that had to be cleared by hand axe for the survey line.

Surveying in the North in the 1940s was very different from what it is today. There were no roads, no permanent camps, no electricity, no telephones, no showers. The men who worked on the survey crews were largely cut off from civilization and communication for months. The survey equipment might seem archaic to surveyors today, as surveying was all done with a transit and chain and the clearing mostly by hand with an axe. Many local Metis were hired to clear the right of way. Stanley Smith of Fort Vermilion had worked as an axeman clearing the original right of way for the winter cat road in 1939. In 1946 he was hired again, this time as a rodman on a survey crew. Thus, he had worked on both the cat road and the Mackenzie Highway.[6]

The surveying equipment and techniques produced very accurate results. The preliminary survey that was done for the Mackenzie Highway in 1945 is essentially the route of today's Mackenzie Highway. The new route bypassed the community of Keg River about 18 km [11 mi.] further west. The survey work did not go off without a few hitches. Jack P. Church, Assistant Chief Maintenance Engineer, who had taken part in the survey work on the winter cat road in 1939-40, recalled:

"We had some difficult times during our final survey. I remember on one occasion our cache of supplies at Indian Cabins was found to be rotten, so we had to live on short rations for about five weeks, until we could get provisions from Lower Hay. On these surveys we were away from civilization for five months at a time and had to carry our provisions with us."[7]

Ed Zack of Stony Plain was a surveyor on one of the crews. He had started with the Department of Highways in 1941, then joined the Canadian Forces during the war. When he came back in 1945 he joined the department again. He got orders to go to Peace River to survey the new road.

"We set up four different camps. Each camp had about 20 men and complete survey parties. We were responsible for about 55 miles [88 km] each. We had to have all the work done by March before spring break-up.

"We arrived in Peace River by special train, a coach at the end of the passenger train. We hired a lot of local people. From Edmonton there were approximately 20. We had to build the cabooses and cook shack so we could live. When we arrived at Third Battle [Meikle River], we had nowhere to sleep. I think there was one caboose and we all slept on the floor. We had the material, hammers and saws, and the first day we started building."[8]

W.C.F. "Bill" Beattie describes the same incident in his article "Construction of the Mackenzie Highway – December 1945 to October 1948" in *Tales of the Mackenzie Highway.*[9] He went to work for the Department of Highways in 1945 when he decided to take a year off after his first year in engineering at the University of Alberta. He was hired to work in one of the survey crews for the princely sum of $90.00 a month.

"I learned at this point that four survey crews had been assembled from various parts of the province to complete the preliminary survey of the Mackenzie Highway north of the Third Battle....On December 5, 1945, I was picked up in Grimshaw by a truck hauling supplies to the starting point of the survey at the Third Battle and arrived to a scene of total chaos. A crew of carpenters had been hired earlier to con-

struct the cabooses which would form the cat trains for each of the crews; however, when the [survey] crews arrived a few days before me they found virtually nothing done. It was therefore necessary to start building the cabooses to have a place for approximately 50 people to sleep....

"The next morning I joined the others in the camp construction, and as the cabooses were very similar to the granaries we built on the farm, the job was not too difficult. The first step was to go into the bush with a cat and get logs for skids and then construct the cabooses, which I believe were 8 feet wide and 16 feet long [2.4 x 4.8m]....Most of the surveyors had no construction experience, and as tools were very limited, much of the carpentry was done with axes and swede saws with some rather crude results. Each camp consisted of an office caboose, cookhouse, two bunkhouses, and a halftrack which was half food storage and half fuel for the cat."

Collecting snow to melt for a hot drink. Jack P. Church, assistant Chief Maintenance Engineer, survey of the Mackenzie Highway, winter 1945-46. Bill Beattie collection.

Ed Zack described the conditions under which the crews had to live and work:

"The only transportation we had was a D7 [Caterpillar] to pull the cabooses. We were all on our own. We didn't have the facilities that they have now. No showers. You know how we got our showers the first winter? By rolling in the snow, running to the bunkhouse and wiping it off, that was our showers, once a week. We didn't have water at -40 below all winter.

"It was really quite primitive. Bathrooms? Outside. You'd find a log...There was a lot of snow that winter. It was a cold winter too. All we had was air tight heaters.

Imagine that! And the cook shacks weren't even insulated. I had a chunk of ice under my bunk. It never did thaw out.

"Although we did have a man to cut wood, at times we had to cut our own wood. It was six days a week, six full days, from daylight to dark, because the days were short. Toward the spring the days got longer. The conditions we worked under, nobody would work under now....By the time we had our supper, it was seven o'clock and we'd lay on the bunk for an hour and then be ready for bed, because you had to get up in the morning."

Bill Beattie was on the crew headed by resident engineer Jack Church, an experienced and respected man who knew the area. The crew left the Third Battle on December 16, 1945, and arrived at Upper Hay River, where they were to start surveying on December 24.

"The only settlement we had seen enroute was the Metis colony at Paddle Prairie and the only other habitation we would encounter later was the small group of Indians at Indian Cabins, a short distance from the NWT border. A small community also existed at Keg River [Post], which was approximately 10 miles [16 km] west of the highway and the Hudson Bay post a short distance west of the highway on the bank of [Upper] Hay River. High Level did not exist at that time, nor did Manning, which is now south of where we started."

The following day the crew celebrated Christmas, and for some it was the first time they had ever spent it away from home. "We had the day off," wrote Beattie, "and celebrated with a traditional dinner of turkey, etc., and Jack Church presented each of us with a package of cigarettes and a bottle of beer." The day after Christmas it was back to work six days a week from morning till night. "Most of us had no experience on snowshoes but Church was a real expert as well as being in great physical shape, and after a few lessons we all managed to master them."

Christmas in the bush, 1945. Survey crew on the Mackenzie highway, Bill Beattie on the far right. Bill Beattie collection.

The little communication the crew had with the outside world was of utmost importance. Beattie writes:

"During the day our cat skinner would move our camp approximately one mile, and when we arrived back at night, one of the first projects was to cut two tall trees and erect a radio antenna for the Forestry radio. It was very unpredictable, depending on location, weather, etc. However, it did provide some communication with Peace River and the other engineers during our scheduled period."

The crew was also visited periodically by a convoy of trucks hauling supplies to Yellowknife – a welcome break from isolation. And every two weeks a supply truck from Peace River would bring fresh supplies for the four crews.

Beattie describes the responsibilities of the crew:

"We had two crews – a transit crew made up of an instrument man, rodman, chainman, and two axemen, which established the location, chained out the stations at intervals of 100 feet [30m]*, located intermediate stations where required by the terrain, and frost-pinned all stakes into the frozen ground so they would remain until needed at a later time. This crew was followed by a level crew made up of an instrument man, rodman, and two chainmen, who ran bench levels and cross sections at right angles to the base line at each stake installed by the transit crew. Normally we would complete*

Mackenzie Highway survey crew, 1945. Back row, left to right: Bill Beattie, Frank Morgan, Ed Pope, Fred Mercredi, Jack Church. Front row, left to right: Earl Danchuk, Ed Boecher, Bob Sharp, Bill Bradley, Bill Hartfield, Ken Hurlburt, Ted Shewchuk. Bill Beattie collection.

approximately one mile a day; however, there were many times when we had to aban-
don several days' work and revise the location due to unfavorable terrain, muskegs,
etc."

Work was not finished in the evenings. Locations had to be plotted that had been done during the day, level notes checked, and plotting cross-sections plotted. To confirm their location, Church would occasionally take a star shot. "We eventually completed the survey to the NWT border, where Ken Hurlburt and I erected a home made boundary sign, and we commenced our 12-day trip back to the Third Battle."

Beattie tells a story about another section crew leader named "Silent" Joe Kelland.

"Kelland earned his 'silent' moniker because he rarely spoke, and transmitted all
instructions to his crew by notes. Church stopped our train at Silent Joe's camp and
asked if he required any supplies and got the abrupt answer 'No!', so we continued on
our way. We had been at the Third Battle for three or four days when the last truck
leaving the North before break-up delivered a note to Church from Silent Joe, stating
he was out of groceries and could we send him some.

"The road was now impassable for a vehicle, so Church decided the only way
would be to build a sloop and haul the supplies with the cat. The only problem was that
our cat skinner had left, although the cat was still there. Church asked if any one of us
could drive it. Not yet having learned to not hold up your hand, I was soon the cat
skinner, and we set about going to the bush for skids and building a sloop. We loaded
up all the available supplies and I set out early in the morning for the approximately
50-mile [80 km] trip, arriving at Silent Joe's camp late at night. I pulled up to the cook-
house and went in to get something to eat when shortly after one of his surveyors came
with a note that stated, 'We're out of fuel – go back down to our fuel cache and bring
back a load of fuel.'

"Next morning I headed back down the road about 20 miles [32 km], loaded up the
fuel and returned to Joe's camp, where I again went into the cookhouse for supper. Joe
looked out his door, saw that I was back, and wrote another note which he sent with a
runner that said, 'That's all, you can go home.'"

Once the preliminary survey for the right of way was completed at the end of March, Zack and Beattie continued with surveying for the construction of the highway. Beattie was having second thoughts about returning to university.

"I soon learned that none of the four engineers were graduates, but had earned
their positions after many years of practical experience. I later learned that there were
very few graduate engineers in the Dept. and most people in senior management posi-
tions right up to and including the Deputy Minister were there because of their expert-
ise in a particular aspect of highway work and not because of any political affiliation.
I was also advised in some of our hot stove sessions (around the airtight heater) that
most of the engineers were very strict and extremely hard to work for, with Church
being one of the worst. I had learned during the course of the winter that he was a hard

task master, expected excellence, demanded a full day's work, but was very efficient and fair. I got along fine with him."

Beattie stayed on to work with Church, who picked his new crew from those in the four crews who wanted to stay on. Many men did not remain, as they had wives and girlfriends back home. Beattie was promoted to rodman and his salary increased to $110 per month. The new crew spent the spring designing the highway and preparing for construction.

"Dutton & Mannix were awarded the construction contract as the prime contractor and they employed three subcontractors, so we had four crews actually clearing and building the road. This kept us very busy keeping four construction crews going. Although we had an army 4x4 for transportation, we walked and carried our work stakes almost as much as we drove because of the impassable conditions. Ed Zack and his crew stayed in Church's camp behind the construction and carried out the remeasurement survey to establish pay quantities for the contractors."

Surveying in winter had its difficulties, but spring presented an all new set of problems. Construction in muskeg required a great deal of dragline work.

"I recall one section of muskeg approximately three miles [5 km] long that we constructed in the winter by dozing all the available trees into the centre of the grade and then truck hauling material to cover them to a depth of approximately four feet. We constructed what appeared to be a good grade. However, in the spring it settled to the point where we had a light grade in some spots and some areas it entirely vanished."

Working in spring also meant longer hours, from daybreak to sunset. "We worked long hours and in many cases all weekend; however, we had little else to do....I learned a lot and it was much more rewarding than building a road on a road allowance in the prairies." Mosquitoes, the bane of the North, were a constant reminder of the good times in winter, when they were gone.

"A real problem were the mosquitoes...Food had probably been scarce before we arrived and they sure liked surveyors and construction workers. Many times I saw the dragline operator climb to the top of his boom to have a smoke, and all the cat skinners had smudge pots on their cats."

Norm Mytron, from Pouce Coupe, worked as a catskinner for Bond Construction in 1947 on the Territories section of the highway. He was at times all too intimate with mosquitoes. "If you had to go to the bathroom, you had to build a smudge. Otherwise, the mosquitoes would eat your butt."[10]

After the summer construction period of 1946, Jack Church asked for volunteers to stay through the winter to supervise the clearing crew. Beattie wrote, "I still hadn't learned to keep my hand down, so I spent the winter there while the rest of the guys went to other jobs in civilization or helped Jack Church in the Edmonton office." So Beattie stayed the winter, but this time he had transportation and managed to get to

Grimshaw once in a while and go home for Christmas. During the following spring of 1947, road construction continued.

"By fall we had completed grading to near the Hay River. When freeze-up came Church and his crew again left and I remained to supervise the balance of the clearing and to assist the bridges crews with any engineering required on either of the steel bridges on the Hay or Steen rivers."

Bridge Construction

Tom Dixon worked on the bridge construction, which started in the early winter of 1947. Don Brown and Fred Guest were the foremen of the steel construction crew. The northern Alberta crew that built the wooden bridges were directed by Nels Jorgensen. The three main bridges were over the Third Battle (Meikle), Upper Hay (Meander), and Steen rivers, and several smaller bridges over creeks.

"Tom drove the boom truck and pounded the pilings. In order to keep it running throughout the bitter cold, he got up at night and ran it every two hours, to the great irritation of the rest of the crew. They were pounding pilings one cold morning on the Steen River when Bill Beattie drove up in his jeep from Guest's camp on the Hay and inquired why they were working. He said it was 60 below [-50°C]. It was standard procedure to shut down activities when the temperature dropped below 50 below, but they didn't have a thermometer and were none the wiser."[11]

Beattie enjoyed watching the bridge crew construct the steel bridges.

"What intrigued me the most was the expertise of the forge-man, who heated the rivets down on the deck. Every joint had several different size rivets which had to be the proper temperature when required. When the rivets were ready, he would take the proper rivet from the forge with his tongs and throw it to a steel worker, who caught it in a funnel-shaped bucket with a handle, [then] remove it with his tongs and place it in the proper hole for riveting. Very seldom did the forge man make a mistake or the receiver fail to catch the rivet."

Sometimes one of the heated rivets would go astray. In *Tales of the Mackenzie Highway*, Tom Dixon, who worked with the bridge crew, told his wife Mary about the time foreman Fred Guest got his whiskers seared with a hot rivet when the receiver missed catching the rivet in the bucket.[12]

All the bridges were nearly completed when spring arrived. Beattie was responsible for taking the crews out.

"We made the trip without too much trouble, but we were crowding our luck with spring break-up....The bridge foreman wanted to get his trucks out and as there was no possibility of them travelling under their own power he had them towed by a cat. The frost was coming out so fast that in many places the new grade was totally impassable. Travel was better in the ditch, except in many places the ditches had two or three

feet of water – some with a layer of ice on top. We were grossly overloaded with eight or ten men in the back of each jeep and to say the least it was a terrible trip."

While Beattie was in Grimshaw, he woke up to a message that the newly-constructed bridge over the Hay River [near Meander River] was out. He returned to find the two spans of the bridge lying on each side of the river. A temporary bridge had to be built out of timber by the bridge crew. "We signed a release that the government would be responsible if the bridge collapsed and the contractor lost any equipment. We breathed a sigh of relief when the last cat got across, and [we] had a party." The bridge crews proceeded to rebuild the bridge, this time higher.

Newly-constructed bridge at Upper Hay River washed out when the river flooded in the spring of 1946. Bill Mueller collection.

A number of men from the North Peace worked on the highway. Jim Glen of Grimshaw and his brother Charlie worked on the highway from January 1947 until September of 1948. Frank Blakley also hauled bridge timbers from the Blakley's stopping place at Mile 230.

George Predy of Hotchkiss helped haul bridge timbers from stock piles to specific sites from Meikle to Steen River during the winter of 1947. Between 1948 and 1952, George and his father owned a sawmill and were contracted to saw and deliver timbers for highway culverts between Peace River and Keg River.[13]

Homer Dickson worked on the highway in 1948, between Upper Hay River and the NWT boundary, at first helping mechanic Frank Wallace overhaul the Cats. "The parts were packed for overseas shipment in wax and canvas. To remove this the parts had to be placed in hot diesel fuel."[14] Later he worked operating a Cat, putting in 12-hour shifts, seven days a week.

Jack Landry, who was raised along the Third Battle, joined school friends Leonard Sexsmith and Jim Harbourne in 1946 to work for Dutton & Mannix on the section from Meikle River to Paddle Prairie. The following year he went north to Lower Hay River, NWT, to work for Bond Construction on the Territories section. He worked on the Cats, and that winter he hauled timbers for culverts and bridges along the right of way. Years later, in the late 1950s, he would again work on the reconstruction of the Mackenzie Highway. In 1980 he worked for Wells Construction on the black topping of the Highway. Thus, Jack Landry was to work on the construction of all three phases of the Mackenzie Highway.[15]

Road Construction in the Northwest Territories, Summer 1947

The contract for constructing the road from Hay River to the Alberta/Northwest Territories boundary was awarded to Bond Construction, an Edmonton-based company. Norm Mytron of Pouce Coupe, B.C., worked on the NWT section of the Mackenzie Highway during the summer of 1947. He had gained experience the year before working as a catskinner on the Hart Highway, under foreman Alec McClarty. When work became available on the Mackenzie Highway in the summer of 1947, Alec McClarty got a job as grade foreman and took Norm and another young man with him. Norm Mytron was 18 at the time and looking for adventure. The three of them drove from Dawson Creek to Peace River and from there caught a flight to Hay River.

The construction of the highway at the northern end was delayed because of a big flood that spring, and the airport at Hay River was flooded out. The barges carrying some road equipment also sank in Great Slave Lake during bad weather, while enroute to Hay River. So while construction was more or less completed on the Alberta end, the completion of the NWT section of the road was not finished until late summer of 1948.[16]

The three men arrived at the Hay River airport around June 15th, 1947, to begin work on the highway.

"The first job we had to do was work our way through and cut off about three tributaries [from] the main river [Hay River]. It was quite a job. I was a catskinner. We operated old equipment from the Canol Road, up at Norman Wells. International TD-14s, TD-18s, and one old Cleatrak for pulling the elevating grader. We had some old

Caterpillar RD-8s that were used to clear the right-of-ways and to push the old burnt brush off. We also had Letourneaus."

Constructing a road through muskeg was like trying to spread icing over a layer of pudding. It had no solid base. Mytron described the difficulties:

"Up there it was all muskeg. That's why they built the road along the river. Most of the highway was built along the river as far as they could. I know one night there, we had three D-8 Cats stuck in the muskeg that were working at night, pushing logs off the right-of-way and getting ready for the scrapers. You went over the muskeg once or twice, then you just dropped in. I can remember stopping and I was the only one that was not stuck. I had to put some logs under the Cat to back out. Then I winched the other guys out, on our day shift in the morning."

Where the ground was dry, the road crew used the Cleatrak, an apparatus that had wide tracks and was used for pulling the elevating grader that made the ditches and threw the dirt in the middle, for the grade.

Mytron started out earning $1.10 an hour, working 12-hour shifts, seven days a week. After a couple of weeks his pay was raised to $1.25 an hour, fairly good wages for the time. By the end of the summer he had saved about $1200. He and the rest of the road crew lived in two camps, one at Hay River, NWT, and the other at Alexandra Falls.

"Our bunk houses there [Hay River] were terrible. They were double deckers, with no windows. It was so hot up at Hay River, and there were mosquito nets over the beds to keep out mosquitoes so you could sleep. When you were on night shift and slept during the day, it was so hot. When you woke up, you were just shaking, you were so hot and tired."

The section of the road that spanned one of the tributaries was particularly difficult to build.

"It was quite large, a river by itself. As we got closer to the other side, about 40 feet or so [12m], the water was so swift it was washing the banks away on the other side. We got that far and couldn't go further. It was just sandy soil. So we ended up putting 45 gallon [170L] drums full of sand, laying them down to divert the water from the bank. We built up a whole big bunch of rock, big boulders, on the other side. We put in some big trees that we swung across the river and let them hit the other side of the bank to slow the water down. Then we had three Cats to push the gravel and rocks in. We finally got it, but man, you could hear these big boulders going clunk, clunk, clunk in the river."

One man almost lost his life when he went out on the logs and fell off. "Right under all this stuff, the logs. He came out the other side all right, but if he had gotten snagged up in those trees, he would have been a goner."

Mytron spent that one summer helping build the highway. The poor construction of the road would later come back to haunt him. In 1950 he got a job driving a truck for Joe

Kostiuk Trucking, hauling pipe for Dawson Creek Natural Gas. The pipe was loaded from the barges at Hay River and shipped by truck to Dawson Creek, where the pipe was needed for the natural gas field. It was a particularly rainy year, and Norm experienced first-hand the problems all the rest of the truckers were having at that time.

"It was slippery. One trip there were trucks and pickups in the ditches. I was coming along, going as fast as I could. But that wasn't very darned fast, maybe 30 miles [48 km] an hour. I didn't stop because I knew I couldn't get going again, so I just kept piling through and made it."

A Little Gravel's a Dangerous Thing

Once the clearing and grading of the Mackenzie Highway was completed, the road was graveled. Hauling gravel was a lucrative job for local men who had their own trucks. Tons and tons of gravel had to be loaded at gravel pits along the route and stockpiled. The gravel pits were spread out widely along the route and gravel had to be hauled as much as 50 miles [80 km] to its destination. Sources of gravel were hard to find, according to Bill Mueller, who worked with the survey crew between Keg River and the NWT border.[17]

"After the survey job I looked after the gravel hauling and stock piling along the Mackenzie Highway. Gravel was hard to find, most of it coming from the Peace River. The pile at Keg River was hauled from east of Keg River 25 miles [40 km] (Carcajou); the second pile was at the 27th Baseline and was hauled from 13 miles [20 km] east. The next pile was at Mile 163 and it was also hauled all the way from the Peace River."

Other locations were a gravel pit close to the road near High Level, a large pit at Upper Hay River (Meander River):

"The road went right through the middle of it. Fifteen miles [24 km] south of Steen River more gravel was located, and it was right in the middle of the muskeg, but the muskeg was not too deep, so we were able to get the gravel out fairly easy. The last pit was located north of Steen River; the road ran through the pit there as well, and there was a lot of gravel taken out of that pit."

In some places, the road had to be resurfaced each year, partly because there was not an adequate road base to hold the gravel. In the spring when the frost came out of the ground, the gravel base would sink into the road. Another problem was that the road was spread with only about 2 or 3 inches of gravel.

Many, like Fred Lorenzen, hauled gravel in the summer and grain in the fall and early winter. In 1948 he hauled gravel in the summertime on the Mackenzie Highway from the Third Battle (Meikle River) to High Level.[18] The next year he purchased a larger truck, a 5-ton GMC, from the GM Dealer in Grimshaw and hauled gravel for Bond Construction on the NWT section of the highway. From 1950 to 1954, he continued to haul gravel in the summer and freight in the winter. Although Fred would haul just about anything, from oil barrels to horses, gravel hauling became a mainstay in his business. "I think I can safely say that at one time or another throughout my life I have hauled gravel to every mile of the highway."[19]

The Kapchinsky brothers, founders of Kaps Transport Ltd., had gravel trucks. Al Hamilton, founder of Grimshaw Trucking & Distributing, also got his start in trucking hauling gravel, first on the Alaska Highway and then on the Mackenzie Highway in 1946.[20] "I had two gravel trucks. I graveled for three summers while the Mackenzie Highway was being built. Then I decided to start freighting when the highway was completed."

Notwithstanding the many tons of gravel that were poured and spread on the highway every summer, by the following spring a good portion of the road had to re-graveled. There was not a good enough road base, and the gravel, along with the trucks, sank into the mud. By the late 1950s the Mackenzie Highway would have to be completely reconstructed, this time to higher standards.

Naming the Mackenzie Highway

The Mackenzie Highway was originally planned to be completed by 1947, but because of the loss of equipment on the barge that sunk in the Great Slave Lake, the completion of the NWT section was delayed for a year. The town of Grimshaw had anxiously awaited the completion of the highway so that it could stage a grand opening. In the Peace River *Record-Gazette*, August 12, 1948, the following announcement appeared:

> *"No effort or expense is going to stand in the way of making this opening a red letter day in the history of not only the southern terminus of the road, Grimshaw, but every village and stopping place which in some measure has been connected with its building."*[21]

But gravel crews continued to pour gravel on the road bed into early October 1948. The opening was delayed again.

David A. Harrison, in his article "The Opening and Naming of the Mackenzie Highway," explains some of the reasons why the official opening of the highway never took place. That summer there was a polio ban notice issued by the Peace River Board of Health, which prohibited all children under 16 from assembling in public places, to prevent the spread of the disease. By October it was too late to hold the opening, because of freeze-up.

There is evidence that the Federal officials had discussed having an opening the following spring. In January, 1949, there was discussion between the governments suggesting possible names for the highway. W.A. Fallow, Minister of Public Works, had used the name Great Slave Lake Road, which had been shortened by most to just "Grimshaw Road." On March 10, 1949, Premier E.C. Manning and James A. MacKinnon, Federal Minister of Mines and Resources, discussed the various names that were put forth, which included the Hay River Highway, the Territories Highway, and the Mackenzie Highway. "They agreed that the Mackenzie Highway would seem most

Ben Peters on his No. 3 Massey Harris tractor, ready to haul hogs overland to Grimshaw by tractor train. Ben Peters collection.

"Tractor Train to Peace River in 1950"[25]

Ben Peters tells a story about another memorable trip, by a rubber tire tractor train, from La Crete to Peace River.

"Back in the 1930s and 40s, shipping grain by boat was very limited, so most of the grain was fed to hogs and cattle. Cattle were not too bad, as they do not have to be just a certain weight. Since hogs must go by a certain weight to get the best price, we always had two litters a year. One litter was ready for the first boat in spring and the other litter for about the last boat in fall.

"We had to depend entirely on water transportation from the Fort Vermilion area, (there was no La Crete in those days). We would try to have the hogs ready and booked for the last or second last trip in fall.

"The Hudson Bay Company put a new boat in to run from Peace River town to Fort Vermilion and Vermilion Chutes that were about 50 miles [80 km] downstream from Fort Vermilion town. The first boat in spring of 1950, they brought some freight but not nearly all that was to come down, mostly store goods, etc. Many hogs and cattle were booked for the first trip to Peace River.

"It was about mid-May and many of us sat at the river landing with our hogs and cattle waiting for the boat. I do not remember how long we waited but when the boat came, they refused to take any hogs or cattle, so we had to take them home.

"Six of us farmers decided to do it our own way. Whoever did not have a wagon box fit to haul hogs made one, and others had two. The 95 miles [153 km] from Buffalo Head Prairie to High Level [on the Mackenzie Highway] was only bush or prairie trail and a lot of mud holes, so we all joined together. At times we had up to three tractors hooked to one wagon to get through, but we were on our way to Peace River with our hogs and to bring our freight in.

"For those of Buffalo Head Prairie it was a trip of about 300 miles [482 km] and the ones of which is now La Crete area, about 285 miles [458 km]. We were fortunate to have fair weather all the way."

(continued next page)

"There was John Harms with a 44 Massey Harris tractor, Jacob Wieler with a Ferguson tractor, and P.I. Friesen with a 70 Cockshutt tractor and a one ton truck. These were all from Buffalo Head Prairie. Jacob K. Peters with a 22 Massey Harris tractor, Jimmy Ward with a 44 Massey Harris tractor, and my dad, my brother John, and me with a 30 Massey Harris tractor. P.I. Friesen's tractor only went as far as High Level; there he caught a truck going to Peace River and sent the hogs along with it.

"The other five all went to Peace River and back. I do not remember just how long it took us, but I think five or six days. We had more drivers than tractors, so we did not stop too much. It was not a luxury trip sitting on a wagon full of hogs and eating out of a grub box, but this little pig went to market!"

appropriate as the new highway would eventually serve the whole District of Mackenzie…Thus the council in recommending the name was not looking back to commemorate previous explorations of Sir Alexander Mackenzie but forward to future development of the whole district."[22]

Government representatives also discussed the location of an official opening. "Officials at several levels discussed the date and place of the opening. Federal officials suggested Alexandra Falls as a suitable location." A tentative date was suggested as the end of May or beginning of June. However, Mother Nature put a damper on that. Warm spring temperatures caused the highway to thaw and softened the roadbed so that it could not hold the weight of the trucks. On April 1, 1949, a road ban was put in effect from north of Grimshaw to the boundary. Writes Harrison:

"The worst section lay between Steen River and the border in northern Alberta where water rose to the level of the road surface. This section of the highway had a weak substandard sandy base and lacked the correct gravel surfacing which should have been completed the previous fall."

The poor road conditions lasted well into the summer, as rains further weakened the road bed. At one point the rains were so heavy that trucks were stopped at the border for 30 hours. "Many of these trucks carried fresh fish to southern markets and holdups on the highway were critical. At the end of July, the Federal Department of Fisheries had to suspend fishing on Great Slave Lake for a week because trucks could not travel down the highway."[23]

The road continued to deteriorate. "At one point, 30 trucks were immobilized in a sea of gumbo. Truckers called the section 'The Hole' and renamed the Northwest Territories 'The Promised Land.'"

Any plans for an official opening had to be cancelled during the summer, as it would have been too embarrassing to the governments to have guests and important officials experience first-hand the soft gumbo that swallowed up the trucks and cars that attempted to travel down the highway.

Harrison remarks that the change in the Federal government may have been the death knell to any official opening. The Federal Liberal government called a general election for June 28, and MacKinnon, who had been so much a part of the building of the highway, resigned and Colin Gibson replaced him.

Fifty years later, on Thursday, August 20, 1998, the Mackenzie Highway was finally officially opened by a host of dignitaries, politicians, pioneer truckers, and old timers who had worked on the original highway construction. It was a historic gathering at the Visitor Information Centre on the boundary of Alberta and the Northwest Territories. But that's another story, told in a later chapter.

Transportation in Isolated Communities

The Mackenzie Highway opened much of northern Alberta in 1948, but the people of Fort Vermilion and the Mennonites in the Buffalo Head Prairie and La Crete areas were still dependent upon river transportation and wagon trails. An all-weather road into Fort Vermilion was not opened until 1952.

On one trip in the spring of 1948, Ben Peters of La Crete travelled by every which way but air transport to Edmonton and back.[24] He and two friends first travelled by the HBC boat upriver from La Crete Landing to Peace River with a load of 30 head of cattle. The water was high, they had to battle a strong current, and they had many adventures and problems with the boat along the way. After nine days from La Crete Landing to Peace River, he travelled by a steam-powered freight train in the caboose. At McLennan they boarded another train to Edmonton. On his return trip on a passenger train, he stopped again at McLennan and got to travel the rest of the way back to Peace River with the engineer on the locomotive.

Ben had planned to go downriver by HBC boat, but he would have had to wait a few days. Instead he bought a bicycle and headed to Grimshaw and north on the Mackenzie Highway for the rest of the 400 km [250 mi.] back to Fort Vermilion. He caught a ride with a tanker truck at Notikewin and tied the bicycle on top of the tanker. At High Level he walked most of the 30 miles [48 km] overland on a trail that was mostly not fit to ride his bicycle. "The return journey had taken about 38 hours, during which I had ridden my bike or walked about 160 miles [257 km] and rode a truck for about 120 miles [193 km]."

Legacy of the Mackenzie Highway

The Mackenzie Highway was the first all-weather road that linked the Northwest Territories to the southern part of Canada. It may have been poorly constructed; it may have been cursed roundly by every trucker who drove the route, got bogged down in the mud, choked on the dust, or was eaten alive by mosquitoes. But it had served its purpose, to provide a conduit for northern resource development on an unprecedented scale.

Ed Zack, surveyor who had put so much of his time and effort in surveying the Mackenzie Highway, has this to say about it:

> "Nowadays we'd call it a tote road. It was a very cheap road to get us through....It was not built properly to standards we have now. Now we have high standards we didn't have then."[26]

Bill Beattie's assessment of the Mackenzie Highway:

> "This road with a 20 foot [6m] top was primitive by present day standards, but it served as a major connection to the north and carried an enormous amount of truck freight before it was finally rebuilt and paved to a good standard many years later. I believe that the major portion of the present highway is located on, or very close to, the original survey, and I have always been glad I was part of the development of this artery."[27]

Jim Glen of Grimshaw and his brother Charlie worked on the highway from January 1947 until September of 1948. "The right-of-way was cleared to the border by Watson Construction of Airdrie. The first year the road was completed to about eight miles north of Paddle Prairie."[28] Jim went on to drive trucks along the Mackenzie Highway for 21 years, working for various companies, including Grimshaw Trucking, Hay River Truck Lines, Horne and Pitfield, and Peace Trailer Industries. About the Mackenzie Highway, Jim writes: "It sure opened the north for everything from freight, fishing, farming, lumber, and oil exploration."

Perhaps one of the most important legacies of the Mackenzie Highway was the start of commercial trucking. Bernice Lorenzen, in her foreword to *Tales of the Mackenzie*, writes,

> "Hundreds of tons of freight could now move from the railway at Grimshaw to Hay River, where it was stored in huge warehouses, to be moved down the Mackenzie River at a later date to serve all points North. This led to the birth of a new industry in the North. Trucking companies grew overnight."[29]

Freight which used to be shipped by air or water could now be hauled overland. Food, supplies, and equipment destined for the mines in Yellowknife or on Great Bear Lake could now be hauled year-round by truck over the highway to Hay River, where the supplies were transferred onto barges. Thus the chief launching point for barge traffic on Great Slave Lake and the Mackenzie River shifted from Waterways and Fort Smith to Hay River, NWT.

Fish, destined for eastern markets, became the chief backhaul for many a trucker. Previously, fish had been hauled in the summers over the water route via the Slave and Athabasca rivers. With the new highway, winter fishing became viable and the fishing industry expanded to a year-round activity. In one year, 1951, 8 000 000 pounds [3 628 800 kg] of whitefish and trout, valued at $612 000, were backhauled by large trucks from Great Slave Lake down the Mackenzie Highway, compared to 1 000 000 pounds [453 600 kg] hauled previously over the water route.[30]

The fur industry also benefited from the new highway. Pelts which used to be sent by air or by water were shipped overland by truck to Grimshaw. Trappers, once isolated from services in towns, could now have their food and medical supplies shipped in by trucks, and occasionally trappers and their dogs would hitch a ride with truckers.

Agriculture expanded further North during the 1950s, especially after the connecting graded and gravel road to Fort Vermilion and La Crete, and another to Keg River, which were both completed by 1952. New homesteads were carved out of the bush for growing crops. Farmers could now haul wheat and barley by truck, rather than just feeding the grain to their hogs and cattle.

The Mackenzie Highway changed the trucking industry as well. Over the winter road, individual truckers or small family-owned operations had hauled anything and everything they could get their hands on. The trucks were 2-tons and 3-tons, small and versatile, and there was not that much investment in specialized equipment. But after the completion of the highway, several trucking companies became more specialized.

The Mackenzie Highway gave access and thrust to resource development. Gravel trucks, log trucks, tankers, and heavier tractors for hauling oilfield rigs began to appear in the 50s and 60s. Some companies, like Grimshaw Trucking & Distributing, Byers Transport, and Hay River Truck Lines, stayed with general freight, while others, like Papp's Trucking and Kaps Transport Ltd., became specialized in oilfield and industrial hauling when the oil activity moved into northern Alberta. Hank Thompson (High Level Construction), John King (King's Construction), and Vern Estabrook (Estabrook Construction) combined road construction with their hauling activities.

The Mackenzie Highway brought in the beginning of the tourist industry. Adventurous tourists seeking new experiences began travelling in the summer over the highway to visit the scenic Alexandra and Louise falls and Great Slave Lake. "In addition, tourists were able to see many typical sights of the north – trappers' cabins, settlements, Indian camps and miles of wild, uninhabited country."[31] Tourist camps and, later, motels were built to accommodate the tourists, as well as the truckers.

The opening of the highway had its downside, especially for the northern Native peoples, whose traditional lifestyle of trapping and fishing was now threatened by competition from white trappers and commercial fishermen. The Dene people had almost no experience operating equipment at the time when the highway was built. Their chief forms of transportation were canoes, wagons, and dog teams. Some were hired to help with brushing out the bush right of way, but the more lucrative construction and trucking jobs went to others. However, many Cree and Metis people, with their long tradition of involvement in northern transportation, adapted to motorized transportation.

The increase and spread of disease, particularly tuberculosis and measles, could be attributed in part to the building of the all-weather highway, which made communities more vulnerable to contagious diseases brought in from the outside. The concentration of Native peoples in communities on or near the highway, however, made much-needed medical services more accessible.

A growing problem affecting northern Native people was the increase in the availability of illegal booze that was smuggled into northern Alberta and the Territories along the Mackenzie Highway.[32]

The increased traffic overland into the NWT required both governments to maintain the highway. The Alberta Department of Highways maintained the section between Grimshaw and the Alberta boundary, and the Dominion Government maintained the 130 km [81 mi.] of highway in the NWT. Snow clearing in winter, between 1948 and 1954, could be slow, despite the optimistic tone in the *Motor Truck and Coach* article.[33]

> *"In winter two snowplows keep the road open – one working out of Peace River and the other out of Upper Hay River…Since the road was opened, maintenance work has kept the road open all year round, with only the occasional filling in of muskeg areas necessary in the summer to prevent settling of the road bed."*[34]

Perhaps the greatest legacy of the Mackenzie Highway was the end to the isolation of hundreds of people living in the North. The completion of the highway marked a new era of transportation and communication. It changed the lifestyle of the average person living in proximity to the highway. Manufactured goods ordered through mail-order catalogues could reach customers more quickly. Fresh fruits and vegetables could now

One of the legacies of the Mackenzie Highway was the development of new communities like Manning, beginning in 1946. This photo was taken in the early 50s. Fred Lorenzen collection.

be hauled in by truck, enriching the diets of many northerners. And the highway effect-ed many changes in education, medical care, and social services. One-room schools were gradually replaced with consolidated schools in larger towns, and children were bussed from surrounding districts. New towns like Manning in the mid-40s and High Level in the late 50s were built after the construction of the highway.

Dr. Mary Percy Jackson of Keg River spent 20 years trying to give proper medical attention to her patients that were spread over a huge territory. She welcomed the new highway like a friend whose arrival was long overdue:

> *"We were thrilled when the Mackenzie Highway was built after the war; even though it was only a rather narrow graveled road, it was passable year round. By 1955 there was even a bus service three times a week from Peace River to Fort Vermilion, and once we had the Keg River Road built up and graveled, we were able to get three mails a week. That was quite different from the eight mails a year we had when I first came to Keg River."*[35]

Notes

[1] The Fallow Papers, Dept. of Public Works, Provincial Archives of Alberta, 68.307, box 87 and 88.

[2] Ibid.

[3] Ibid.

[4] "Mackenzie Highway Vital to North," *Motor Truck & Coach*, July 1952.

[5] David A. Harrison, "The First Winter Road Ever," *Up Here*, March/April 1990, p. 57.

[6] Interview with Stanley Smith, High Level, August 19, 1999.

[7] "Mackenzie Highway Vital to North," *Motor Truck and Coach*, July 1952, p. 9.

[8] Interview with Ed Zack, at Hay River on August 20, 1998.

[9] A special thanks to Bill Beattie for permission to quote extensively from his story, originally published in *Tales of the Mackenzie Highway*.

[10] Telephone interview with Norm Mytron, August 11, 1999.

[11] From Mary Dixon's story "Tom Dixon" in *Tales of the Mackenzie Highway*, p. 40.

[12] Ibid.

[13] Letter from George Predy to Bernice Lorenzen, August 1, 1999.

[14] Ibid.

[15] *Tales of the Mackenzie Highway*, p. 21.

[16] David A. Harrison, PhD, "Opening and Naming the Mackenzie Highway," *Alberta History*, published by the Historical Society of Alberta: Vol. 38, Number 2, spring 1990, pp. 24-29.

[17] From "The Bill Mueller Story," in *Tales of the Mackenzie Highway*, p. 36.

[18] "Fred Lorenzen Story," an unpublished story written by Fred Lorenzen, June 1999.

[19] Fred Lorenzen, "Fred Lorenzen Recalls," in *Tales of the Mackenzie Highway*, p. 13.

[20] Interview with Albert Hamilton, April 24, 1996.

[21] As quoted in David A. Harrison, "Opening and Naming of the Mackenzie Highway," p. 24.

[22] Ibid., p. 26.

[23] Ibid., p. 28.

[24] From Ben Peters, "A Trip to Peace River That I'll Never Forget."

[25] Unpublished story by Ben Peters, February, 1999.

[26] Interview with Ed Zack, Hay River, August 20, 1998.

[27] *Tales of the Mackenzie Highway*, p. 8.

[28] Op. Cit., p. 16.

[29] Op. Cit., p. 2.

[30] "Mackenzie Highway Vital to North," *Motor Truck and Coach*, p. 9.

[31] Ibid.

[32] Prohibition may have ended for most Albertans and Canadians in 1923, but it was still illegal to sell liquor to Natives until the 1950s and 1960s. Illegal trade in booze, however, flourished in the North, and the Mackenzie Highway became a conduit for the transportation of liquor.

[33] *Motor Truck & Coach*, p. 10.

[34] According to Stella Friedel, by 1954 there were grader men every 50 miles [80 km] to clear snow, as traffic increased. High Level had a blacksmith shop, where Mike Papirney re-capped grader blades. "Bobby Gray and Howard McKay were the 'toast of the north' for years." As services expanded grader men were posted at the Upper Hay and Steen rivers.

[35] *The Homemade Brass Plate*, p. 189.

🚛 Chapter 5 – Pioneer Truckers Before 1948 🚚

This chapter recognizes truckers who started trucking companies in northern Alberta and the Northwest Territories prior to 1948. Some of these pioneer truckers expanded their operations into larger companies, while others remained one-truck owners. Some family trucking companies had started hauling before the Mackenzie Highway opened in 1948. They cut their teeth on the Grimshaw-Hay River winter road and the Canol roads.

Most men who started trucking in northern Alberta before the completion of the Mackenzie Highway in 1948 were local. Many were homesteaders, or children of homesteaders, who had arrived in northern Alberta, to the North Star, Battle River Prairie, Keg River, and Fort Vermilion districts in the late 1920s and early 1930s. They had started driving horse-drawn wagons, hauling grain to the railhead at Grimshaw. It seemed a natural transition to learn to drive tractors and trucks, which began to appear in the early 30s.

The Dirty Thirties held little fear for northerners. It was pretty much a continuation of the conditions that existed in the 20s. They had survived with little cash, no electricity, no telephones, poor roads, no indoor plumbing, few doctors and nurses. These were all conveniences that people living in urban areas of southern Alberta took pretty much for granted. Many children of northern homesteaders did not have the luxury of acquiring a secondary education. A grade school education in a one-room schoolhouse was the extent of their formal education. Before the North had consolidated high schools, the nearest high school was in Peace River. Most families in northern districts could not afford to pay for their children's board. Also, youth were an important part of the family economy, and they were needed to work on the farms.

Trucking on the Grimshaw-Hay River Winter Road

A few hardy (or foolhardy) truckers had ventured over the winter cat road between Grimshaw and Hay River in the tracks of cat trains, almost as soon as the right-of-way had been cleared. Trucks followed the cat trains; if they got into trouble, they had the tractors to pull them out. During the spring of 1941, the first truck convoy left Grimshaw enroute to Hay River and ran into all kinds of difficulties. It wasn't until the American army widened the winter road for the Canol Project the following year that freighting by truck was viable.

During the Second World War, in the north, any man who had a truck, or who had access to a relative's or neighbor's trucks, could find work hauling for the American army – first on the Alaska Highway, then on the Canol 6 Road between Peace River and

Mills Lake, NWT. They made good money, more money than they had ever dreamed of making. Some used this nest egg to buy their own truck and start a general freighting company. They hauled whenever they had a load to haul, whether it was grain, hogs, horses, perishable foods, fuel, machinery, backhauls of fish, or gold ore or pitchblende from the northern mines.

Once the Mackenzie Highway was completed in the fall of 1948, the people of northern Alberta, particularly those who lived north of the Third Battle, could now transport their grain, potatoes, hogs, and cattle by truck to Grimshaw instead of depending upon the uncertainties of river transportation on the Peace. They could have fresh vegetables, dry goods, farm equipment, and other merchandise delivered to their door, and receive mail more than two or three times in winter.

Trucking in the Lower Peace

Fort Vermilion, La Crete, and Rocky Lane, however, were still virtually isolated from the Mackenzie Highway in 1948, and did not have an all-weather road connecting them to it. There were only winding, narrow wagon trails. Farmers still had to depend upon water on the Peace River, between break-up and freeze-up. Tompkin's Landing (later La Crete Landing) east of Paddle Prairie provided access across the Peace River. But the ferries only operated from break-up until freeze-up. After freeze-up, only winding wagon trails linked these communities to the outside world.

A fairly good wagon trail existed between Grimshaw and Notikewin in the early 30s, called the Battle River Trail. Other trails wandered through the bush to Native settlements. A well-used wagon trail existed along the telegraph right-of-way, which had been brushed out in 1930 between Paddle Prairie and Fort Vermilion. Another trail wandered between Fort Vermilion, Rocky Lane, and Eleske and joined the winter road at "The Crossroads," where the town of High Level would be built beginning in the mid-1950s. It was not until 1952 that a gravel road was extended between High Level Crossing and Fort Vermilion.

Tony Tretick, Tony's Truck Service

Tony Tretick arrived from Saskatchewan in Peace River in October 1928. He bought Palace Transfer, a freighting outfit with two teams of horse and drays, and began hauling general freight.[1]

A few farmers in the Fort Vermilion district had small farm trucks, but most still used horse-drawn wagons to haul freight and livestock to Grimshaw or Peace River town. Because the telegraph right-of-way was too narrow to take a two- or three-ton truck over, Tony Tretick and Dick Randle decided to widen the trail in 1943 so that they could take Tony's International truck over the route. They also had to corduroy several creeks, because the ice was not thick enough to hold the weight of the truck. Tony

Tretick and Dick Randle were the first drivers to haul freight by truck into Fort Vermilion.

On that first memorable trip in 1943, it seemed to Tony that everyone had something they wanted him to bring back from Peace River. "I had a list a foot long, everything from nuts to whiskey for Christmas, a few cases of bread and even ice cream, if I thought it was cold enough so that it wouldn't melt."[2] After that first trip to Fort Vermilion by truck, Tony switched from horses to trucks. He sold Palace Transfer in 1944 to devote his time to his new trucking business.[3]

Tony's Truck Service provided the first mail delivery by truck to the area. Before that, mail had been delivered first by wagon or sleigh by Louis Bourassa, from 1916 to 1935, between Peace River and Fort Vermilion, and then by airplane. That first winter of 1943, Tony and Dick Randle made five trips before the snow got too deep to travel. The following year Tony bought a new truck and installed a snowplow on the front so that he could plow the snow as they drove along at 10 or 20 miles an hour [16-32 km/hr]. By 1945, Tony Tretick expanded his service with two trucks, which hauled freight to Keg River, Paddle Prairie, Meander River, and Hay Lakes, as well as Fort Vermilion. Several local men worked as drivers or helpers for Tony's Trucking, including Doug Stranaghan, Dick Randle, Buster Lambert, John Ward, and Clifford Smith.

When the snow was particularly deep during the winter of 1945, Tony was unable to make deliveries to Hay Lakes (Habay-Assumption). An arrangement was made for him to deliver 10 tons of supplies to 'The Crossroads'. Tony recalls: "When we arrived at this point there were 10 teams with sleighs to pick up the freight and one team with a caboose which had smoke curling from its chimney." It gave Tony some second thoughts about the wisdom of driving a truck, especially the next day when it was -54° F [-47°C].

> "Inside this cozy caboose was a wood burning stove and everyone was comfortable…I thought to myself, I might be smart to know how to drive a truck but they were smarter at hauling freight. There was no snow shoveling, no frozen gas lines, no worries about breakdowns as there is with the truck a hundred miles from nowhere…Yes, many times I wished I was driving a team instead of a truck."[4]

Tony's Truck Service hauled the first combine by truck into the Fort Vermilion area in 1947. Tony continued to operate his trucking service in the North Peace after the Mackenzie Highway was completed in 1948. He took Doug Stranaghan as a partner in 1949 and, in 1961, Les Stranaghan became the third partner.

In 1967 the Stranaghan brothers bought Tony's Truck Service and continued to operate the business under the same name. At that time they had three single-axle trucks – one with a 20-foot [6m] van and the other two with open boxes which were tarped. The Stranaghans built a garage, warehouse, and office in Peace River.

Before the Stranaghan brothers purchased refrigeration vans, frozen foods were a worry. They had to wrap frozen foods in blankets and tarps to keep food from thawing.

"Sometimes the ice cream was running out when we delivered it," wrote Les Stranaghan.[5] "All loading was done by hand and flour and sugar came in 100 pound [45 kg] bags...All the stores gave the drivers their orders for the wholesale, there were no telephones. You'd deliver these orders so that the goods would be ready for your picking up for the next trip."

In 1985 the Stranaghans disposed of the company's trucks and retained the warehouse for awhile.

Henry "Hank" Thompson, High Level Construction

Hank Thompson was a pioneer, not only in northern trucking but in many other fields of transportation and road construction. He was one of the most respected northerners, remembered with fondness by many people in the North Peace.

Hank Thompson arrived in Grimshaw in 1929; he stayed on with friend Lorne Harlson and the two trapped together for a month at the Third Battle. "I then decided I was not a trapper, so returned to Grimshaw and accepted the job that Bill Miller had offered me as mechanic in his garage."[6] He helped Miller build a snowmobile, which came in very handy, as there was a lot of snow that winter. The snowmobile was used to take people to Fairview and back. It was also used to take Dr. Matas to his patients.

Hank Thompson bought this Diamond T in 1942. Hank Thompson collection.

He got his first truck in the 1930s and started to haul grain and other freight for local farmers and businessmen. When the winter road was completed, he got a contract from the Hudson Bay Company to haul freight into Upper Hay River, Fort Vermilion, Indian Cabins, and Hay Lakes.

After the U.S. Army came into the Peace River Bloc in 1942, Hank went to haul freight on the Alaska Highway for eight months. "I used a Diamond T truck that stood up better than any make of truck to the tough conditions up there. I came back from there with $1200 in my pocket and bought a farm and went farming as well as trucking." When the American Army moved into Peace River in 1942-43, Hank hauled material for the Canol pipeline, from Peace River to Lower Hay River and Mills Lake.

"Hank, along with many truckers from the Grimshaw and Manning areas, worked around the clock to complete the winter haul before break-up. Every winter after for several years, Hank was trucking north to Lower Hay and Mills Lake."[7]

He got into the road construction business when he went into partnership with Vern Estabrook during the Second World War. The two of them bought two D-6 Cats, had a brush cutter built, and began to cut and pile brush.

One of the more unusual hauls Hank Thompson made was a wrecked airplane and lighting plant.

"I loaded my truck on Jack O'Sullivan's boat and we went to Fort Vermilion to pick up the airplane and lighting plant that had been left behind. We hauled it out with the freight and my truck to Fort Vermilion, where it was loaded on the D.A. Thomas …and then to Peace River. This was one of the most difficult missions I had ever encountered, what with mosquitoes, black flies, and practically no roads. I had to hire the Regus brothers with teams to assist me."[8]

After the war, he hauled fresh fish for Menzies Fisheries, from Great Slave Lake to Faust, Alberta, for the Chicago markets. He also got a contract to haul freight into Upper Hay River, Fort Vermilion, Indian Cabins, and Hay Lakes. In the winter of 1948-49, the Catholic Diocese contracted Hank to open a road from High Level Crossing to Hay Lakes and to haul supplies to the new mission at Assumption.

"It was necessary that I take a Cat in and make a road from High Level to Hay Lakes following an old bush road. When the road was completed I hired a number of trucks to help haul the freight in."

In 1954 he took over the agency for Imperial Oil at High Level and had Doug Rule manage the bulk plant. Hank and his wife Pat moved to High Level and, in 1955, he started his own construction company, High Level Construction. Thus he was one of the earliest residents in High Level, along with Jim Jones and Don Staples, who operated a stopping place. Hank built a shop, a house, and later a café and motel, called the Blue Top, and got Valle Gray from Fort Vermilion to come and manage the operation.

Hank had always had an interest in aviation, ever since he flew with Punch Dickins in 1926. He had soloed in 1947, and flew several times. He and Vern Estabrook had bought a Seabee to use for bush work in the north and Hank used to fly with his friend, Bourke "Tack" Tackaberry, who had been a fighter pilot in the Second World War.[9]

It must not have been easy to get the Department of Transport to finally give Hank a legitimate license to fly in 1960. Gordon Reid wrote, in *Notes of the North*, "Hank had a problem when he approached the Department of Transport to get a license to fly. He had only one eye and one-eyed pilots were rare in Canada."[10]

In 1960 Hank bought a Super-Cub C-FMNE, and built an airstrip and hangar to house it.

> *"His foresight in building an airport was greatly appreciated by the oil companies and charters when oil was discovered [at Rainbow Lake] in the 60s. Some days it saw more traffic going in and out of Thompson Airport than the Edmonton Municipal had."*[11]

His company continued expanding through the 50s and 60s, especially with the purchase of heavy road building equipment, which he used to build roads for Alberta Forestry, Alberta Transportation, and various oil companies. In 1971, Hank retired, and he and his wife moved from High Level to Grimshaw. He is fondly remembered by many friends, especially John King, who had worked for him. "Hank loved to play practical jokes on his friends and he was well known for his wit and generosity, and …his flying exploits….Hank Thompson was everybody's friend."

Ed Dillman, Dillman Transport, North Star, and L & D Carriers, Manning

Ed Dillman of North Star started hauling grain for local farmers between Battle River Prairie and Grimshaw in the mid-30s. In 1935, Ed bought his first truck, a Rugby. The Dillmans moved to B.C. for a short while but they returned to North Star in 1936, where Ed started trucking grain to the railhead with a D-30 International. A year later he started the first garage and service station in North Star. Oldest son Lawrence remembered, "He had Imperial Oil pumps out front and UFA bulk oil right behind the garage." At the time he also took over the International Harvester dealership, which was in the same building. Dillman's Garage was a fixture in North Star for many years, until Ed sold it in 1949.[12]

During the war from 1942 to 1946, Ed Dillman hauled for the American Army, mostly to Mills Lake. He continued trucking after the war and running the Dillman Garage and IHC dealership. In the late 40s, Dillman bought a KB-8 tandem and hauled grain and machinery under the name Dillman Transport. One time he hauled a D7 cat with dozer and winch, and a Hobart welder bare back from Calgary to west Hotchkiss.[13] He also had four or five barrels of fuel behind the welder, for Slim Moulson. Lawrence stated, "We were a long time coming down old Peace River hill."

Ed Dillman and son Bob, ca. 1939. Dillman had the International Harvester agency in North Star from 1937 to 1951. Ed Dillman collection.

In 1953 Ed went into partnership with George Levine, who used to work for him off and on. L & D Carriers hauled general merchandise between Edmonton and Hotchkiss, about 15 miles [24 km] north of Manning. Lawrence recalls, "I think at the time we had three semis, a body truck, and a pickup that George used to drive in Edmonton." Lawrence, who had a chauffeur's license, also drove for L & D Carriers.

> *"At that time it was regular freight, basically groceries, and that included every-thing from cookies to ice cream, slabs of meat and meat that was wrapped. We'd go to Edmonton, load up and leave Edmonton at 6:00 p.m. And we'd have to be back to Grimshaw the next morning because the people expected it, even though the roads were the way they were in those days. The pavement only ran to Clyde Corner [about 75 km or 46 mi. north of Edmonton]. The rest of it was just gravel, if you could call it grav-el. Some places along Lesser Slave Lake it was terrible."[14]*

Starting in the 60s, Ed Dillman went into oilfield construction and built forestry roads. Second son Henry continued to operate Dillman Transport Ltd. In 1962-63, Henry hauled the first train engine to Pine Point in the Northwest Territories, for the construc-tion of the Great Slave Railway. The locomotive engine was needed for laying track from the north end, to speed up the completion of the railway line. In the late 60s tragedy struck the family when another son, Clem, was killed. At the time he was work-ing for his brother Henry. Clem was driving a fuel truck when he hit a grader on the Third Battle bridge. The truck went over the bridge and blew up.

Ed Dillman retired in 1970 and died in 1971. Henry Dillman continued to operate Dillman Transport Ltd. until 1978.

George Frith, Mail Hauler – Grimshaw to Notikewin

George Frith of North Star started trucking in the 1930s, hauling grain from the North Star area to the railhead at Grimshaw, and backhauling freight. In 1942 he got the contract to pick up and deliver mail from Grimshaw to Notikewin. The K-5 International truck could also haul passengers. He charged $1.00 per passenger to ride from Grimshaw to North Star, thus providing one of the earliest bus services in the North Peace. If a passenger did not have the money, George let him or her ride anyway.

His day was a long one: up at 3:00 a.m, he would pick up mail at the Battle River Hospital, Notikewin, then head south, pick up mail at North Star, Lone Star, Dixonville, Chinook Valley, and on to Grimshaw. At Grimshaw he collected the mail bags and sometimes passengers, and made the return trip, usually arriving home by 5:00 p.m. His wife Clara wrote:

> *"In Grimshaw the general mail was previously sorted into bags for each place along the way. The registered mail was all placed in one bag, and at each stop the postmaster opened the bag and took out the mail for the particular spot. The bag was locked and carried in the cab of the truck. George did not have a key, only the postmasters were allowed to open the bag."*[15]

Joe Ursulah, the Trucker-Banker of the Fort Vermilion District

Early truckers had to wear many hats. They were asked to deliver the mail, pick up groceries, backhaul tractor parts, or give a trapper and his dogs a ride to a trading post. Joe Ursulah wore another hat – as a local banker.[16]

Joe Ursulah was one of the earliest truckers in the Fort Vermilion district. After the War he got a job on the Mackenzie Highway hauling gravel. He took a side trip over the rough trail to Rocky Lane with his 1945 Reo 2½ ton truck and started hauling for the local farmers. While trucking, he rented Mrs. Andrew Donecz's farm, and in the 1950s he settled permanently on his own homestead.

In the summer of 1947, Joe hauled the first overland truckload of grain from the district to Grimshaw – 255 bushels of No. 1 hard wheat for Arthur Simmons Sr. For other farmers he hauled hogs, cattle, stags, and sheep to the W.J. Lampley Livestock Co. in Peace River. He would also bring supplies of fresh fruit from the market gardens at Peace River.

In *Notes of the North*, Gordon Reid lists one of Joe's bills of sale from December 1949:

Sold to: Einar Malmquist, Fort Vermilion

1 Box Pears	$ 5.10
1 Box Peaches	$ 2.40
1 Box Plums	$ 1.90
Twine	$ 9.75
1 Box Apples	$ 3.50
1 Box Pears	$ 5.10
Freight	$ 1.90
Paid Total	$26.65

One of the more unusual hats he wore was as a banker. Because farmers did not get into Peace River town very often to cash their cheques, they asked Joe to do it for them. He cashed the cheques at a bank in Peace River. When he returned to the Fort Vermilion district, with approximately $5000 cash, the farmers met him at Ponton Landing (near Rocky Lane) to pick up their money. Joe had it carefully sorted out in piles of bills and anchored down each pile with a rock.

Larry Sheck, Sheck Brothers

Lawrence "Larry" Sheck is a respected pioneer of northern transportation. He was reputedly the first in the North to haul freight by water, tractor trains, and trucks.

Larry decided to go north in the spring of 1937. He was 22 years old when he went to work for the Yellowknife Transportation Company, after Harcourt, McLeod, and Nieland moved operations from Great Bear Lake to Yellowknife.

In the spring of 1937, Larry worked with 12 or 13 other men helping Bert Nieland build a tugboat and barge at Taylor Flats, B.C. The work was completed in June, and Larry joined the crew to take the *Little Chief* tugboat and barge down the Peace River. At Fort Fitzgerald, the boat and barge were trucked by Ryan Brothers over the 16-mile portage [25 km] around the "Rapids of the Damned" on the Slave River between Fort Fitzgerald and Fort Smith; then they continued across Great Slave Lake and down the Mackenzie River.

It was a memorable trip for Larry.[17]

"We had 50 barrels of [airplane] gas for Fort Nelson. We went into Resolution. We delivered some freight at Pine Point. There was a prospector's camp then. And we went to Hay River, over to Wrigley Harbour [on the west end of Great Slave Lake], and we left the barge at Fort Simpson with all the barrels of gas around the edge of the tug boat. Then we went up the Liard…and went right up to Nelson River, but we couldn't get

into the Nelson River because of the sandbar. So there was a bunch of us, and we had lots of rope; we stripped naked and took the anchor across, sunk it in the sand, and we threw in the barrels of gas. Grant McConachie [the bush pilot who ordered the aviation fuel] would have had a fit! Three barrels at a time, we tied them together and waded across. We had all 50 barrels of gas floating in the middle of the river. But they were well sealed. Then we turned the boat backwards and put it in reverse and washed the sand away. Of course the boat came up when we took the gas [barrels] off. When we got the boat across, we put the tow rope on the anchor and swung them all into shore, and we had to lift all these barrels off the water and reload them. Everything was done by hand. A barrel of gas weighed 425 pounds [193 kg].

"We got up to Fort Nelson and delivered the gas. Then we went back down [north] to Fort Simpson, on to Fort Wrigley and Fort Norman. We did some work for Imperial Oil at the oil wells, 20 or 30 miles [32-48 km] down the river. Then we went back to Fort Norman and up the Bear River. It took us nine days. We winched the tugboat up the Bear River Rapids into Bear Lake and went across to the El Dorado Mine. After El Dorado Mine, the tug took a load of radium ore to Fort Smith. And we made two trips to Yellowknife for Northern Transportation."

After the trip, Larry moved to Yellowknife, which was booming at the time. The first winter he worked as a cook for Sunbird Diamond Drill, which were subcontractors of Negus Mines. In the spring he got a job as foreman with Negus, where he hauled all the freight that came off the boats to the Negus Mines. "I was 22 years old and I was surface foreman of the Negus Mines. I was all through the Negus Mines, all under construction then until they went into production. Then the Negus Mines financed me into the cat trains."

Negus's little Caterpillar tractor, a D-4, came on the first boat that arrived in Yellowknife in the spring of 1938. "It had a winch on it. That's all we had. We didn't have a truck. Just a little Cat to haul all that freight. And we had to haul it 1500 feet [457m] up over the rocks to where the mine was – lumber, cement, sand, everything."

In December of 1938, Negus Mines purchased another Caterpillar D-4 tractor, which had come on the boat to Fort Resolution. Larry and Carl Werner flew over to Fort Resolution to bring it back to Yellowknife. It was the first time a tractor had made a trip across the ice of Great Slave Lake.

"We didn't have a caboose or nothing…we had a sleigh with a tent on it. We had a stove made out of a 45-gallon [170l] gas barrel. We'd light a fire, and we'd run the tractor right up against the stove and put the tent over it to keep the radiator from freezing. We didn't have any antifreeze then, just water in the radiator. We'd put planks on the ice on either side of the tractor. I slept on one side and Carl slept on the other. It was the first tractor that came across Great Slave Lake in 1938."

In the winter of 1938, Larry and Hans Hansen cut and hauled wood with the little Cat by night. Bill Stewart of Negus Mines told Larry about another Cat that was available in Edmonton. Bill Stewart made the arrangements, and Larry bought the RD-6 Cat for $3500, which he picked up in Edmonton. It was his first Cat, which he used as his freighting Cat. It was the start of his tractor train business.

Larry continued to trouble-shoot for Negus Mines. In 1940, Larry expanded his cat train business and made his first trip over the winter road to Grimshaw. He would continue for several years to bring the cat trains across Great Slave Lake each winter. "In all the years I used tractors, I never had one break down on me in the winter time. And when they went out in the winter, they never stopped till spring. We ran them 24 hours a day."

Sheck Brothers cat train arriving at Yellowknife, spring 1943. Larry Sheck collection.

In 1945 Larry and his brother Don Sheck bought a sawmill near Fort Resolution, and a lake boat named the *Guy* and some barges from Al MacDonald, who had originally purchased the *Guy* from the Oblate mission at Fort Resolution. Sheck Brothers sawmill was one of several sawmills on the lake at the time when Yellowknife was expanding and needed a lot of lumber. Sheck Brothers sawmill was located about four miles [6 km] upstream from the mouth of the Slave River, on the east shore. "We had two barges. We could push 100 000 feet [30 480m] of lumber on the barge across to Yellowknife from our sawmill."

In 1945, '46, and '47, Sheck Brothers started using trucks over the winter road, as well as tractor trains. In 1946 disaster struck when two of their Cats sunk to the bottom of Great Slave Lake. *News of the North* covered this event on January 6, 1946:[18]

> *"The first 'cat train' of the season to leave Yellowknife in 1946 met with misfortune Sunday afternoon about 50 miles [80 km] from Yellowknife and ten miles [16 km] northwest of Outpost Island while crossing Great Slave Lake en route to Hay River. A freak accident – and the two Caterpillar tractors …were under 300 feet [91m] of water.*

"The outfit, which comprised 14 sleighs and a light load, left Yellowknife on Friday afternoon of last week with a seven-man crew under the supervision of Don Sheck, a partner in the firm. They were followed closely by the Grimshaw-Yellowknife Transportation company's winter train. All went well until Sunday afternoon.

"Halting at a wide crack in the ice, the two tractors, a RD-4 and a RD-6, were uncoupled and a pressure point was tested and successfully crossed. The crew were preparing to again hitch the tractors to the sleighs and one tractor went ahead a distance of only a dozen feet or so. Suddenly the ice gave way and one tractor broke through, then the other broke through the ice as well. Every attempt was made by the drivers, Bill Greer and Bill Coburn, to reach safe ice with their machines, but this was impossible. Fortunately they jumped to safety when the tractors plunged into the icy water. Bob Seddon, who was between the tractors at the time, also leaped to safety."

The loss of the Cats was only partially covered by insurance. No attempt could be made to raise the tractors because they were too deep, so Larry replaced them with other tractors. The loss of the RD-4 and RD-6 Cats to the deep waters of Great Slave Lake is still vividly remembered by Larry. "I cried when they went down."

Sheck Brothers got into truck transportation as well as cat trains. In 1945 Larry bought a new three-ton Fargo for $2500. In 1946, they worked on the construction of the Mackenzie Highway during the summer, and hauled freight in the winter, with trucks. The fleet included Fargos, Internationals, and Diamond Ts. At the peak of their transportation business they had nine trucks. Sheck Brothers also contracted other trucks and drivers.[19]

One of the worst parts of the Mackenzie Highway was 280 Hill (Jackpot Creek).[20] Many pioneer truckers have their own horror stories about this hill. As Larry wrote in *Tales of the Mackenzie Highway*,

"We had to go down this side and turn sharp at the bottom; there was a dirty little creek and we couldn't get a run at the other side. Those trucks [Diamond Ts and Internationals] had all kinds of power, but no speed. We managed to get up with one of the Fargos and Ray Lutman had an old 1939 Ford, and he managed to get up the hill. By cutting down three poplar trees and tying the trucks together end-to-end with logging chains, we pulled the other trucks to the top."

When Larry Sheck sold his transportation business, he continued his love affair with Cats. He moved to Grimshaw permanently in 1949 and started working as a Caterpillar mechanic and sold Caterpillar tractors for a number of years.

Vern Estabrook, Estabrook Construction Ltd.

Vernon "Vern" Estabrook came of age during the Depression. He started working in the North when he was 17 as a catskinner for Yellowknife Transportation Company Ltd. During the Second World War he drove a Cat on the Canol Project, and hauled freight a short spell on the Alaska Highway. By the end of the Second World War, Vern was a seasoned northerner and an experienced Cat operator. These experiences would help him later in life when he started his own construction company, Estabrook Construction Ltd. Although Vern did not run a trucking company, he was closely associated with truckers and had trucks to haul his equipment in his construction business. He was a true pioneer in northern transportation and construction.

In February of 1940, Vern got a job, along with the family's small 2-Ton Caterpillar crawler tractor, working for Bert Nieland of the Yellowknife Transportation Company. Vern towed trucks over the winter road to Hay River and Yellowknife.

> "It turned out to be a tough undertaking; some trucks broke down or were in too poor a shape to continue, so dropped their loads and returned south. I finally reached Lower Hay with the Cat; a larger diesel Cat and several sleighs went south from Hay River to pick up the freight the trucks had to abandon at Indian Cabins."[21]

Since Vern was only 17 at the time, he was very much the youngster on the cat train crew. Vern's son Miles remembers his dad telling him that he got teased a lot by the crew when he first started catskinning.[22]

> "He was just a young lad, and he was always sitting on the edge of the seat, scared to drop through [the ice]. So they'd always give him a hard time about being a little bit of a chicken his first few trips north. Of course, if you broke through the flood ice,[23] you just crawled your way out of it and kept going. You tried to steer wide of it, one way or the other, so the cat train that followed behind you, with all the guys on it, wouldn't go into the hole.

> "One time he went into a hole, crawled his way out of it. You're supposed to turn one way or the other so the bunkhouse doesn't go into the hole. Well, he put the bunkhouse straight into the middle of it. He said the front of the bunk went down, the windows flew open, and the guys were bailing out left and right. He turned around, then he never looked back. He just kept pulling. That was the last time they called him chicken."

About this time, Vern and Hank Thompson formed their partnership.[24]

Vern got a job as a tractor operator with Bechtel, Price, and Callahan, on the Canol Project, in December 1942. He worked on the Canol road between Upper and Lower Hay River and from Lower Hay River to Norman Wells. During this period his letters to his father reveal many details of life for civilians working on the Canol Project. (See Chapter 3).

Miles remembers his father telling him about one unusual haul during the war years:

> "With the 2-ton Cat, they left here and went up to Yellowknife to pull some old army trucks back to Grimshaw. They pulled the trucks all the way back and hand-bombed these sacks in the railway cars. He asked a guy, 'What is this stuff?' The guy

Vern Estabrook looking very cold. Canol Project, 1943. Vern Estabrook collection.

told him, 'It's uranium.' He figured it was probably some of the uranium that went into the bomb."

After the war ended in 1945, the need for goods in the North continued, and Vern got a job hauling for the U.S. Army. By September 1945, Vern was working for Vic Ingraham, who was starting up another freighting business, Grimshaw-Yellowknife Transportation Ltd. Correspondence from Vic Ingraham to Vern Estabrook during the fall of 1945 suggests that Vern held a foreman's position, overseeing the building of sleighs at Grimshaw, while Vic was in Edmonton getting financing in place and purchasing some Cats.

One of Vic Ingraham's letters posted from Edmonton reflects a sense of urgency of getting the sleighs put together. He obviously put a lot trust in Vern in Grimshaw to carry out his directives:

"Vern: What I would like to know is, how many sets we could make up if we had the runners shod? What width shoe? And have we got cross chains enough? I wish to set up at least another 10 sets of sleighs and get them to Lower Hay as soon as possible. I thought we would ship them here for shoeing as it is a hell of a lot cheaper and quicker. Let me know what you think of this by wire. Deal all settled with the Vancouver people and expect to be going full blast in a few days – got a D-6 and a D-4. Both have blades, will get delivery here about the 10th and will ship to Grimshaw at once and send 2 cats instead of one down the road. For Christ's sake send me down a deer or a moose. This meat business is the shits. Regards, Vic.

By this time the Mackenzie Highway was being surveyed, and the days of cat trains pulling freight between Grimshaw and Lower Hay River were numbered. Trucks soon replaced the cat trains, and the need for winter roads and connecting roads to the Mackenzie Highway created job opportunities for tractor operators.

In the early 50s, Vern started his own construction company.[25]

When the Rainbow oilfield opened up northern Alberta in the late 50s, things got pretty frantic. Off-road construction work was needed to cut brush, make roads, and clear the oil leases. Vern's business expanded. When the Great Slave Railway to Pine Point, NWT, was being constructed in 1962-63, Vern's construction company did a lot of work building the right-of-way.

Many young men got their start working for Vern Estabrook. He would often finance them into their first Cats, and shared his years of knowledge catskinning in the north.

In 1983, Vern's son Miles had started working for Estabrook Construction Ltd. He eventually took over more and more responsibility in running the company as Vern took an interest in placer-mining gold. Today he is the general manager of Estabrook Construction Ltd. The company continues to do road building and oilfield work on seismic lines and lease building on pipelines. Says Miles, "In the summer time we do a lot of road building with the scrapers and a lot of water, sewer, and underground utilities. We keep busy pretty much year round." When DMI pulp mill was built in Peace River in 1988, the company got involved in logging operations. "There's probably close to 100 people employed by us." Estabrook Construction Ltd. runs about 50 Caterpillars, among which are small dozers, D-8s, and LTP Cats for seismic work. Equipment includes feller bunchers, skidders, log loaders, and a fleet of scrapers. This equipment is hauled by the company's own fleet of Kenworth trucks. The company does work all over northern Alberta, including Lac La Biche and Fort McMurray, and the Rainbow and AMA oilfields.

Vern died suddenly of a heart attack in April 1999. At Vern's funeral, many old friends and former employees gathered to say their last good-byes to Vern. Audrey Brown, minister of Grace United Church in Grimshaw, gave a reflection on Vern's life, comparing him to the precious metal that had fascinated him in his later years. Below is part of her talk:

> "As elements that occur, gold is relatively rare and I think that men like Vern Estabrook are too. Especially in the times that we live in. He was honest, generous, and very forgiving. He still believed that in a deal, a handshake was good enough. …He was easy to work with because as part of his nature he did give a lot of people their start in business. He looked at others in business, not as competition, but as a sign of prosperity to all. He cared about those who worked with and for him….

> "The book of Revelation, chapter 21, says that the streets of heaven are paved with gold. Now, I don't know about you, but the thing that occurs to me is that Vern is right now there trying to make a deal with God to see if he can't get that stuff off the ground and do something with it. And because he's still working at making a deal, that means he's happy and will be all eternity."[26]

John King, King's Construction (Grimshaw) Ltd.

John King is one of the earliest men to combine three different forms of northern transportation – trucks, cat trains, and airplanes – in his construction and transportation business. For over 45 years he worked in and out of the Canadian North and along the Mackenzie Highway.

John got his first driving job when he was 15, during the winter of 1942, hauling on the construction of the Canol 6 road.

> *"Nobody had any money back then. I guess my Dad mortgaged everything he had to get this truck, and everybody did the same. You could make big money with the American army. Wages went from 15 dollars a month to a dollar an hour – overnight!"*[27]

John remembers the old mile posts along the road. The mileage, he explained, started at Peace River, which added another 20 miles [32 km] to the current mileage used today.[28]

The following summer John and his brother Donald headed for Dawson Creek to haul lumber and supplies on the Alaska Highway for the American army.

> *"For the next several years I hauled grain, lumber, wood, etc. for farmers and businesses in summer. In winter I hauled for Ingraham Bros. Freighters and Sheck Bros., from Grimshaw to Lower Hay. I also drove for Hank Thompson, who had all the Hudson's Bay freight along the road."*

In 1948, John helped Hank Thompson haul lumber and materials for new buildings at the Catholic mission at Assumption. It was no picnic. West of High Level it was just a bush road, with no grade. "That's when I fell through the ice on the Upper Hay River!"

John King would often give a ride to a trapper and his dogs. He'd stop sometimes to visit the trappers along the way.

> *"Many a night I stopped, I'd see a fire in the bush, and I'd see Indians, trappers, with a tarp and tent up. They might not even talk English. You'd stop there and they'd give you tea. Once in a while we'd come along and there'd be a dog team on the road. If we were empty, we'd stop, load their dogs on the back of the truck. We used to bring them down to High Level. It was a stop-off point to Fort Vermilion. We'd drop them off and then they had about 45-50 miles [72-80 km] to go. We'd sometimes haul them for 150 miles [240 km]. That was great for them."*[29]

Around 1947 oil companies began sending seismic crews into the North. John got a contract with Imperial Oil Exploration to haul seismic camps and drilling rigs. About that time John also got involved with cat trains for a couple of months.

> *"I was up there cat training part of the winter with [Vern] Estabrook. I was cat skinning on Great Slave Lake. We were hauling fresh fish from the North Arm to Hay River. Just that one winter. But we used to truck a lot of fish on our back hauls later on, from Hay River to Grimshaw. "*

By 1952, John King had three trucks he operated under the name "King's Truck Service." (He later incorporated under the name "King's Construction.")

Imperial Oil party #75 crossing the Kakisa River, fall 1954. John King collection

In 1955, John added another type of transportation to his business. He went to Edmonton to learn how to fly at the Edmonton Flying Club and got his license. He bought his first airplane, a Cessna 170, and later bought a Cessna 180 and a 185. "The aircraft were invaluable over the years, hauling men and supplies to remote sites as far north as Inuvik, miles from any highways. Hank Thompson Airport at High Level was one of our main bases when the Rainbow Oilfields were discovered in 1965."[30] He would later purchase a Beaver and a single Otter. "If something broke down, you'd fly in the parts. If somebody got hurt, you'd go pick them up...We used to go to High Level and go west for two or three hundred miles [321-482 km]."

In the mid-50s, John bought his first Cats, two D7s, and started the next phase of his business – oilfield hauling and construction. While he was working for Imperial Oil Exploration in northern Alberta, he bought several more Cats, which he used in northern Alberta, B.C., and the NWT. The seismic crews started working in the Rainbow Lake area, and John, working with Hank Thompson, used these Cats to build roads and oilfield leases. Later he ran Cat trains in the Arctic.

"In 1965, oil was discovered at Rainbow Lake, and things really broke loose. Trucks and Cats worked around the clock to keep up with all the oil activity...In the late 60s oil was discovered in the Arctic. We were hired by Imperial Oil Exploration to supply Cats and camps for projects north of Inuvik.

"The first winter we trucked Cats and camps to Yellowknife and loaded them on PWA [Pacific Western Airlines] Hercules aircraft for the flight to Aitkenson Point on the Tuk peninsula on the Arctic coast. This happened in January; temperatures were -55°F [-48°C] and windy.

"The next two summers we hauled more Cats and camps to Hay River, then barged down the Mackenzie to the Arctic Coast via Inuvik. One of these crews travelled along the Arctic coast sea ice for 630 miles [1013 km] to Point Barrow, Alaska in the winter of 1973. Once there we worked for the U.S. government on petroleum reserves in Alaska. I worked there for four years, then sold the equipment. The Arctic oilfields finally died down in the late 70s."

When the oil activity slowed down in the north, in the late 70s, John King returned to northern Alberta.

"We all headed home and worked in northern Alberta again, utilizing the Mackenzie Highway for access to remote drilling sites for the oil companies. We had now worked for Imperial Oil Exploration every year for 31 years, a lot of it up and down Mackenzie Highway. Imperial at this time started cutting back on northern operators, so for the last 10 years Husky Oil Exploration were our main clients."

In 1989, John King retired from trucking and oilfield construction. About the highway that has been so much a part of his life, he states: "The Mackenzie Highway has been a lifeline for the north since the late 30s and still is. Activity in the north just would not have been feasible without it."

Fred Lorenzen, Lorenzen's Gravel and Water Service, Ltd.

Fred Lorenzen hauled just about everything and anything that could be loaded on the back of a truck. He started driving trucks when he was 14 years old.

In the winter of 1941 and 1942, he hauled freight for the U.S. Army, north to Hay River and Mills Lake, in a 2-ton truck owned by John Myshyniuk. In 1944 Fred purchased a 1940 D-30 International from George Grimm of Notikewin; he freighted for Sheck Brothers, from Grimshaw to Hay River, where the freight was taken across the Great Slave Lake to Yellowknife by cat train. The following year Fred bought a new KB7 International for $3919 from Charlie Kay, the IHC dealer in Berwyn, Alberta.

During the period of construction of the Mackenzie Highway, he hauled gravel. He handled anything that needed to be transported over the highway.

"I hauled grain that fall and winter, and also hauled empty barrels to Mills Lake, approximately 30 miles [48 km] west of Fort Providence on the Mackenzie River, for Bruce Rome. Bruce had a contract with the U.S. Army. The barrels were shipped [by barge] from Mills Lake to Norman Wells to be filled there. In 1948 I hauled gravel in the summertime on the Mackenzie Highway from the Third Battle (Meikle River) to High Level."[31]

During the winter of 1948-49, he hauled cattle from the Battle River Country for Josie L'Hirondel of Little Buffalo to Edmonton, with a 28-foot [8.5m] trailer and a KBS7 tractor unit. "The roads were terrible; they were narrow bush roads in God-awful condition." He also hauled fish brought from Hay River to Peace River, where they were loaded onto refrigerated cars and shipped to New York and Chicago.

In the winter of 1947-48, Fred Lorenzen and Peter Keleman hauled freight and empty barrels for Bruce Rome, from Grimshaw, Alberta, to Mills Lake, NWT. Fred Lorenzen collection.

In 1949 Fred purchased a larger truck, a 5-ton GMC, from the GM Dealer in Grimshaw. That year he hauled gravel for Bond Construction on the NWT section of the highway. For the next two years, he continued to haul gravel in the summer, and general freight in the winter, which included fuel and gas for Walter Chubb of Grimshaw, who was the Imperial Oil Dealer. "We hauled orange gas from Hay River, that had come in on the barges from Norman Wells, and hauled diesel fuel from Grimshaw north to Hay River."

Jim Mabley had Fred haul logs and pulp wood from Chinook Valley to Grimshaw. In 1952 he freighted lumber from Paddle Prairie to Hay River, where the lumber was loaded onto barges for shipping to Bromley and Sons in Yellowknife.

Although Fred would haul just about anything, from oil barrels and logs to horses and fish, hauling gravel was the most important part of his trucking business. "Hauling gravel was my main job, and I can safely boast that I hauled gravel on every mile of the Mackenzie Highway." Fred hauled gravel for Tim Kostiuk on the Fort Providence to Yellowknife highway in the early 1960s. Now called NWT Highway 3, it is mostly paved all the way to Yellowknife.

When the oil and gas was discovered in the area of Rainbow Lake in the 1960s, Fred started to expand his business. By the early 70s he owned two trucks. He hauled fuel for Bill McClarty to the oil rigs at Rainbow Lake, Zama Lake, Caribou Mountains, Steen River, and Bistcho Lake for several winters. "In the winter I worked for larger trucking companies hauling and moving oil rigs and camps. About that time I started using tank trucks and hauled water for the oil companies."

He recalls one trip when he had to take a load of horses to Fort Chipewyan.

> "When we arrived on our first trip, the teachers declared the day a holiday and all the kids came running to watch us unload. Some of the horses got away and were running around town, with us and the little Indian kids chasing them. It was quite a round-up."

Hauling water for the oil companies became a mainstay when activity in the oil industry heated up in the North. Fred's business, Lorenzen's Gravel and Water Service Ltd. of Manning, expanded along with the oil activity. By the time Fred sold out in 1994, he had 17 trucks, two loaders, a gravel crusher, and a 40-man camp.

> "During my younger days, I worked at just about any type of trucking job that was available for me. Living conditions were really terrible as compared to this day and age, but I guess we didn't know any different, so we fared quite well and always managed to have a lot of fun. We made many very good and lasting friendships. I believe that we have seen more change in our generation than any other has seen or will ever see. Things were not easy in our day, and we mostly had to fend for ourselves. If we broke down on the road we could not phone for service or tow truck, so had to do the best we could with what was at hand and the help of our fellow travellers."[32]

Fred and Bernice Lorenzen moved to Grimshaw in 1997 to start a truck museum to house their collection of antique trucks, mostly K-line IHCs, and to interpret trucking history along the Mackenzie Highway. Many of these trucks can be seen at the Grimshaw Antique Truck Museum, just north of Grimshaw. The Lorenzens also started the Annual Truckers Reunion in Grimshaw. As of 2000, the Truckers Reunion has been held in August every summer for six years.

Terry Baxter, Terry's Trucking Company

Terry Baxter was 15 when he left home to work for the American Army Engineers on the Alaska Highway. Later he drove trucks going north between Grimshaw and Hay River on the winter road.

In 1946, at the age of 20, Terry started hauling lumber from Battle River Lumber Company to the new town of Manning, where the lumber was used in several buildings, including the Bank of Commerce.[33]

Terry drove for various trucking companies hauling general freight, and for Bob Mitchell hauling bridges that were used across the Boyer and Steen Rivers. He hauled all sorts of freight north to Hay River, and brought fish south on the backhauls. "Then there was that other, mysterious cargo. In those days Hay River had no liquor store and very few other stores, so the items hauled were often ill-assorted and unmentionable."[34] He would often have a passenger or two on some of his trips, as there was no bus service as such in the north.

Terry's experiences with winter roads were like those of many other truckers who were hauling before the Mackenzie Highway was completed. Much of his driving was over treacherous ice roads and ice bridges.

> "Some places could only be reached in the winter, on ice bridges over frozen lakes. Cats would cross the ice in a sort of train. Terry said that they would often break through the ice and then the drivers would have to scramble to safety, though they didn't always make it. He recalled a friend who died when his cat broke through the ice. They were never able to recover the cat or the operator from the icy waters."[35]

In 1950 Terry hauled fish for Clark Fisheries, one of several fisheries on Great Slave Lake at the time. He had one of his own fish stories, with a different twist. Bette Baxter writes:

> "The fish were destined for the U.S. market, and with only a narrow road to travel on, things often tended to be more than a little exciting when it appeared that they might miss connecting with the train. On one memorable occasion Terry lost his brakes going down the Peace River hills. Despite his best efforts, [the truck] rolled,

Part of the fleet of Terry's Trucking Ltd., 1957. Terry Baxter collection.

spilling fish and ice all over the lawn of a homeowner who was surprised when he returned empty handed from a fishing excursion."[36]

In 1953, Terry started his own trucking company, "Terry's Trucking." His fleet eventually grew to include eight trucks. He and his drivers hauled freight into Hay River and backhauls of fish packed in ice for the eastern markets. Bobby Dodds, renowned in the North Peace River Country for his recitations of ballads and poetry by Robert Service, was one of Terry's drivers. Another driver was John Richard.

After 10 years running Terry's Trucking, Terry decided that he needed a change. After discontinuing his trucking business, Terry bought a farm in Warrensville. He still has fond memories of almost 30 years of trucking.

"He used to like going up north, even in the winter, but he said the best time was right after the last full moon in September when it was still warm during the day but all the bugs had died off."[37]

Bruce Rome, Entrepreneur in Northern Transportation

How did Bruce Rome, a farm boy from Manitoba, end up in Yellowknife in 1945 and later become one of the North's pioneers in transportation? Like other men of his age group, he was looking for work. Any work, at the time.

After the Second World War, the switch from wartime to peacetime was not an automatic process and jobs were few and far between. Men coming home from overseas were trying to pick up the pieces of their lives and find meaningful work. Employers were encouraged to hire these returning servicemen. Those who had been too young to have gone to war picked up jobs wherever they could find them. For a farm boy from the prairies, that meant working in the fields during the harvest season in the summer and fall, and then looking for any type of work in the winter that would keep beans on the table.

In 1946, Bruce wound up in Edmonton "trying to decide what to do with the rest of my life."[38] One morning Bruce met a young man at a café near the King Edward Hotel where he was staying. Noticing he was unshaven and looked pretty tired, Bruce suggested he get some sleep. When the man explained he couldn't find a room in Edmonton, Bruce handed him his keys. "'Go have a shave and a shower and a nap and you'll feel better.' Then I worried for the next few hours, because all my worldly possessions were in that room."

The two men met later that afternoon. Bruce found out the man's name was Don Sheck, of Sheck Bros. Transportation, a company that operated cat trains from Grimshaw to the mines at Yellowknife. He gave Bruce a note to his brother Larry, at Grimshaw, to give him a job. Bruce took off for the Peace River Country on the Northern Alberta Railway and arrived the next morning at 10:00 at Sheck Bros. office and got a job as swamper on the next cat train north.

Sheck Bros. were hauling dynamite and caps and diesel fuel for Consolidated Mining and Smelting, Negus Mines, and Discovery Mines; and beer for the bar at the Yellowknife Hotel, owned by Vic Ingraham. A good part of the freight was aviation fuel for Canadian Pacific Airlines, which had a fleet of single engine Mark V Norseman planes.

"In the late winter of 1945-46 we hauled well over 6000 barrels of aviation gas just for the airplane industry in Yellowknife....We'd load on 45 barrels of fuel, then we'd double-deck them and have another 45 on top."

During one of the early trips, Bruce Rome nearly lost his life.

"We stopped at Alexandra Falls and walked in a few hundred yards to take a look at it. It's a sheer drop about 127 feet [39m], and the snow had drifted out and cut back underneath the drift. We were standing out on the drift and didn't know it had cut back so steeply. As I was putting my camera back in my case, the French cook we had gave me a little friendly shove. I went ass over tea kettle and started to go down the 127 feet. But for some reason the snow held. I couldn't move because every time I moved, I'd feel the snow shift. Some of the men ran back to the cat train for a rope. Others ran out in the bush, got a tree and cut the end of the tree and passed it down for me to hold onto. Anyway, they pulled me out of there. I lost my mitts and my toque, but no big harm was done. It scared me, but not half as much as it did the cook, although I did need to change my underwear."

In Hay River the crew met up with the other cat train coming south from Yellowknife. They rearranged the freight loads and took off with about 55 sleighs and five or six Cats across the ice of the eastern shore of Great Slave Lake. After dropping off some freight at Fort Resolution, they continued on to Yellowknife.

In Yellowknife the young, inexperienced Bruce Rome learned that taking initiative nearly cost him his job.

"Most of the catskinners went on a binge, or went looking for a poker game, the bosses as well as the catskinners. I was young and inexperienced. I didn't drink much in those days, still don't. After a couple of days of doing nothing, I dug up the manifests and the bills of lading and decided where all the freight went. So I hired some men. I had a couple of deaf-mutes, great guys. I had to converse with them by written note."

Rome's crew unloaded the sleighs and got ready for the return trip, just about the time when the regular crew started showing up. "The boss wasn't there yet. So after waiting for awhile, I decided to go without him. That was probably a mistake and pretty near cost me my job." The next afternoon his boss arrived in a plane that landed beside the cat train. Bruce had told the pilot to wait while he went back to the bunkhouse to collect his duffel bag and sleeping bag. His boss asked him, "'Where do you think you're going?' I said, 'Well, I'm fired, aren't I?' He told me to put my stuff back in the bunkhouse."

Bruce spent the rest of the winter and spring before breakup working on the cat trains. He stayed in Yellowknife that summer hauling gravel with Larry Sheck's Fargo truck, for the construction of an airport. Beecher Linton was also working on the airport and had a 3-ton Ford he wanted to sell. Bruce bought it. "So I ended up with this 3-ton Ford and worked at the airport and unloading barges at McInnis Fish all that summer. Northern Transportation Company was the giant in northern transportation. There was always something to do down at the wharves."

From Cat Trains to Trucking

Bruce Rome saw opportunities opening up in northern transportation, but with trucks, not with cat trains. By the summer of 1946 he knew all the mine managers and lined up some contracts to haul freight for the mines. He had more freight than he could manage with just one 3-ton truck. He had read somewhere that War Assets were selling off a bunch of 6 X 6 army trucks out of Winnipeg.

> "I got the brain wave that the 6 X 6 would plow the road across the ice and snow on Slave Lake. Instead of unloading the 3-ton trucks in Hay River and having to reload, I could just meet them there and transport them across the Great Slave Lake by plowing the road for them. So, that I did. I went to Winnipeg, bought this 6 X 6 International....It had a soft cab, which means that it had a canvas top. It was probably warmer than the metal tops, but the wind blew through it. It was colder than a bitch, about 70 below [-56°C] in the middle of Great Slave Lake."

In Winnipeg he also purchased a couple of heavy duty bush sleighs from Greg Manufacturing that would hold 20 tons of freight. With the International 6 X 6 he headed west through a blizzard across Saskatchewan, and it took him a week to reach Edmonton.

> "I went to Edmonton and delivered my truck to Nordheimer Manufacturing and had them build me a big snowplow for it. In Grimshaw, I had to assemble sleighs and build boxes. I parked a week or ten days there and travelled on another 400 miles [643 km] to Hay River, where I had to finish building the racks and loading and getting the freight and trucks all lined up.

> "I had lined up 30 to 35 3-ton trucks, every make of truck in the Peace River Country. I had some from as far away as Edmonton. They all lined up behind me and took off the first four or five miles [6-8 km] out of Hay River. The ice was really broken and piled up. It was tough going. But once we got through that, it was fast sailing. Two days, day and night, we were in Yellowknife and unloaded. I plowed them back and made a half dozen trips that winter."

The next winter, Bruce acted on another idea of his. Instead of hauling everything across the lake by truck, he leased freight planes from CPA, a couple of C-46s, which, Bruce explained, were actually DC-3s with freight doors. When the trucks arrived in Hay River, everything that could be flown was loaded into the planes and hauled to

Snow plow on the front of Bruce Rome's International 6 x 6, crossing Great Slave Lake to Fort Resolution, 1946. Bruce Rome collection.

Yellowknife by air. "The oversized equipment – the boilers and stuff that couldn't go through the doors of the airplane – we stockpiled in Hay River for the last trip in the spring, when I'd plow across the ice to deliver the oversized freight."

Edmonton-Yellowknife Truck Lines

The following year, in 1948, Bruce went into partnership with Gordon Papp and formed a company called Edmonton-Yellowknife Truck Lines. "That year I bought a couple of pretty good GMC 6-tons and a couple of Trailmobile trailers, 35 feet long [10.5m]. I was the first owner-operator of semi trailers north of Edmonton."

In the summer they were hampered by poor road conditions. But in the winter they could haul roughly 30 000 lbs. [13 600 kg] on each load. There were no weigh scales then. "Les Stranaghan was one of our drivers. He'd back into a freight car, take a carload of freight on one and I'd take a carload of freight on the other." On the backhauls they would haul fish from Great Slave Lake to Peace River.

"In 1947 and '48 there was a big fishery – whitefish coming out of Great Slave. They were shipping express out of Peace River. We expanded far too fast. After coming out of Hay River one trip we had 30 tons a piece. We were told the railroad strike was on and for us to re-ice in Peace River and to haul the loads to Winnipeg, where we would be met by U.S. trucks that would take our loads from there. However, we were far too heavy to go south of Edmonton, so we hired two more trucks in Edmonton to take half our loads. All four of us proceeded to Winnipeg.

"Once we got to Winnipeg, the American trucks failed to show up, so we had to re-ice again. Without any sleep, without any sleeper cabs or anything, we hired extra drivers, and we took those two loads all the way to Chicago. Even though I was young and used to it, I was so stiff and sore that when we got to Chicago I could hardly get out of the cab. After a day off, a bath, and a change of clothes, we were pretty near as good as new. So we turned around and headed back to Peace River."

Oilfield Hauling

By 1949 there were four partners, after John Denison and Bob Seddon joined Edmonton-Yellowknife Truck Lines. Differences arose between the partners, and Bruce Rome decided it was time for him to leave. He started again as an owner-operator with one truck, a brand new KB8 International.

"I took it to Edmonton to Lennox and company, had an oilfield deck put on it, live rolls, gin poles, a headache rack, wheel guards. I decided I'd move oilfield camps. Oil companies were starting to move into Peace River. We had a lot of oil exploration camps that we moved around the Peace River Country. One truck wasn't enough, so I bought another 3-ton GMC. I expanded from two trucks to 20-some trucks."

In 1952, he moved operations to Fort St. John, when Scotty Tache, drilling superintendent for Inland Pacific, made him an offer he couldn't refuse.

"What Scotty wanted was that they had a half dozen medium-sized drilling rigs out of Fort St. John. Two or three were Commonwealth. Regent had a rig or two and Trinity Canadian Drilling had three or four. He assured me that I would get all their work if I would move to Fort St. John."

In 1963 Bruce Rome purchased a number of Cats and other the equipment off the DEW Line. He sold his trucking company to Bannister Construction of Edmonton and went up to the Arctic for a few years to move all the equipment off the Dew Line.

"The equipment in the western Arctic I moved by Yellowknife Transportation Company along the shore of the Arctic and down into Tuktoyaktuk. From Tuk, up the Mackenzie River for 750 miles [1200 km]*, across Mills Lake and to the southern shore of Great Slave Lake, and across the lake into Hay River."*

In 1963, Northern Alberta Railways had just completed the Great Slave Railway line between Roma Junction north to the mines at Pine Point, NWT. Bruce Rome shipped a full trainload of D8 Cats that came from the western Arctic into Edmonton by train, where he refurbished and overhauled them and re-sold the Cats. The equipment that came from the eastern Arctic was loaded on a Norwegian icebreaker and moved around the eastern Arctic to Montreal.

This marked the end of his pioneering activities in the Arctic. As his son was becoming interested in mining projects, Bruce turned his attentions to mining in the Alaska panhandle, and he is still involved.

John B. Denison, C.M., Denison Brothers Trucking, Northern Freightways, Byers Transport Ltd.

On October 22, 1999, John Denison of Kelowna, British Columbia, was invested as a Member of the Order of Canada. This is the most prestigious honor Canada can bestow upon a civilian citizen. The fact that the honor went to a trucker gives special recognition to all truckers who pioneered truck transportation in one of the world's most forbidding and unforgiving environments. John's comment regarding the honor was, "It was great, having that. You never think this could happen to you. Especially an old truck driver."[39]

If you look on the internet, you'll find a brief description of the reason given for John Denison's investiture:

"Well-known in the North for his legendary and revolutionary work as a transportation pioneer, for more than 40 years, he has been responsible for building the ice road each winter that carries cargo and supplies between the Northwest Territories and Alberta. The 510-kilometre ice road, which is used to transport a variety of materials that supply the region with invaluable items, is essential to the local economy. Considered a hero for keeping the vital route open, he overcame many obstacles and risks, often braving temperatures of minus sixty degrees [-50°C] and intense winter storms."[40]

While the citation may be a fitting tribute to John Denison, it has a number of inaccuracies. The geography is very confusing (the ice road was wholly within the Northwest Territories, from "Fort Byers", near today's Rae-Edzo, to Great Bear Lake), and it implies that John Denison is still building ice roads.

A Pioneer in Northern Transportation

In the mid-40s, John Denison and Bob Seddon bought an army truck that had been used on the Canol Project and took it overland to Peace River town.

"We bought this old four-wheel drive army truck in Yellowknife, a 1942 Army Model Marmon-Herrington that came in from Norman Wells to Hay River. We came out [with it] to Peace River. That was when there was no highway yet. We met these people who were in the freight forwarding business and they used to hire trucks and cats to haul the stuff to Hay River to get it to Yellowknife across the lake...They sent us back to Hay River with some freight.

"I remember when we went to Yellowknife the fall of '47, with that old model army truck. We didn't have any windows on it. We were ten days on Slave Lake – went straight across to Outpost Island as quick as we could. All we had to cook with was a frying pan and some frozen eggs and [we] used a blow torch to cook the eggs."[41]

This was the start of D&S Trucking Service. In 1948, they bought one of the first refers [refrigerated trailers] in the Mackenzie district, a Fruehauf refer trailer. D&S

Trucking hauled meat from the Burns packing plant in Edmonton to Yellowknife, and backhauled fish to Edmonton. Later Denison and Seddon decided to join with Bruce Rome and Gordon Papp of Edmonton-Yellowknife Truck Lines, which in turn merged with Northern Freightways, owned by R. Forsythe and S. Forsythe of Dawson Creek, B.C., in February 1950.

Northern Freightways had the Alberta rights between Edmonton and Yellowknife as well as rights in B.C. along the Alaska Highway. The rights along the Mackenzie Highway were later sold to Grimshaw Trucking & Distributing after the Hamilton brothers incorporated GT&D in 1953.

Northern Freightways ran between Edmonton and Alaska by way of Dawson Creek and up the Alaska Highway to Haines Junction, Alaska. John recalls, "I went to Dawson Creek for eight or nine years. I was troubleshooter, road superintendent, salesman, the works." Northern Freightways hauled a lot of freight for the DEW Line during the 50s, north on the Alaska Highway. "We had a contract out of Fort Nelson. We had about 25 or 30 trucks working. I spent most of my time with the airport, supervising loading the airplanes that flew out of there."

Later Northern Freightways got involved with the first piggy-backing venture out of Vancouver.

> *"The highway along the Fraser Canyon was closed off, and it was hard to get stuff up to Dawson Creek, so we put the trailers on the barge [at Vancouver] and shipped them to Squamish, then loaded them on the train and sent them to Prince George, and then up from there. That was quite an experience. It didn't work out too well, but we put the first trailer on the train in B.C. and tied it down."*

The trucking industry in Canada in the 50s and 60s was a continuing saga of companies starting, expanding, and selling out, or merging with larger companies. The process continues today, of course. Some trucking companies continue to get larger and others disappear into trucking history. In 1956, Northern Freightways sold the B.C. portion of its business to Canadian Freightways, a subsidiary of Consolidated Freightways in the United States. The Alberta operations into the NWT were bought out by Byers Transport Ltd. Jim Chapman, owner and manager, hired John Denison on a salary plus commission. Later, John became a partner of Byers, with a 20% ownership. John was put in charge of the company's northern operations in Yellowknife.

Building Ice Roads with Trucks

John Denison began building northern ice roads in 1959, when Northern Freightways put in a winter road to Fort Simpson. In the winter of 1963-64, Byers Transport built an ice and snow road into Discovery Mine, a gold mine 60 miles [96 km] north of Yellowknife. Jim Chapman recalled the decision to build the winter road:

> *"There was a lot of building material, fuel tanks for fuel storage – all had to be taken in there. Between John Denison and two of the Natives up there at Yellowknife*

they came up with the idea of building this ice road with trucks instead of using the cat trains, which was a slow, ponderous way."[42]

The haul involved moving some houses out of Rayrock Mine to Discovery Mine. John recalls, "They were 24 feet wide and 40 feet long [7 x 12m]. We put them on a trailer and moved them all the way through the bush into Yellowknife."

In 1964, Byers Transport Ltd. got a contract with Echo Bay Mines to put in an ice road to Port Radium on Great Bear Lake. John Denison was in charge of the construction of the ice road and the haul of big generators from Echo Bay Mines. John and his crew started from what was jokingly called "Fort Byers," a garage facility and launching point for the ice road located about 90 km west of Yellowknife on today's Yellowknife Highway. Most of the road construction was on ice, over a string of lakes – Faber, Hardisty, and Hottah lakes among some of the largest. Trucks equipped with snowplows and drags were employed to build the ice road. The bush roads between the lakes were put through initially with Cats with snowplows, and trucks with drags were used to keep the snow clear.

John Denison used trucks in ice road construction. He knew that trucks could do the job faster and cheaper than the traditional use of cats. Ice roads across lakes and rivers became much thicker than the surrounding ice as the season went on. They checked the depth of the ice by testing it, using an ice auger, every 100 feet [30m]. When the ice was about three feet thick, it was ready for the trucks to roll. The actual techniques Byers Transport Ltd. used in building the ice road are described in detail, in *Denison's Ice Road*.[43]

John Denison and the crew cleared and maintained a 520-kilometre [323 mi.] ice road into Great Bear Lake for several winters, starting right after Christmas and continuing through to break-up, which came in late April or early May. Once the road was in place, Byers' trucks and other trucking companies hauled freight north almost non-stop to the Echo Bay Mine at Great Bear Lake.

With an established road in place, trucks could make the trip there and back in around 24 hours, travelling at an average speed of 40 kilometres [25 mi.] an hour. Truck convoys travelled at 55 km/h [34 mph] maximum. At higher speeds they risked the danger of a blow-out.[44] But that speed was only during the best of weather and road conditions. When the weather fell below minus 40, or if there was a blizzard or white-out, the trip could take a good deal longer. Truckers had to be prepared for delays. Seasoned northern truckers had a real contempt for the truck driver from the "outside" who came unprepared for the severity of northern winters, without proper footwear, extra clothing, a sleeping bag, or food.

When Byers Transport Ltd. sold its operations to Pacific Western Airlines in 1969, John Denison retired (the first time) to British Columbia. But Dick Robinson of Robinson Trucking Ltd. (RTL), brought John out of retirement on a few occasions to work for RTL. John's experience in building ice roads was very useful to the company.

John Denison with the Right Honourable Roméo LeBlanc, Governor General of Canada, at Rideau Hall, Ottawa. John was invested as a Member of the Order of Canada, 1998. Photo by Sgt. Christian Coulombe. GGC98-527.23.

John looks back on the 40-odd years that he was an integral part of northern transportation.

> *"I wonder sometimes now how the hell I did it. If I knew then what I know now there was no way I'd do it. Everybody else told me I couldn't do it, but if you don't take no for an answer, how are you going to know you can or can't do it?"*

Ambrose Parenteau, owner-operator, Paddle Prairie

Ambrose Parenteau spent most of his life as a trucker, hauling on the Mackenzie Highway. In 1945, Ambrose bought his first truck and started hauling grain from Paddle Prairie to Grimshaw. It was the first of many different models of trucks he would purchase over the years. "I bought my first truck, a used KS5 International. I hauled grain from Paddle Prairie to Grimshaw, also lumber from Williamson's Mill [between Manning and Keg River] on winter roads to wherever it had to go." On one trip, he was at High Level when he had engine trouble. It was miles from anywhere, and he figured out a way to keep the truck going.

"It was about 35 below (F) [-37°C] and I took the oil pan and head off, pulled the piston and rod out, taped the crankshaft where the rod fit, wrapped string around it and ran it without the piston and rod back to Notikewin, to Sharp's Garage. When they took it apart they found that it had the wrong crankshaft; from a small motor. That's why it didn't have any power when it was loaded. The motor didn't vibrate too bad at 20 m.p.h. [32 kph]. They put the right crankshaft in and it had more power."

Ambrose, like many truckers, had trouble getting up 280 Hill, between Steen River and Indian Cabins.[45]

"I had a load of lumber on this International KS5. The lumber was a little bit long for the wheel base, and it wanted to lift up in the front. Going up the hill, the front end would lift, and I couldn't get up the hill. I couldn't steer it, so I turned around and backed up the hill and managed to get going that way."

In 1947, Ambrose sold his KS5 International to Elton Murphy at Williamson's Mill and bought a brand new 1947 GMC. He started hauling gravel for Standard Gravel, from Paddle Prairie to the NWT border, helping to put the first coat of gravel on the new highway between Paddle Prairie and the NWT border.

"We hauled right from the crusher. We stayed in a tent camp wherever they were crushing. We graveled from Mile 140 right to the border, all summer, with them little single-axle trucks in '47. We had hydraulic boxes then, and we just hoisted the box and spread it. And then they had small graders to spread it. At that time the highway was pretty narrow. It was only a 22-foot [7m] top."

One day when he had unloaded his gravel and was heading back for dinner, he had a close call with another truck coming the other way.

"This one day I happened to be first in line, so I went about 10 miles [16 km] to unload. I was coming back, and it was about two miles before I met the first truck. The road was dusty and I eased toward the centre of the road, as I couldn't see. First thing I saw was a Ford grill, so I cranked the steering wheel as fast as I could. When I got stopped and got out of the truck I couldn't see anything for dust. I didn't know whether he tipped over or not. All of a sudden I heard a door slam. When the dust settled, Bruce Hagen was standing on the road, and his truck was sitting in the ditch, right side up. Our duels had just missed each other by 6 inches [15 cm] and piled gravel to a peak. Bruce was driving for Jack Frith at the time. I was sure glad it was Bruce driving. If it had been somebody else, maybe they wouldn't have turned the wheel."

Ambrose also hauled fish for Menzies' at Hay River, with his '47 GMC.

"I fixed the hot water heater from the motor to the front end of the box to blow warm air to keep things from freezing. I had it all tarped in and it worked good. I also hauled empty barrels, for Bruce Rome, to Mills Lake. Then I traded the '47 GMC for a

1949 GMC. I hauled gravel and lumber with it as well as timbers to go on the barges at Hay River."

In 1949 Ambrose hauled lumber from Ken Fischer's sawmill, west of Manning, to Grimshaw. Later he and his wife Evelyn moved to Peace River, where Ambrose hauled shacks to oil camps for Fortier and Northey[46] with a four-ton 1958 Ford truck with a winch.

"In the spring of 1958 we moved back to Paddle Prairie and moved from the farm to an acreage of land, which we purchased from Lawrence Lariviere, near the settlement of Paddle Prairie. We built onto the house, and this addition became a café. We also had a service station and garage, and Evelyn cooked for many of the road crews. In the winter I hauled fuel to oil rigs in the north. Evelyn ran the café for about eight years, but it was too much work for her. So she closed the café down and then got the post office and had a little confectionery and bus stop. It was a very busy place. It was

Ambrose Parenteau, hauling logs for Boucher Brothers Sawmill, Nampa, Alberta, early 1980s. Ambrose Parenteau collection.

a lot easier for her than running the café, because truckers would stop in all hours of the night with the café."

By 1963, Ambrose bought a new Fargo that he used to haul fuel locally and from the refinery in Edmonton. He helped to build the airstrip at Footner Lake, north of High Level, and the new highway between High Level and Fort Vermilion. "I helped re-gravel the Mackenzie Highway many times and also helped build the base and repave the highway as years went on."

Ambrose had always driven on his own. Then in 1973 he got a job driving trucks for Grimshaw Trucking & Distributing.

> *"I drove for Grimshaw for three years. I hauled just about everything. I hauled powder and dynamite caps way up to a mine north and west of Yellowknife, where they were building a dam. Grimshaw had only two trucks that were licensed to haul all that powder, dynamite, and caps. I was driving one of them, and another guy was driving the other. We went up to Hay River and we had the vans backed up to the train.[47] They told us we had to take those loads. We were the only two trucks that was licensed to haul the powder. They called it powder in them days, for dynamite blasting."*

Ambrose continued trucking through the 80s, hauling logs for Boucher Bros. of Peace River and hauling gravel. In 1990 he retired.

Today he lives in Peace River. He is still involved with trucks, but now he hauls his two black horses to parades and gives rides. "We take a wagon in summer and go to the Manning rodeo, usually from Paddle Prairie in a covered wagon. It takes four days and we camp out along the way. The grandchildren really like that."

Notes

[1] From *Peace River Remembers*, Sir Alexander Mackenzie Historical Society, 1984, p. 284.

[2] Gordon Reid, *Around the Lower Peace*, Lower Peace Publishing Co. Ltd., 1978, p. 30.

[3] From *Peace River Remembers*, p. 284.

[4] *Around the Lower Peace*, p. 31.

[5] Les Stranaghan, "Tony's Truck Service," *Tales of the Mackenzie Highway*, p. 35.

[6] From, *Land of Hope and Dreams: A History of Grimshaw and District*. Grimshaw: Grimshaw and District Historical Society, 1980, p. 374.

[7] *Tales of the Mackenzie Highway*, p. 23.

[8] *Land of Hope and Dreams*, p. 375.

[9] Mike Papirney from Keg River also flew for Hank Thompson. According to Stella Friedel, Mike was decorated by the Governor General for heroism in rescuing an American couple off Margaret Lake in the 1960s.

[10] Gordon Reid, *Notes of the North*, Lower Peace Publishing Co., 1977, p. 26.

[11] Pat Thompson and John King, "Hank Thompson," *Tales of the Mackenzie Highway*, p. 23.

[12] Information about Ed Dillman is from Lawrence Dillman and from *Saga of Battle River – We Came, We Stayed*. Battle River Historical Society, Manning, 1986, pp. 160-161.

[13] Lawrence Dillman explained the term bareback: "If you pulled the sides off the back of the truck and just have the floor, and put a load on top of that, it's referred to as 'bareback'."

[14] Telephone interview with Lawrence Dillman, February 16, 2000.

[15] *Tales of the Mackenzie Highway*, p. 28.

[16] *Notes of the North*, p. 16.

[17] Personal interview with Larry Sheck, Grimshaw, August 17, 1997.

[18] Quoted in *Tales of the Mackenzie Highway*, p. 18.

[19] Ibid.

[20] This is by the old mileage, which commenced at Peace River, not Grimshaw.

[21] Vern Estabrook, "The Estabrook Family," *Land of Hope and Dreams: A History of Grimshaw and District*, p. 622.

[22] Interview with Miles Estabrook, January 31, 2000.

[23] Flood ice is the thin layer of ice that forms over the melt water on top of thicker lake ice.

[24] *Land of Hope and Dreams*, p. 375.

[25] *Land of Hope and Dreams*, p. 623.

[26] My thanks to Rev. Audrey Brown of Grace United Church in Grimshaw for allowing me to quote from her presentation titled, "Reflection on the Life of Vern Estabrook 'Good as Gold.'"

[27] Interview with John King at his farm near Grimshaw, August 18, 1997.

[28] From *Tales of the Mackenzie Highway*, p. 22.

[29] Interview with John King.

[30] *Tales of the Mackenzie Highway*, p. 22.

[31] "Fred Lorenzen Story" an unpublished story written by Fred Lorenzen, June 1999.

[32] Op Cit., p. 2.

[33] Sources about Terry Baxter and his trucking company are from Bette Baxter's article, "Terry Baxter" in *Tales of the Mackenzie Highway*, p. 17, Sharon Reichert, "Trucking in the North – The Last Frontier," *Mile Zero News*, August 13, 1997, p. 1, and *Land of Hope and Dreams: A History of Grimshaw and District*, p 555-56.

[34] *Land of Hope and Dreams*, p. 556.

[35] Reichert, p. 1.

[36] *Tales of the Mackenzie Highway*, p. 17.

[37] Reichert, p. 1.

[38] From Bruce Rome's taped memoirs, recorded in December 1999.

[39] Telephone interview with John Denison, June 22, 1999.

[40] Http://www.gg.ca/cgi-bin/oc.

[41] Telephone interview with John Denison, June 22, 1999.

[42] Alberta Trucking Association interview with Jim Chapman, 1981. Tapes are deposited at Glenbow Archives, Calgary.

[43] See Edith Iglauer, *Denison's Ice Road*, pp. 38-39.

[44] An ice blow-out happened when trucks travelled too fast over the ice. The ice starts to bend, creating a wave under the ice, and when the wave reaches shore, it blows through the ice.

[45] There are many horror stories about truckers trying to make it up Mile 280 hill north of Steen River. When the highway was reconstructed, the road was straightened and the hill was bypassed.

[46] Fortier and Northey, based in Peace River, catered and supplied camps to oil rigs.

[47] The Great Slave Lake [GSL] railway was built by CNR from Roma Junction, 8 miles west of Peace River, to the mines at Pine Point, NWT. The first steam train arrived at High Level on November 2, 1963, and launched the development of High Level as a town and major distribution and service centre in northern Alberta. Until then, trucks hauled everything, from bulk fuel to mine ore. After the GSL railway was completed in 1965, bulk cargo, primarily ore, grain, and lumber, was freighted by rail. Since the Pine Point mine was closed down a few years ago, the trains now run infrequently. Trucks, once again, are the prime movers of freight for the North.

![car icon] Chapter 6 – Stopping Places ![truck icon]

The original stopping places in the Peace River Country were early trailside inns, where travellers could find a meal and lodging for the night and hay for their horses or oxen. The term "stopping place" has remained in the vocabulary of many old-timers, long after paved roads have replaced trails, and freight is now hauled by trucks instead of horse-drawn wagons.

Before 1900, stopping places in the Peace River Country were mostly fur trade posts, Native and Metis dwellings, homesteads, and missions. When the Edson-Grande Prairie Trail was cut through the bush in the spring of 1911, log-constructed stopping places were quickly established along the route, every 10 to 15 miles [16-24 km], and were ready for the following season's traffic.

The accommodations were very basic. Some stopping places were no more than one-room log shacks with dirt floors, where travellers competed for floor space and ate whatever was the meal of the day. They had to reach these stopping places early to find room. If a traveller was lucky enough to get a bed, he or she risked a night's misery from "pilgrims of the night" – fleas, lice or bedbugs. However, the hosts of these stopping places were usually friendly and helpful, and most of the time one could get a decent meal.

Meals were served family style. There was no set menu. One ate what was cooked that day, whether it was moose stew or beans. In the annals of local history, some early stopping places became famous for their meals, such as Pa and Ma Brainard's ranch,

between Hythe and Pouce Coupé, B.C. Ma was noted for her chicken dinners, and she was known to never let a stranger go hungry. If she ran out of chicken, she just went out in the back and killed and plucked another one for the pot.

Everett "Ed" Blakley ran a stopping place between Grimshaw and Berwyn, when he first

This derelict house near Grouard was once a stopping place on the Grouard-Peace River trail in the early 1900s. R.L. Hursey collection.

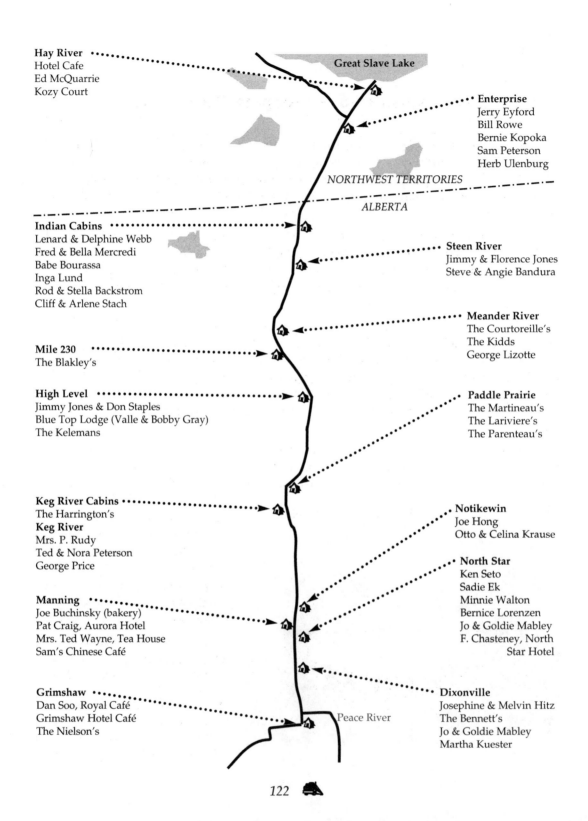

Hay River
Hotel Cafe
Ed McQuarrie
Kozy Court

Great Slave Lake

Enterprise
Jerry Eyford
Bill Rowe
Bernie Kopoka
Sam Peterson
Herb Ulenburg

NORTHWEST TERRITORIES

ALBERTA

Indian Cabins
Lenard & Delphine Webb
Fred & Bella Mercredi
Babe Bourassa
Inga Lund
Rod & Stella Backstrom
Cliff & Arlene Stach

Steen River
Jimmy & Florence Jones
Steve & Angie Bandura

Meander River
The Courtoreille's
The Kidds
George Lizotte

Mile 230
The Blakley's

High Level
Jimmy Jones & Don Staples
Blue Top Lodge (Valle & Bobby Gray)
The Kelemans

Paddle Prairie
The Martineau's
The Lariviere's
The Parenteau's

Keg River Cabins
The Harrington's
Keg River
Mrs. P. Rudy
Ted & Nora Peterson
George Price

Notikewin
Joe Hong
Otto & Celina Krause

North Star
Ken Seto
Sadie Ek
Minnie Walton
Bernice Lorenzen
Jo & Goldie Mabley
F. Chasteney, North
Star Hotel

Manning
Joe Buchinsky (bakery)
Pat Craig, Aurora Hotel
Mrs. Ted Wayne, Tea House
Sam's Chinese Café

Grimshaw
Dan Soo, Royal Café
Grimshaw Hotel Café
The Nielson's

Peace River

Dixonville
Josephine & Melvin Hitz
The Bennett's
Jo & Goldie Mabley
Martha Kuester

122

came to the Peace River Country from Nova Scotia back in 1913. Guests would pay for their meals by donation, placing their money into a large enamelware sugar bowl kept on the table.[1] Other stopping places became obsolete when trails were re-routed or new roads developed. A popular stopping place along the Grouard-Peace River trail on the Pakishan Reserve fell into disuse after the arrival of the Edmonton, Dunvegan & B.C. [ED&BC] railway in 1916, between High Prairie and Peace River. The log building is still intact along the old trail.

In the 1930s, when settlers began to homestead further north along the wagon road between Grimshaw and Notikewin, stopping places and cafes were also established to accommodate farmers and ranchers travelling to and from the railhead. Places along the trail – Chinook Valley, Dixonville, North Star, and Notikewin – soon had cafés and stopping places.

After the provincial government cleared the Grimshaw winter road north of the Third Battle (Meikle River) to Hay River in 1939, the cat trains carried their own cookhouses and bunkhouses, and had their own cooks. There was little reason to open stopping places for the cat trains. When the American Army widened the winter road in 1942 and built camps at Paddle Prairie, Alexandra Falls, and Mills Lake, some civilian truckers would sometimes stay at the camps. Most ate out of their grub boxes and slept in their trucks to keep the motors running all night in severe weather. Now, 50 years later, truckers still sleep in their trucks, which now have heated and air conditioned bunks, and they still eat out of grub boxes too, as stops can be 200 miles [321 km] apart.

Dan Landry making tea by the side of the Mackenzie Highway. Dan Landry collection.

Blakley's Stopping Place, Mile 230

One of the earliest stopping places on the old winter road was the Blakley's Stopping Place at Mile 230 near Upper Hay River (Meander River). It was opened in September 1942 by Everett Thomas "Ed" Blakley from Grimshaw. Frank Blakley was 14 years old when he went north with Frank Smith in his dad's International 1½-ton truck, to stay with his dad and help him build the stopping place. "I didn't help him that much. I wasn't old enough to."

They lived in a very small shack until the stopping place was built. That winter, trucks driven by U. S. Army personnel and civilians began to come through, hauling supplies and materials to Mills Lake for the Canol Project. Many of them were black soldiers from the Deep South who suffered from the severe cold.

"I felt sorry for them. They couldn't stand that cold weather. They were really abused. They made the soldiers ride in the back of the trucks with no heaters, in the back with a canvas over the top."

Frank recalls a time when some of the black soldiers stopped by at the shack.

"I remember one night, there was five of them coming down from the north in this army truck. They were all in the front and they were cold. They stopped at our shack when we were ready to build the stopping place there. They came in and wanted some antifreeze. Well, the old man knew what they wanted. They wanted alcohol.

"He had a great big 40-ounce [1.18 l] bottle of overproof rum. It was 90 overproof, something like that. Oh, it was strong stuff. He just set the bottle out there and gave them a glass. And each one of them took a full glass of that stuff and downed it....About two weeks or so later, my dad and my brother were sitting in a café in Grimshaw having dinner. In walks these Negroes, a couple of them he gave the liquor to. They walked in and they said, 'Well, you're not paying for your dinner...What you did for us up there. That meant so damned much to us. We never forgot." [2]

There wasn't much to do at first, so Ed and Frank went out hunting moose and they had no idea how cold it was. It got down to 65 below [-54°C]. They also tried commercial fishing. E.T. Blakley and his sons Therman and Frank, along with Blackie Chase, went to Hay River to try commercial fishing on Great Slave Lake. "We got the first commercial fishing license ever issued on Great Slave Lake." They hadn't planned on getting a license, but when a local RCMP officer at Hay River explained that he could seize all their equipment – two trucks and all their fishing gear – they went with him to the telegraph office to apply for license from Ottawa. They thought this was going to take a long time. They no sooner got back to the stopping place when word arrived that their fishing license was in Hay River. But fishing on Great Slave was not to Ed's liking, as the lake was too big and the ice was five feet deep. They chiseled down through the ice with a needle bar, and when they put the jigger in under the ice, they couldn't see it because of the snow on top of the ice. After spending four or five days of frustration, Ed figured a way to find the jigger. [3]

"He was sleeping this one night and he got a brain wave. 'I know how I'm going to find that jigger,' he told Frank. 'We'll cut a hole in the jigger and we'll put a quart sealer in there, with the bottom up against the ice and turn it so it's water tight. And put a flashlight in there.' All he was interested in was getting the line through under the ice...we could go anywhere, we just followed it along."

The following summer, Frank's mother Mabel and some of his sisters and brothers came to help at the stopping place. Although there was a bunkhouse for truckers to stay in, most of them slept in their trucks. They also had a big garage, mostly for their own use, but occasionally truckers would need to do repairs on their trucks and would borrow the space to work on them. Most of them stopped at the Blakleys' house for the meals. Mabel and the girls did the cooking.

At the Blakley stopping place, Mabel beside the Blakley's 1941 1½ ton International truck. This truck was used to haul freight for the American Army between Grimshaw and Mills Lake, NWT. Frank Blakley collection

"They didn't have a menu. They just put on the table what my mother was used to cooking. If it was roast beef or stew, that's what they served, as well as baked bread, pies, or cakes. At breakfast time you got bacon and eggs." The family ordered their supplies from Grimshaw or Peace River, and the supplies came on the trucks.

Like many families in the North Peace, the Blakley's have their own interesting story about the infamous 280 Hill on the old winter road. In trying to make the hill, Woody

Van Natter, son-in-law married to eldest daughter Evelyn, blew the engine in the International D30. Ed and Woody went back the following summer to try to bring it out. The trip turned into an adventure that is still talked about in coffee shops.

"My dad was so determined, when he set his mind to do something. There was nothing that would turn him back. They went down river from Peace River to Fort Vermilion on O'Sullivan's boat and overland with a team of horses and wagon to the stopping place. They had a new motor and everything to put into it. When they went through Fort Vermilion, the people had bets placed on him that he'd never bring that truck out. When my dad found that out, nothing would turn him back. He said he would have hung his hide on a tree before he'd turn back..."

An accident with the team and wagon almost ended the trip. In the story "The Saga of the Old D30 International," Woody and Evelyn Van Natter wrote:

"Back along side of Devil's Lake, now called Haig Lake, we had a slight accident. The front of the wagon slapping back and forth caused the tongue to come out of the neck-yoke ring, and going down a slope the tongue dropped down, causing the wagon to run up on the horses, and they took off. The wagon rolled down the hill and stopped in the bush. The horses got tangled up in some trees about a quarter of a mile down the trail, the neck-yoke held them together. When the men got everything straightened out they hitched the horses up to the wagon again and started on their way. This is where we had our first drink out of our Hospital Brandy."[4]

From the stopping place they continued on to Upper Hay River, where they forded the river, and went down to where the bridge crosses today. There they built a raft big enough to carry the truck when they came back. Then they headed to 280 Hill, where they put in the new motor into the truck.

Evelyn Van Natter wrote how Woody and E.T. Blakley got over a big muskeg:

"There was an air strip at the Post approximately where the ranger station is now. They crossed that and about one half mile further on they came to a big muskeg that they had to cross. They had to build four pontoons, each 30 feet long. These were made by lashing three poles together. They would take two pontoons and stake them down and drive the truck on, then drag the other two pontoons around in front of the truck with the horses, stake them down and then drive the truck onto the second set of pontoons. Then they had to drag the first set around to the front, stake them down and repeat the performance. They continued to do this for 14 hours nonstop before they finally got across the muskeg. All the while they were doing this, Woody, Dad, and the horses were knee-deep in mud, not to mention the bugs and mosquitoes that they must have had to contend with."

When they finally got to the stopping place, they had another "big shot of Hospital Brandy."

While the Mackenzie Highway was being constructed, Duncan McPhail had a sawmill on the property at Blakley's stopping place. McPhail sawed timber for the

The Blakley stopping place at Mile 230 (near Meander River), ca. 1944. Frank Blakley collection.

bridges; the Blakleys hauled the logs to the mill and the sawn timber to locations along the road.

The completion of the highway marked the end of the stopping place. It was on the old winter road, which meandered almost as much as the Meander River did. The new highway bypassed the stopping place and ran along the top of the ridge above it. Nineteen forty-seven was the last year for the Blakley's at Mile 230. "We pulled out pretty well in '47. I don't remember being there after that. We were off the road then, so there was no reason to be there."

The Blakleys returned to their farm southwest of Grimshaw. The buildings at the stopping place were sold to Mr. Draglands, who in turn sold them to Jimmy Jones. Jones had the log bunkhouse hauled to High Level the following summer. Thus the log bunkhouse and the shingle-sided stopping place were two of the earliest buildings in High Level. The Department of Highways used the stopping place for a number of years as a home for employees.

Stopping Places along the Mackenzie Highway

It was not until after the Second World War and the construction of the Mackenzie Highway that there was a need for stopping places to accommodate the increase in trucking and construction traffic. The decline in the use of cat trains after the winter of 1946-47 and the emergence of trucks as the primary freighters created the need, and several enterprising men and women began to provide services along the highway. These stopping places, which came into existence during and after the construction of the

Mackenzie, differed very little from the earlier stopping places, except that some had better stoves and kitchen facilities. Most of them still did not have indoor bathrooms, running water, or electricity. Because trucks travelled faster and covered longer distances in a day than wagon teams had done, the stopping places were located farther apart and not necessarily in the hamlets and towns along the way. The meals varied in price, averaging about 50 to 75 cents in the 40s and $1.00 to $1.25 in the 50s.

Let's take an imaginary historical journey, beginning at Grimshaw, and visit some of these early stopping places along the Mackenzie Highway. Some of you pioneer truckers who hauled in the 40s and 50s will no doubt recall stopping to have a dinner at Dan Soo's Royal Café. The Royal Café was perhaps the longest-running café owned and operated by one person.

Dan Soo Der, Royal Café, Grimshaw

Dan Soo Der ran the Royal Café in Grimshaw from 1928 until his death in 1966. "Dan Soo" immigrated to Canada from China in 1916, when he was 23 years old. He remained a bachelor all his life. Perhaps in part because he had no family in Canada, or because he was just a naturally friendly and gregarious person, he took an active role in community affairs. He loved to go goose hunting and became a curling enthusiast. He also had a fondness for children, who came into his restaurant for ice cream. Aurelia Vangrud, long-time teacher and local historian in the North Peace, grew up in the Grimshaw area. She remembers as a child going to Dan Soo's for ice cream. At times she didn't have any money to buy an ice cream cone, but he gave her one anyway.

Continuing north on the Mackenzie Highway, we stop at the Dixonville café run by Josephine and Melvin Hitz. Also in Dixonville were cafés run by Goldie Mabley and Martha Kuester. The Bennetts had a garage and café as well. At North Star there was Joe and Sadie Ek's place, and Doris Chastney's Hotel as well as Ken Seto's café. And later, in the 1950s, Bernice Lorenzen operated the North Star Café.

Bernice Lorenzen's Story [5]

The North Star Café was a neat little café in the 1950s. In this day and age it would be considered quite crude. The main item in a restaurant is your stove. The stove in that café had a griddle, like today's, and four burners. The only difference was that it was fired with wood. So consequently we had a big wood box beside the stove. When some customers came in, we had to hurry up and poke wood in the stove to get everything heated up, so we could cook them a meal. The other unique item was a barrel sitting at the end of the stove, which was the warmest place in the kitchen. And we kept that full of ice throughout the winter. In the summertime we hauled water from nearby dugouts, or the river or whatever was the best water at that time of year.

Then for disposing of all the dish water, we had a pail under the sink, and, of course, that had to be emptied quite often. A five-gallon pail. In order to dispose of this, Fred dug a hole – he had a cat at that time – in the backyard of the restaurant, and he shored it up with railroad ties. I believe he cut some timbers at that time and put [them] across the top, then put dirt on the top of that. He had cut a hole about 2' x 4'. So, we just poured the slops into this hole. We used to throw our ashes down there, and bleach. We all had bleach in those days to keep it smelling sweet, in our backyard in the middle of town. Imagine in this day and age getting away with that. You wouldn't be open for an hour.

Anyway, we did just fine. Pie and coffee was 25 cents. You got a good-sized scoop of ice cream for a nickel. The meals were, maybe, $1.50, $1.75 for pork chops. Of course we always had our specials. I think they were probably a dollar. A cup of coffee was a dime. We did what we had to do. But I'm sure I worked much harder than we do today, but I didn't have the government breathing down my neck, with all the rules and regulations. As to whether my cook had a hairnet, I doubt if I could have afforded the ten cents for the hairnet.

But, it was a good life. Because my husband was always a trucker, I served a lot of truckers. I made a lot of lunches. They'd come through heading north and I'd make them sandwiches and a thermos of coffee for them and away they'd go.

Business always depended on who was around. If there were no crews in or people working in the area taking their meals there, then I might be up at 6:00. Regular hours were mostly 8:30-9:00 o'clock, because the farmers still came to town with teams of horses. It wasn't a fast-moving society like we have today. So not too much was moving until after dinner.

Saturday night was the big night. Everybody came to town and, at that time, Manning was alive and well. They'd go to Manning and do the shopping and they'd stop at the North Star Café on the way home. And they'd all stop there, so they'd visit till 2:00 or 3:00 in the morning!

I used to bake pie on Saturday afternoon, for this Saturday evening affair. I always made a lot of pies. I never could win, because all the bachelors came in and bought a whole pie and took it home. It finally came that I had no pies. So I'd be up Sunday morning making pies again. Apple pie, pumpkin pie, cream pie was always the best seller, as they are today. Raisin pie, apple-raisin, blueberry, and mince. And cream pies. We did all our own baking. There was no having things shipped in.

About the same time, the telephone service came to North Star. There was one community phone, and I had the phone in the back of my café. People came from all around to use the phone. And many, many nights they'd be knocking on the door, and I had to get up because they needed to phone, perhaps the doctor or an emergency of some kind. Sometimes the guys would come in and want to phone their girlfriends. But I wouldn't get up for that. I wasn't too popular, and they probably went someplace else for their coffee.

I had two sons at the time. Bruce would have been first year in school; he was six and Bob was four. That was before the girls, Cheryl and Susan, were born. The boys

129

used to play in the back of the café. There were living quarters there. There were a lot of little rooms, and they'd bring the friends there, and I'd be constantly trying to make them be quiet, which was a losing battle. They soon found out if they ran through the café that they could sometimes talk me into giving them an ice cream cone, or something, and they'd be good then, if I did. I'm sure that's where my profit went. It must have gone somewhere, because I don't remember making much money. I think if I made $35 in a day, I was having a good day. But then, of course, things didn't cost a lot then. Cigarettes were 33 cents a package.

We had a friend, an older fellow who had the bulk fuel station down on the corner. He was Fred's friend as far back as Fred could remember, because they came into the North Star area around 1928 as well. And he used to come down to the café every day and play cribbage with me for a package of cigarettes. And I never won! I'm not going to say that he cheated me, but there was something odd, because I never won.

I was there at least two years. And then I sold the café to my brother and his wife, Goldie and Jo Mabley. I'm not sure how long they were there, probably two or three years. I believe after they left, the café closed, because Manning then was the place to go. North Star, as with Notikewin, and the little places along the road, died. Dixonville stayed much the same and remains the same. It's still a place to go. It's further away from Grimshaw and Manning, more in between. North Star was just next door to Manning.

We continue north on our historical journey. Just south of the hamlet of Notikewin was Pat Craig's hotel and beer parlor, the first building in the location of the new town of Manning, in 1946. At Notikewin Joe Hong had a restaurant and rooming house. When he decided to go back to China in 1946, Otto and Celina Krause bought his business and operated it for a number of years, as well as establishing the first bus service between Manning and Peace River.[6] At the Third Battle (Meikle River), Dan and Ellen Landry's farm was not a stopping place as such but they often fed and housed truckers who came by to stay at their homestead. Ma and Glady Harrington had a stopping place on the new highway, at Keg River Cabins.

Glady and Eva Harrington, Keg River Cabins

Glady Harrington had been a telegraph agent at Keg River Post for several years. He and his wife were very much involved with the local community. Eva, affectionately called "Ma," gave sewing lessons to the young girls in the area, and she had a piano, the only one in the area. If anyone wanted to learn to play, the Harringtons would let them use the piano. During Christmas season, the piano was moved carefully to the local school for the Christmas concert.

In 1945 Glady and Eva decided to build a stopping place where the new highway was being surveyed, 18 kilometres east of Keg River. Glady still had a couple of years running the telegraph office, so the stopping house would be run by "Ma" Harrington until he could join her there after retirement. In *Way Out Here*, Anne Vos described the stopping place:

> *"The main building was built with logs for the lower portion and the second floor was a frame construction. The store and café were downstairs, while the rooms for rent were upstairs, as well as Mrs. Harrington's living quarters....Fred Martineau and Louis Houle were hired to start building the cabins. When completed they were single-room cabins equipped with bunk beds, airtight heater and washstand. You had to get your own water. The bathroom was the little brown shack in the back."*[7]

The stopping place was open for business in 1946, and many early truckers remember stopping by for a meal and a much-needed rest. At first "Ma" Harrington managed it on her own, with a couple of helpers. Louis Jackson, son of Frank Jackson by his first wife, was "chief cook and bottle washer for several years. Some of the helpers were Susie Parenteau and Shirley Martineau." George Chadwick Watkins, Eva's nephew, remembers visiting the stopping place as a boy, and had a boy's memory of Eva's 5-gallon crock behind the stove filled with floating raisins.[8] Susie (née Parenteau) Fischer, who went to work for Ma Harrington in February 1946, remembers, "It was a fairly busy place, a truck stop with rooms and a café." In 1952, a separate café was added on.

The Harringtons ran the stopping place until Glady died in 1958. Eva died the following year. By that time new owners, "Skinner" Tardiff, his wife Dorothy, and daughter Peggy from Fort Vermilion, ran the stopping place. In the 60s, the place changed

In the late 50s, Ambrose Parenteau and his first wife Evelyn had a café, store and post office. Evelyn Parenteau working in the kitchen at their café at Paddle Prairie. Ambrose Parenteau collection.

hands several times. In 1986, Mark and Sondra Viau bought Keg River Cabins; as of 1996 they were still operating it.

On the road again, our next stop is at Paddle Prairie, where the Larivieres and Martineaus operated cafes.

North of Paddle Prairie there were two stopping places at the High Level Crossing before the town of High Level even existed. One of the first buildings in the location was the stopping place that Jimmy Jones and Don Staples operated beginning in 1950. Gordon Reid wrote in *Notes from the North*:

> *"Jimmy Jones with his wife Florence and Don Staples established the first café and cabins at High Level in 1950. They lived in a tent while they were building the café. After the building was completed, they moved into the rooms upstairs above the café. In 1951 they built the cabins, which became known as simply the High Level Motel.*
>
> *"When they arrived in High Level there was only one shack-like structure which was owned by Trader George Clarke for storing supplies on trips from Fort Vermilion to Hay Lakes.*
>
> *"Don sold his share of the business to Jimmy in 1953, who in turn sold out to Steve Keleman in 1954. Jimmy and Florence moved to Meander River for a time, where he purchased the pool room/store from Sam Fedorus. Later they moved to Steen River."*

Fred Lorenzen remembers staying at Jimmy Jones' stopping place at Steen River. Truckers knew that Jimmy didn't like to get up early in the morning, so they would cook their own breakfast, leaving enough money to cover the cost of the food they used. Later Jones sold the place to Steve and Angela Bandura in 1970, who ran the service station, sold tires, and later had a switching yard for Hay River Truck Lines.[9]

Another favorite stopping place for truckers was the Blue Top Lodge at High Level.

Valle Gray – The Blue Top Lodge, High Level

In 1954, Henry "Hank" Thompson, an agent for Imperial Oil, built a service station and restaurant, called the Blue Top Lodge Cafe and Cabins. Hank asked Valle Gray and her husband Bobbie to come and run the Blue Top. The Grays arrived in November 1954 from Fort Vermilion.

> *"Hank asked me to take over the restaurant for $100 a month. I helped plan the interior and went to Edmonton to buy my own equipment and supplies, then opened it November 24, 1954," explained Valle Gray.[10] "Everybody was busy. About that time they were building the DEW Line. In February 1955 is when the first trucks came through with the line equipment."[11]*

The Grays provided a 24-hour service to their customers, who were mostly truckers. The Grays also depended upon truckers who delivered groceries from Horne & Pitfield and meat from the Burns packing plant, both of Edmonton. The deliveries came once a week; if important items were not on the order list, or if the order was delayed for some reason, the menu for the week could be pretty limited.

"In 1957 we bought the restaurant and added cabins, then added bulk propane and filled bottles." Valle recalled that it was hard work. "We had few facilities. Water was a difficulty, as we didn't have running water. We had to haul it. We built a double wall ice house and filled between the walls with shavings from the sawmill. We'd put up ice and that ice did us all summer." They collected ice in winter from Footner Lake, "hardly more than a glorified slough" but the ice was "just as blue and nice as it could be. But if you cut a little bit too deep, God help you." They melted the ice and stored it in barrels. It was hard work.

When a woman came in one time and asked to have her thermos filled with water, she balked at the price when Valle told her that it would cost 25 cents. The woman got upset, insisting that "God gave us water." Valle's reply was, "God didn't give it to us. We put up ice last winter, and this is the result of the ice we put up."

The meals at the Blue Top were pretty plain, according to Valle. "For breakfast, there was the usual bacon and eggs or ham and eggs. Pies and cinnamon rolls were baked fresh. For noon day we always had roasts of some kind, chops and all the vegetables....I always tried to have a salad." Bread was a problem. "We only got bread once a week and it would get pretty stale....If the weather was very damp it would start to get moldy."

The cabins were furnished with a bed and dresser. "It was a regular room but no facilities," said Valle. "You had to go out to a biffy to go to the bathroom. There was no running water." She charged $4.00 for a single and $6.00 for a double room. There was also a bunkhouse for the men. "It was cheap – two dollars a night. But we supplied the bedding, changed the sheets, pillows, everything. I spent a lot of time doing laundry. I had washing machines and a gas-propane dryer, but in the summer I'd stretch them out, line after line after line. They would be dry in no time."

Valle remembers another incident, when an English couple, a Captain and Mrs. Cooper, arrived in a Land Rover. They registered for a cabin, but the next morning when they came in, the captain asked how much for the room. When Valle said $6.00, he handed her a five-dollar bill and wanted one dollar back. She refused to accept the money, telling him, "It's not going to break me. So put that in your wallet and leave." And they did, without paying a cent.

Valle's regular customers were mostly truck drivers. "And you know something? The truckers were nicer people than those just travelling through. You remember the ones that were gentlemen."

The stove, lights, and other machinery operated on propane, but later on the Grays got their own power plant. "A Lister Diesel, a big 'one banger' electric power plant," said Valle. "We had 50-some batteries stacked on step shelves to store power. We could

The Blue Top Lodge at High Level, built by Hank Thompson in 1954. The Grays arrived from Fort Vermilion to manage and operate the café. In 1957, after Valle and Bobby bought the café, they added the cabins. Hank Thompson collection.

use the power during the day, and in the evening we'd start up the plant again. That was a godsend."

From 1954 to 1968, the Grays ran the Blue Top Lodge. "I was up about eight o'clock and I'd be there till midnight, one o'clock. And the final cleanup at night, I did." The hired help had to come from elsewhere, as there were no local girls. The whole family, which included two of their three daughters and a son, had to pitch in. "They helped out a lot. High Level wasn't a good place to be when you've got two or three young daughters."

Although Valle has no regrets for the hard work of running a stopping place in the bush, she was glad when it ended. "I thought I couldn't live without it, but when I got out, what a relief! Now I don't want to cook a meal for myself."[12]

Continuing north from High Level to Upper Hay (Meander River) there was a stopping place run by George and Mary Courtoreille. Also Mrs. C.J. Kidd ran a café, which Stan Smith of Fort Vermilion used to frequent. "She made ice cream the old fashioned way, not the milky water you get today," remembered Stan. "It was just wonderful. If it melted, you had real cream too."

For the time being, we'll pass through Indian Cabins and return there on our backhaul later on. Instead we'll go on to Enterprise, NWT, where Jerry Eyford and his wife ran a stopping place for awhile. Bill Rowe also had one. At Hay River there was the Hay

River Hotel and café and a coffee shop run by Ed McQuarrie. Heather Knauf remembers visiting there with her husband Gunnar back in the 50s.

> "It was just a wee tiny place. They served coffee and delicious cranberry pie. Wild cranberries. He looked a bit like Churchill, and he dipped the coffee out of a basin. It was so different, now that was years and years ago. Before the highway was finished. And the others were playing cards. And of course those were the days when you didn't play cards in public places. It was really enlightening to go in and see that."[13]

On to Yellowknife, where we visit several early stopping places and cafés: Alex Morrison, who was part of the crew of the first cat train in 1939, remembered that Yellowknife had the Wild Cat café, the Nugget Café, and the Squeeze Inn.[14]

Vic Ingraham

Yellowknife has had its share of memorable personalities, but one of the most unforgettable was Vic Ingraham, who started Yellowknife's first hotel.

In 1922, Vic Ingraham went to the Northwest Territories to prospect for gold. He later joined forces with another unemployed former government clerk, Gerry Murphy. The two of them opened a store at Echo Bay on Great Bear Lake, to serve the local miners. Vic also ran a small tug and barge business between Echo Bay and Fort Franklin on the west end of the lake. For the next 10 years, Vic was involved in water transportation.

On a fateful trip in late October 1933, Vic Ingraham, Captain, and Stewart Curry were returning from Fort Franklin to make the 195-mile [313 km] trip back to Echo Bay on the Murphy Services boat, *Speed II*. The gas-powered open boat was pulling a barge loaded with freight and 11 men bound for Port Radium. During normal weather the trip would have taken no longer than a day and a half, but the boat didn't arrive on the 25th of October as expected. The temperature had dropped to -25°F [-32°C] and a storm brewed on the lake. Ernie Mills, who worked for Murphy Services, and Harry Hayter, a bush pilot who operated a Curtiss Robin, waited anxiously for the boat to show up. Hayter had just switched over from floats to skis and had to wait until there was enough ice on the lake to take off. Harry and Ernie took off at 10:00 a.m. on October 29th to look for the missing boat and crew. For the next 11 days they went airborne and searched the frozen shores of the lake. They finally found the barge on the north shore at the mouth of the Katseyedie River. The boat had exploded and sank, killing two of the crew. Vic Ingraham was seriously burned trying to rescue the two. It was only the beginning of an ordeal that would have killed the average man; but Vic Ingraham was no average man. Curry and Ingraham drifted about in a rubber life raft for two days until they reached shore. By then Ingraham had suffered severe frostbite. When Harry Hayter finally found them, Vic was more dead than alive. He was flown to the hospital at Aklavik, where he received emergency care. Eventually, after several operations, Vic had lost both legs below the knees and the first joint of three fingers on each hand.[15]

Murphy Services at Echo Bay, Great Bear Lake, ca. 1933. Vic Ingraham is third from left. Harry Hayter, the pilot who saved Vic Ingraham's life, is on the far left. Len Ingraham collection.

In 1938 Ingraham moved to Yellowknife at the start of the gold rush. He built the Yellowknife Hotel, a small place and the first of three hotels he eventually built in Yellowknife. The hotel was a favorite stopping place and watering hole for miners, catskinners, bush pilots, trappers, and truckers.

By 1943 Vic was also running a freighting business with his brother Harry. Ingraham Bros. Freighters operated cat trains and a fleet of trucks. Arthur Smith, who had taken the first civilian truck into Mills Lake, was one of the early drivers who contracted with Ingraham Bros. Art had traded his International to Hank Thompson for a larger International tandem. In spite of his disabilities, Vic Ingraham took an active role in both the hotel and freighting operations. Equipped with wooden legs, he still managed to drive a truck.

Ingraham's sense of humor was widely known, and his indomitable spirit and positive attitude toward his disability was remarkable. "Long fingers are not much good for anything but maybe typing," he once said about his hands. He also joked that he didn't have to worry about getting his feet frostbitten, or worry about mosquitoes attacking his artificial legs. He acquired nicknames of "Old Cedarfoot" and "Mr. Yellowknife."

In 1951 Vic Ingraham retired and moved to Victoria, B.C. He died of a heart attack in 1961, at age 65. One of his pallbearers was Harry Hayter, the bush pilot who rescued him after the boat accident. His cremated remains found their way back to Yellowknife, where a special memorial service was attended by so many people he knew and befriended. His ashes were scattered from an airplane over Yellowknife Bay.[16]

Indian Cabins

On our backhaul we return for a stop at Indian Cabins. The story of Indian Cabins exemplifies some of the difficulties and frustrations of people who ran stopping places in the bush and tried to weather the "boom and bust" nature of the economy of the North. Indian Cabins is located a few miles south of the Alberta/NWT boundary and is one of the most remote communities in northern Alberta. When business was good – as during the construction period of the DEW line in the 50s, and the activities of the mines and oil companies – the stopping places made a decent living. When activity in the North slowed down, highway transportation also slowed, and the people would either have to hunker down till the next boom or sell out. Because Indian Cabins was never a very large community – only six or seven families at any one time – the turnover of ownership of the stopping places was fairly frequent.

Indian Cabins started as a permanent community in 1920 when the Hudson's Bay Company established a trading post. There were a few Native families living in the area, mostly trappers, as it was rich in fur-bearing wildlife. Harry Clarke ran the HBC store for many years, and was in charge in 1939-40 when the survey crew came through to stake out the winter cat road.

The chronology of Indian Cabins is not always clear, but one of the first to establish a stopping place was the Webb family, Lenard and Delphine, about the time the Mackenzie Highway was under construction. They built a small house and store and bought furs from the local Natives. One of the most remarkable stories to come out of the North Peace concerns a tragedy that happened to the Webb family.

The Tree Grave

Delphine Webb was alone when one of their three children, Jonathan, died at age seven months. Lenard Webb was away at the time on a buying trip. The local Dene people felt sorry for the family and helped Delphine by building a Tree Grave and giving the baby an Indian burial ceremony. Stella Roman, a daughter born later to the Webbs, related the story in *Tales of the Mackenzie Highway*:

> *"He was put to rest in a Tree Grave at a local Indian burial ground. This Tree Grave was a birch bark canoe built to the size of baby Jonathan. So for years tourists etc., who visited the burial ground got to view the many above ground Spirit Houses,[17] and my brother's birch bark tree grave. The elders of the Natives felt that since Mr. Webb was gone at that time, they, out of respect for my mother and her sons, wanted to do this special ceremony for my family. My parents never forgot that."[18]*

The Webbs stayed at Indian Cabins until 1953, when they moved to Hay River so that their sons could go to school.

137

Fred Mercredi

Fred Mercredi of Fort Vermilion worked at many jobs and trades in Alberta and British Columbia throughout his lifetime. Some of the jobs included driving cattle to Grimshaw, cooking for the American army on the Canol Project in 1942, working on a survey crew that surveyed the Mackenzie Highway in 1945-46, and as a carpenter on the construction of the powerhouse for the Bennett Dam in B.C. He and his wife Bella also ran a stopping place at Indian Cabins beginning in the mid-40s.

Around the time that the Webbs were still at Indian Cabins, Fred built his house and café. A licensed carpenter, he was very skilled at squared-log construction, and his skill at making dove-tail joins can still be observed at Indian Cabins today. Fred talked about his work:

> "I bought a broad axe at Fort Vermilion; I paid $15 dollars for it, got eight blades, a chalk line and I started. Two smudges running on each side to keep the mosquitoes from eating me up."[19]

He salvaged some planks from the bridge that washed away at Meander River, by paddling upriver with a canoe.

> "When I went to the Fort, I bought a whole bunch of rope and rescued these planks and got enough planks to make a floor for my restaurant. I built a well right in the house....The water came right up through the floor. Very sweet water."

Fred was known to many truckers as "Chili Mercredi." They often stopped at the café and stayed the night, rolling out their sleeping bags on the floor of the café. In the morning, Fred's wife Bella had to walk over the bodies to get to the kitchen to cook breakfast.

George and Mary Lizotte

George and Mary Lizotte ran a café in the old Bay house, from 1949 to 1952. This café was very popular with many truckers, perhaps in part because the Lizottes' three lovely daughters – Val, Mabel, and Justine – helped out in the café.

Babe Bourassa

In the early 50s, the Mercredis sold out to Babe Bourassa. By 1952, Bourassa had a post office assigned to Indian Cabins.

On one trip in the early 50s, Gunnar Knauf was driving a tanker truck for Mercier Brothers, hauling gasoline from Grimshaw to Hay River. He had his wife Heather with him on this trip, as well as their two-year-old daughter. It had been a rainy summer, and there was a lot of water running on the roadway and in the ditches. Near Indian Cabins the truck went off the side of the road. Heather got soaking wet getting out of the truck, as she tried to jump across a ditch and landed in knee-deep cold water. Ray Hirondel, another trucker, picked them up and took them to Indian Cabins, leaving Heather and daughter at the café while Gunnar and Ray went back to unload Gunnar's truck and pull him out again.

Babe Bourassa was in charge of the café at Indian Cabins at the time. Heather remembers to this day the good meal Babe served them and the kindness he showed to Heather and her two-year old daughter while they waited for Gunnar to return with the truck. "It was such a welcome sight and that meal tasted really good. He [Babe] was such a friendly person."[20]

Inga Lund

Babe Bourassa later sold out to Inga Lund, who purchased the store and café after her husband died in 1958. She ran the trading post from 1958 to 1972. At the time she was the only white resident at Indian Cabins. She was originally from Norway, and never quite lost her Norwegian accent. Much has been written about Inga, including the following story that appeared in the Edmonton *Journal*.[21]

> "*Everyone knew Inga Lund. Inga was the only white woman living in Alberta's most northern trading post, at Indian Cabins, for many years. She was a 68-year-old great-grandmother at the time.*
>
> "*Inga came to Peace River at the age of 19 with her husband Ole from her native homeland of Norway. Inga and Ole farmed in the Brownvale area for approximately 35 years. After the death of her husband in 1958 she went north and purchased the café and store at Indian Cabins. Her nearest white family neighbors were 15 miles* [24 km] *away to the south. The nearest doctor or police station was 100 miles* [160 km] *south in High Level.*
>
> "*During her years at the Cabins she was host to all sorts of truckers, road crews, oil workers, tourists, and whoever else might drop in.... Her only neighbors were a group of Slavey Indians living nearby. They all became her true friends who would protect her if necessary. She had a huge dog, a Labrador-wolf cross, who was also her companion and protector.*
>
> "*Her greatest concern was that the doctor was so far away. During her period at the Cabins she delivered 3 babies, but to Inga it was just 'one of those things you had to do!'*"

Gordon Reid also paid tribute to Inga in his book, *Frontier Notes*.[22]

> "*The North misses a character who lived with us since 1958 and operated a Trading Post at Indian Cabins....Just about everybody knew Inga Lund. Despite being the only white resident of Alberta's most northerly trading post she claims that loneliness was never a problem at Indian Cabins. 'I had lots of friends'...The bus drivers were 'all my boys' and each day one dropped into her small store at Mile 288 on the Mackenzie Highway to bring her news from up and down the line.*

"Add this to the hundreds of oilmen, commercial travellers, tourists, and road workers who came to know her during her stay at Indian Cabins and it's easy to see why she always kept the coffee pot on."

Arlene Stach wrote that Inga never locked her door.[23]

"When the roads were blown in or muddy or just plain impassable, many a traveller, truck driver, or bus driver came in through the night, fired up the stove, made themselves something to eat, took what they needed and left money to pay. If they had no money they would leave a note and that was okay too. Every person came back and paid their bill or sent the money back with someone else. She traded with the local Natives, buying their furs. She was always their friend and sometimes their care-giver as well."[24]

The Backstroms

Until Rodney and Stella Backstrom bought Indian Cabins café and store from Inga Lund in 1972, it was basically a small trading post and café. But during their tenure, from 1972-78, the Backstroms expanded the services, adding several buildings, gasoline pumps, and a small seven-unit motel.

In 1971 they had visited Inga at Indian Cabins. Rodney was a chum of Ivor's, Inga's son. Inga, over 70 years old, wanted to sell the place to them. The next summer the Backstroms moved to Indian Cabins and Inga retired to Peace River.[25]

"The first year we wintered there. We had oil stoves in each little shack. Our family of nine slept in three different cabins. We kept the fires going. We got a fur trading license and traded in fur. We installed gas pumps. We served gas and food to whoever showed up and we more than made our expenses."

Stella got a teaching job at Steen River School that fall.

"Steve Bandura from Steen River drove up every morning with the van and hauled our children down to school. I had 24 students, from grades one to nine. The second year I didn't teach, because we had a big moving and building project that I had designed and oversaw to completion."

They needed to modernize. Although they had power from Alberta Power, they needed running water, sewer, and more buildings. At the time, the Hudson's Bay Company was closing down many northern posts. The post at Habay was closed down; the buildings were vacant. A friend of theirs suggested they put a bid in on one of the buildings. Their bid on the 60' x 70' [18 x 21m] building was accepted and they contracted Ivan Strom from Fort St. John to come with trucks and skids and move the building from Habay to Indian Cabins. With permits from Alberta Power to raise power lines, "the move went like clockwork." They applied to Alberta Opportunity Company for a grant to bring the whole place up to standard. AOC gave them $50 000 to put in utility systems and complete the motel. "We hired contractors to do the work." By October they had a seven-unit motel, a store and café, and a two-storey Bay house and garage completed on site and open for winter trade. Within two weeks an oil company moved in and stayed for three months. "So we had seven units in the motel occupied right away. We supplied the food to the oil company and the truckers."

Business began to boom, with oil exploration and the many trucks that stopped.

"That winter it went to 60 below [-50°C] for weeks on end. The trucks would run nonstop, parked in the yard. The trucks could move when it was 48 below [-48°C] and go north, but no 'iron' moved anywhere at minus 60 degrees."

However, business on the highway had begun to slow down by the mid-70s. Steve Bandura's station at Steen River was doing most of the business. The seven-unit motel at Indian Cabins came into its own.

"It was actually a lifesaver, because people would just get exhausted and we had showers and bathrooms in each room. The truck drivers would come in and shower and bath for a nominal fee. And sooner or later, going up or coming back, they would have to have a sleep. But the oil company coming in really helped us get on our feet. Our overhead costs were very high. It was nothing to pay $2500 a month for our power bill.

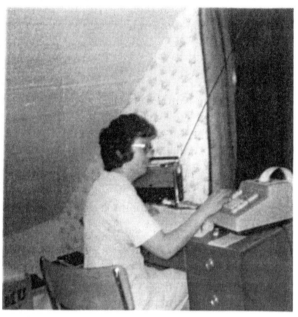

Many wives were jacks of all trades. Angie Bandura did the bookkeeping for the Bandura family stopping place at Steen River. Stella Friedel collection.

"Our heating was mostly wood fuel. The Indian trappers would put up wood for us in the summer. We would pay them by the cord. We would put up about 40 cords of wood each winter. Lovely, efficient, comfortable, and relatively safe." The seven-unit motel was heated by a small boiler that piped hot water through the rooms. There was also a laundry room.

"We kept it open 24 hours a day....The five girls and two boys, they worked. There was no distinction made by sex. The girls would serve gas as well as the boys. The boys could also cook. The girls, also excellent cooks, would go on night shift. They are John, Virginia Hursley, Ralph, Vivian Hallwachs, Jeannette Gardner, Margaret Weir, and Betty Backstrom."

Stella credits the work and skills of the seven children for the successful operation of the Truck Stop. The meals were pretty basic. They served plenty of pancakes, steak, bacon and eggs for breakfast and hamburgers, pork chops, and chicken roasts for lunch and supper. Supplies and groceries came in from Peace River by Byers Transport. They had two large freezers to keep frozen goods. "We had bus service every day, going one way or the other," Stella explained. "One day north going to Hay River; the next day south going to High Level. So we were never really isolated."

They had truckers stop by regularly. Byers Transport always stopped, because they were driving in winter at that time over Denison's Ice Road to the El Dorado Mines on Great Bear Lake. "I got to see what raw gold looked like, when it was being transported south. These [hauls] were supposed to be secret." The Backstroms also saw a lot of trucks hauling fish south. Drivers for Grimshaw Trucking, Northern Transportation Company Ltd. (NTCL), and Robinson's Trucking were regular stoppers. "We saw the usual people most of the time. I think at the time there were about 80 or 90 truckers on the road."

Like the Banduras at Steen River, the Backstroms were also seeing the switching of tractor units. "When the new territorial government was established, there was the fuss over the licensing of the trucks going in and out of the NWT. They put in weigh scales at Enterprise, so they [the truckers]were sometimes doing turn-arounds at Indian Cabins." Before a reciprocal agreement was in place between Alberta and NWT, trucking companies had to switch tractor units with appropriate licenses to haul the trailers and freight over the Alberta/NWT boundary.

In many ways it was a very satisfying life, Stella recalls. It was not all work. In the summers, for recreation, the seven children would go pick wild strawberries along the railroad right-of-way. "I put the strawberries into the deep freeze, and in the wintertime and at Easter time, the Indian people would come by and say, 'Teacher, do you have any fresh berries in that box?' So, life was good in lots of ways." With the long days, the kids had fun on the dune buggy at Steen River. It was made from an old Volkswagen frame and motor. "And six or eight kids would pile into the pickup and go to Steen River to race in the gravel dump." In the wintertime they would go ski-dooing.

Because the Backstroms bought and sold furs, they got very knowledgeable about the quality of over 13 different kinds of pelts the Native trappers brought in. "Bill and Winnie Askin came in and got a trapline at Steen River. She trapped with him, and she was about my age," said Stella. "She could trap, clean, and stretch her own lynx, wolverine, and stuff like that. She was as good a trapper as her husband was."

The lifestyle in the North was not without its dark side. "If you think that booze and belles was the story of the life there, that's true too – heavy on the booze and extremely few were the belles," Stella said. "When you find out that being your own police officer is normal, you know that you are in an abnormal situation." Some of the local people would get injured during a drunken party. If no one was seriously hurt, the police did not bother to come. When she phoned one night at the request of a resident complaining about a drunken party, the police asked if anyone needed to be hospitalized. "No," she replied. "Well, fine, we won't bother to come." Stella said, "In that case, if you are not coming up to shut down this party, I'll phone you next when there is a dead person."

"When you operate a truck stop for three years, and there are only two incidents, that's not bad. When you're up there four years, six years, and there's only one set of stitches from a knife, it is no sweat. Swearing, cursing, and rowdying around at night might be uncomfortable, but I found that you endured three hours of arguing before anybody raised fists anyway. It's called the 'wide-awake drunk syndrome', tiresome to a sane person."

One woman came to Stella and told her she was running away from her husband because she was afraid he would kill her. Stella asked her, "How big are you? How big is your husband?" The woman replied, "Oh, he's about five-foot-two, skinny." Then Stella said, "And you're going to run away from *him*?" Afterwards Stella had second thoughts about her advice to the woman. What if she decided to kill *him*? "She never came to my door again, after her awareness that she was bigger than he was."

In 1978, the Backstroms left Indian Cabins, selling the business to a person from Hay River, who in turn sold the business to Ray Ouellette and the Cliff Stach family.

The Backstrom children all worked at the Indian Cabins stopping place. Ralph Backstrom, age 12. Stella Backstrom collection.

The Stachs

While the Stachs were at Indian Cabins, a switching yard was established. Arlene Stach remembers a truck driver who worked for Cascade being very shy. Another driver was a woman who travelled with a cat and thus her truck's CB handle was "Pussy Galore."

> "[She] lived and breathed for the sole purpose of putting some poor guy on the hook. One day she was waiting for her switch and had time to waste, so she took after the poor Cascade driver. What a show! Finally the poor guy gave up and hid in his truck."[26]

Arlene Stach also wrote an insightful account about the effect of the Mackenzie Highway on the Dene people living in the area. She had observed the changes to their lifestyle:

> "At one time there was a lot of Indian families living at Indian Cabins. The road was a mere wagon trail that wound around the high ground, avoiding the swamps as much as possible...When the Mackenzie Highway was built the younger generation was introduced to the outside world, not just the good stuff but trouble too. The elders were hard working, honest, and good people. Their furs were of the best quality and would bring the highest prices on the market.

> "Although some adopted the Catholic faith, many kept their old ways. One of their beliefs was that the wolves were their ancestors and if they trapped a wolf they had a special man of the community to skin and dress it with respect. The Indian Healers were very powerful in their ways. We have witnessed some of their many cures, which were truly amazing. However they could not cure the white man's diseases and so became unhealthy. For the Indians the progress of the highway was certainly their loss."[27]

It is not surprising, however, that many who ran stopping places operated for only a few years. It was hard work, the hours were long, and the profits, if there were any, did not allow for hiring the help needed to give the owner time off. Those with large families got help from the children, but children grow up, get married, and move away.

The Legacy of Mackenzie Highway's Stopping Places

The people who ran the stopping places usually had to be open 24 hours a day. Owners hired night staff or, if their family was large, each family member shared the responsibility of taking graveyard shifts. Being awakened in the middle of the night by some hungry or tired trucker was a routine occurrence. Stopping places were definitely homes away from home for the truckers and a welcome relief for tourists who had spent hours driving the hot, dusty gravel road, sweltering in cars with the windows rolled up to keep out the dust and mosquitoes.

Stopping places were important centres of communication, since travellers would be coming from either north or south. You could find out what the road conditions were like further along the road, or get emergency help if you were broken down or stranded in the ditch. You could leave a message there for another person coming through behind you. Or just simply find out the latest gossip.

Stopping places often provided emergency help when drivers got into trouble. While the food and accommodations at these places were pretty basic, the friendliness of the owners added spice to whatever meal they served.

Highway improvements and regulation of the trucking industry eventually caused the small family-owned stopping places along the Mackenzie Highway to disappear. They were replaced by larger motels and hotels in towns. By 1980 most of the highway was paved between Grimshaw and Hay River. Truckers could make faster time now and many did not need the stopping places anymore. New regulations required two drivers per truck and they could drive straight through. Most of the small, family-owned stopping places along the highway disappeared.

The people who ran the stopping places were an essential service to travellers in the North and played an important role in northern transportation. They have also added a richness to the history of truck transportation. Even a few romances grew out of a trucker's frequent visits to one of the stopping places. Hank Thompson met his future wife Kathleen "Pat" Nielson, who was waiting on tables at her family's café in Grimshaw.[28]

In *Tales of the Mackenzie Highway*, Fred Lorenzen pays tribute to the families who ran stopping places:

> *"We never left any of these places hungry, even if we had no money; we often slept on the café floor in our sleeping bags. We were treated good by every one of them. These many years later we offer our heartfelt thanks. We've never forgotten you."*

Notes

[1] Interview with Katherine Blakley, October 12, 1999.

[2] Interview with Frank Blakley, October 12, 1999.

[3] Frank Blakley describes, "A jigger is a plank about 10 to 18 inches wide [25-46 cm] and 8 feet long [2.5m] with a mechanism on it so that when you pull it, it goes away from you." The jigger pulled the line under the ice to where another hole was chiseled through the ice, usually about 100 yards [91m] away. The fishing net was attached to the end of the line, and the net could be pulled along and set beneath the ice.

[4] Woody and Evelyn Van Natter, "The Saga of the Old D30 International (The E.T. Blakley-Woody Van Natter Story)," *Tales of the Mackenzie Highway*, p. 32.

[5] Interview with Bernice Lorenzen, September 19, 1999.

[6] "Otto and Celina Krause" story, in *Saga of Battle River – We Came, We Stayed*, pp. 323-325.

[7] Anne Vos, "Keg River Cabins," in *Way Out Here: History of Carcajou, Chinchaga, Keg River, Paddle Prairie, Twin Lakes*. Keg River, Keg River Book Committee, 1994, pp. 59-60.

[8] Op. Cit., p. 190.

[9] In the late 70s the licensing and permits for trucking companies became a bit complicated. Freight from Alberta into the Territories had to be hauled by companies licensed in the NWT, and vice versa. The switching of drivers and tractor units took place at switching yards at Steen River and Indian Cabins until the 80s, when changes in regulations allowed trucking companies to haul freight on either side of the border. This change in licensing seriously affected the businesses in these communities, as truckers no longer had to stop for switching and could drive straight through.

[10] Correspondence with Valle Gray, February 28, 1998.

[11] Interview with Valle Gray, August 18, 1997.

[12] My thanks to Valle Gray, who now resides in Peace River, for sharing her experiences in running a stopping place.

[13] Interview with Mr. and Mrs. Knauf, August 18, 1998.

[14] *Tales of the Mackenzie Highway*, p. 41.

[15] The source for Vic Ingraham's accident and recovery was Bertram B. Fowler, "Earth's Hardiest Creature," Baltimore *Sunday Sun*. The article was condensed in the *Reader's Digest*, October 1946.

[16] A special thanks to Len Ingraham, for providing me with several articles and photographs about his father.

[17] The Dene (Slavey) buried their dead in two ways: by placing them on scaffolds or in crooks of tall trees. The second method was to erect a spirit house, a structure made of wood. Diamond Jenness, in *The Indians of Canada*, page 391, described the method of burial: "...sometimes they buried them with leaves or snow, placed all their property beside them, and erected small huts over the remains to protect them from wild animals. The souls of the dead, aided by loon or otter spirits, were believed to pass through the earth, cross a large lake, and begin life in another world."

[18] *Tales of the Mackenzie Highway*, p. 11.

[19] Interview with Fred Mercredi, August 19, 1998. At the time, he was 89 years old.

[20] Interview with Mr. and Mrs. Gunnar Knauf, August 20, 1998.

[21] The *Journal* article appeared on March 18, 1970.

[22] Gordon Reid, *Frontier Notes*, p. 59.

[23] *Tales of the Mackenzie Highway*, p. 14.

[24] Arlene Stach, "The Stach Family," *Tales of the Mackenzie Highway*, p. 14-15.

[25] Interview with Stella Friedel, May 20, 1999.

[26] *Tales of the Mackenzie Highway*, p. 15.

[27] Ibid.

[28] *Land of Hope and Dreams: A History of Grimshaw and Districts*, p. 374.

Chapter 7 – Life on the Road

People's attitudes about truckers are mixed. Firstly, there seems to be a general ignorance about truckers and the trucking industry, and secondly, there is a lack of recognition of just how vital trucks are to the lives of every Canadian. Truckers are all too often caught up in a world of mythology reinforced by the media and popular culture.

Country and western songs in the 60s and 70s presented truckers as "Knights of the Road," and glorified the freedom and independence of the trucker and the dangers he faced on the highway. About the same time, films about trucks and truckers began to come out of Hollywood, either romanticizing or vilifying truckers. Unfortunately, these images influenced public perceptions. As trucks got bigger, scary films like *Duel* fed upon the nameless fears of many automobile drivers intimidated by trucks on the highways.

Adele Boucher of Peace River is the wife of Mag Boucher, who owns and operates Mag Boucher Trucking, a company that specializes in salvage logging and hauling. Adele has thought at length about Hollywood's images of truck drivers:[1]

> *"There was* Smoky and the Bandit *with Burt Reynolds. That gave trucking this cool look. It moved from cowboys to urban cowboys. They were radio equipped and these trucks were big bucks. Truckers became sexy after Burt Reynolds. You started looking at other truck drivers as not just being a pair of cowboy boots and a ball [cap].*

> *"There was a movie came out in the States about – I forget what it was called.* Back Haul, *I think. It's about this guy and his wife who are stranded on the side of the road and the truck driver stops and picks them up and the man sends the woman to town with the truck driver, and he waits till they come back and the woman disappears. It has destroyed the image of truck drivers."*

These images of the trucker have little to do with real life truckers in the North. They are men and a few women doing a highly skilled job – at times working under extraordinary conditions, at times achieving heroism.

Truckers about Truckers

Truckers in general are a pretty independent lot and most of them treat each other as equals, with the respect and courtesy that they expect from others. However, some truckers are perceived as being more equal than others. Truckers who own their own trucks are just a cut above the hired driver. And those who own several trucks are a bit higher up the ladder. But they all started in the same place.

Adele Boucher explains:

"Owners of trucking companies were truckers. You worked your way up. You got one truck and two trucks, three trucks, and so on. There is a different mentality when you own the truck than when you drive for somebody else.

"Some truckers look at other truckers as not being real. A freight hauler is not the same as an oilfield hauler... Truckers in this area will look at some highway truckers as city slickers because they never get off the paved roads. They don't want to get their trucks dirty. Compare that to the guy who hauls pipe and works out in the camps in the bush."[2]

This attitude of bush drivers about drivers who never get off the highways is expressed in *Denison's Ice Road*:

"Bush and highway drivers are two different breeds...Just like among highway drivers, the tankers think the freight haulers are a cut below them and won't sit in the cafes with them. Well, the highway drivers come in from the Outside and think they're goin' to show us bush apes a lot of things. But when one of those highway fellas has somethin' happen to his truck, even though he knows how to repair it, he's not used to doin' that, so he just sits and waits for someone to come along and fix it. Their first trip up, these here highway drivers don't even like to cross the Mackenzie River. The ice scares hell out of them and it's like prodding a cow into an airplane to get them to go out on the ice bridge."[3]

On the other hand, the highway driver often views himself at the top of the heap. Like most people, he likes to think that his job requires the most skill. Driving a modern-day, heavily-loaded unit on a very busy freeway and having to share the road with amateur drivers – the highway trucker has to plan well ahead before passing anyone or pulling off the road. He may view off-road driving in a log truck down a dirt road as a piece of cake.

Truckers' Wives

The lifestyle of trucking families is often a waiting game for many wives and children when the trucker husband is on a haul. Trucker's wives, like truckers, had to be independent and self-sufficient, because there were long periods of time – days, sometimes weeks – when they wouldn't see their husbands.

Adele Boucher would sometimes not see Mag for weeks at a time.

"Communications comes into it. If you were where you had a pay phone, you were still in civilization. If you got beyond pay phones, and left that area, then you were roughing it. I remember, Mag would be home and he would say he was going to High Level, and he wouldn't come home for two weeks. And I'd never know where he was. At one time you only heard where your husband was if you phoned the truck shop and they had somebody that came in and said, 'Yes, I saw Mag Boucher's truck over there at Red Earth last Thursday.'"[4]

Many early trucking companies were family operations, and, as in farming families, the wives and children were very much a part of the business. Wives of truckers had to be jacks-of-all-trades. Adele commented: "Lots of truck drivers' wives are half-assed mechanics. You've heard their stories for so long you get a little education."[5]

Truckers' wives kept as busy as possible so that there was no time to worry. But at night, the worries would surface. "Is he well? What if his truck is broken down north of High Level? It's minus 40...out there. Will there be someone along to help him?" "He should have been home today. Was he in an accident? Is he stranded someplace along the highway?" These were all too often legitimate fears.

Communication was sporadic at the best of times. There was the telegraph, but only in a few communities along the highway. Telephones didn't come to rural communities in the North Peace until the 60s, and radio telephones in trucks were not a common feature until much later.

Medical and emergency services were also widely dispersed. In the early days on the Mackenzie Highway, it could take several hours for a doctor or ambulance or the RCMP to arrive at an accident scene. Between Manning and Fort Vermilion there was Dr. Mary Percy Jackson at Keg River and at Fort Vermilion, Dr. Hamman and St. Theresa's hospital operated by the Sisters of Providence. But north of High Level there were no hospitals or medical services until you reached Hay River, NWT.

For women whose marriages might be on shaky ground, there were other worries: "Has he taken up with that waitress at Hay River?" "Has he run into that no-good buddy of his and they're out drinking again?"

Truckers' wives had the lion's share of the day-to-day tasks of taking care of a house: fixing that leaky toilet, going to town to pick up the truck parts her husband ordered from Edmonton, taking the kids to church or a hockey game. And the piles of laundry to wash and iron!

Many trucking families were also farm families, so for the trucker/farmer wife there were many other chores to do or supervise. It is a wonder that wives of truckers had time for any other occupation. But surprisingly, many of them did, because there was always a need for extra cash. Some wives, like May Eyford, did the bookkeeping; others ordered truck parts, ran errands, and "trouble-shooted" if their husbands had problems on the road. A few, like Bernice Lorenzen and Evelyn Parenteau, even ran a café or small store.

"You did what you had to do," said one wife. "Looking back, I wonder how we managed, raising big families, making do, and trying to earn a few dollars on the side."

Animals

One of the hazards of driving a truck in the North is encounters with animals on the highway. Moose and deer were especially a problem at night and had the habit of darting out on the road at the wrong time. In the early years, Natives and settlers let their horses wander freely to graze. In *Tales of the Mackenzie Highway*, Bruce Hills wrote about a very unusual encounter with a particular horse on one of his trips, when he was hauling a power unit for one of the seismic camps in the Rainbow Lake area. At the time Bruce was driving a '50 Chevy with a flat deck and gin pole set up to be used to load and unload. Near Paddle Prairie, around 2 a.m., he came around a corner right into a herd of horses.

> "The moon was very high, and as I came around the corner, lo and behold! A herd of horses all on the road. Naturally I did the dumb thing, I hit the brakes. The front ones locked up and nothing happened in the back. Before you could blink, the truck had swapped ends and I was sailing into the horse herd backwards. The moon was bright enough that I could see to keep the truck on the road till I got it stopped. As I was attempting to turn around and head north again, I got one front wheel over the shoulder. I got out to throw a chain under the wheel, and that's when I discovered I had a passenger. I had scooped up one of the horses. His hind-end was up against the power unit, his back legs folded on the flat deck, and his front legs hanging over the deck apron. I climbed up and tried to get him to move, but no luck. I thought, 'Well, I'll get the truck turned and maybe I can shake him off or someone will come along and we can pull him off.'

> "My brakes were still froze up and after backing up, I would roll to a gentle stop. I still had a horse on board and no one was in sight. I got back up on the deck and had a chat with the pony. He didn't pay much attention to me. I started thinking about some of the things old horse handlers had told me. One being, if a horse was stuck in the mud or muskeg and refused to help himself, pour a few drops of water in his ear and he will get right lively. Hey, I didn't have water, but I [did] have coffee. When I put a few drops in his ear, I got his attention all right. The S.O.B. unloaded both of us."[6]

During the early 50s, there was a rabies epidemic in the North, and many animals – especially predators – were rabid. On one of his trips, John King encountered a rabid fox on the road. He stopped, and the fox started to bite the tires on his truck. John could see that the fox "was all froze up" and grabbed his rifle, got out of the truck, and put the fox out of its misery.[7]

Booze and Belles

In the North, life on the road was a lonely occupation for truckers, especially for those who had no families to return to. They had virtually no social life. Sharing a bottle of booze with another trucker or visiting the local "belles" was a way of relieving some of the loneliness.

The history of any frontier follows much the same pattern, and the North was an expanding frontier. In northern towns like Hay River, Fort Smith, and Yellowknife in the mid-30s and throughout the 40s, men far outnumbered the women by a considerable percentage. Most of them were single. Having come from all over Canada, the U.S., and Europe, they worked at a variety of occupations – prospecting, mining, fishing, trapping, fur trading, lumbering, construction, and transportation. Among the latter were bush pilots, river boat operators, catskinners, and truckers. There were also a handful of government workers, store owners, bankers, Anglican and Roman Catholic priests, RCMP officers, hotel and cafe owners, cooks, and moonshiners. This invasion must have been a bewildering mix of humanity to the Natives, the Dene people whose villages were nearby.

Booze

A thin veneer of civilization exists in frontier towns at the best of times, and that veneer is soluble in alcohol. In the North there wasn't supposed to be any booze, or at least not much. Some alcohol was imported for medicinal and sacramental purposes. Prohibition was abolished in the rest of Canada before 1930, but not north of the 60th parallel in an effort to control whisky trading to the Natives. It was well into the 50s before prohibition in the Northwest Territories was finally abolished.

One could get a permit that allowed you to buy five gallons of liquor a year. The HBC or RCMP were the dispensers of the liquor, which generally arrived on the first boat of the summer. Tim Nagle, a prospector who was in the North in the 30s, recalled:

> "The permits had been stored in the strong room along with the other items governed by law. After the privation they had been forced to endure, the men from Fort Fitzgerald considered themselves near illness, so they were taking their permits and heading home to recuperate."[8]

Jock McMeekan, a long-time newspaper editor and resident of the North, recalls that it was only "two gallons" on a permit. He writes:

> "We were allowed to buy...two gallons of spirits a year. This covered light table wines and 60 overproof grain alcohol or 30-proof rum. The result was that every purchaser got the strongest possible potation....This two gallon a year business led, of course, to the drinking of many weird and unorthodox liquids, the least dangerous of which were fruit extracts, which came in many flavors: lemon, orange, vanilla, banana, almond and peppermint. It was grimly humorous to see some of the hardened drinkers, after consuming their legal allowance of medicinal liquors, 'sobering-up' on shaving lotions and other repulsive concoctions.

> "There was, of course, a great deal of 'home brew' made. This not being a standard recipe but likely to have a base of dried fruits, potatoes, or anything fermentable. One of the cooks at the Burwash, one time, made a brew of dried apricots enriched by the addition of moose steaks."[9]

It is not surprising that bootlegging became a thriving business in the North. Illegal booze came in by airplane, boat, cat trains, or trucks. These purveyors had ingenious ways of hiding illegal booze in the most unlikely places, and the RCMP constables had the dubious distinction of upholding the law. It was their job to find and seize the booze before it disappeared down the throats of very thirsty men. Ken Coates, in *North to Alaska*, wrote about the problems during the construction of the Alcan highway:

> *"Bootleggers became extremely adept at hiding their caches: many bottles were smuggled into the camps in hollowed-out loaves of bread or in rolls of tar paper....Men would cut the bottom out of a 45-gallon barrel, empty it, but leave the top looking like a barrel of gas. The rest would be filled with sawdust and whisky. Another truck driver hollowed out a beam, stuffed whisky bottles into the hole and sealed his treasures with padding and a plug."*[10]

Most early truck drivers had a bottle of whisky hidden somewhere in their trucks. During wartime, on the Canol Project, booze was a medium of exchange that could be traded for a pair of tires, or a few hours' use of tools in a warm military garage to repair an engine. The further north one went, the more valuable that bottle of whisky became. What may have sold for $10 in Grimshaw might sell for as high as $50 to $75 in Norman Wells.

Owners of transportation companies usually prohibited any consumption of alcohol while their crew travelled in cat trains or trucks. Svein Sigfusson wrote about inherent problems with alcohol in the bush:

> *"The problem of booze on the cat trains was like that of a brush fire in a drought: no matter how hard we stamped it out, it kept coming back, a chronic recurring evil....From the day we began hauling on Reindeer Lake, we flatly prohibited liquor on the swings. The work of tractor freighting was far too hazardous for intoxicated skinners; one drunk on a swing crew could bring the entire train to disaster and tragedy."*[11]

Many men with drinking problems took jobs in which restrictions of liquor gave them a respite from the temptation of alcohol. Svein Sigfusson mentioned that "some of our best cooks were alcoholics...but abstainers each winter, drying out while working on the swings – though we had to curtail their supplies of vanilla."[12]

When liquor was freely available to all after the 1950s, road construction companies had a difficult time controlling the crew's drinking. Practically all construction companies had very strict rules about drinking on the job, and it was grounds for getting fired if you were caught drunk while operating machinery. It was just too dangerous to have booze around on a job and too many accidents could occur to other men or equipment. Controlling booze in camps was another matter.

Jock Shannon of Shannon Construction Ltd. remembered a time in 1961 when the crew was cleaning up from having completed their section of the Mackenzie Highway reconstruction.[13]

> *"That's something I wouldn't tolerate on the job, but nothing I could do about it during wind-up time. We got finished up at Paddle Prairie in '61. The engineers came*

152

in and they were gravelling to the south of us, as our work had already been gravelled. He said to me, 'Would your fellows consider taking a grader down and spreading gravel for us?' We had a good grader but we didn't have a grader man. We were just winding up, and the superintendent with Stettler Construction was all that was left. I went down where the grader was, and there was some of the crew there in the cab of the grader. I read the riot act. 'Get that off the road and get into camp!' I knew there was a truck coming up from Edmonton to pick up MacGregor-Johannson's Caterpillar tractor, and it hadn't arrived yet at Paddle Prairie.

"I went back to Keg River Cabins, and I was just sitting down to have my supper when all of a sudden in come the boys saying, 'The grader's on fire.' I said, 'What in the world set the grader on fire?' 'Well, a truck ran into it.' This guy that was coming to pick up MacGregor-Johannson's Cat had stopped in Manning and had imbibed too much too. The thing was all dented in and diesel fuel everywhere and the back tires of the grader burning! The fire burnt the grader and the truck, and the fellow in the truck, they had taken him down to Manning to the hospital. So, that was the wind-up of that year. We had to rebuild the whole grader. And then, lots of law suits. Those are just little episodes of the construction business."

Belles

Prostitution in the North was also an integral part of frontier life. Jock McMeekan, in one of his articles for the *Yellowknife Blade*, described the morality of frontier towns such as Yellowknife in the 30s and 40s.

"In those days a Red Light District in a mining camp was a normal and accepted thing. It may surprise some of the residents of Yellowknife, who today are accustomed to the present high moral tone of the community, to know that along the lake shore in the days of 1937-39 there was what is known as 'Glamour Alley,' where five or six houses and log cabins housed from 14 to 16 'filles de joie'....It is doubtful that these houses seriously corrupted the morals of any otherwise incorruptible male. However, the Great White Fathers in Ottawa...issued an edict: 'Clean house in Yellowknife.' The settlement was forthwith, on surface, rendered moral!

"Policing was a difficult business. There was no jailhouse. It was necessary for those early men to exercise great restraint and considerable tact mixed with firmness, to their credit they maintained order."[14]

Earle Harcourt, general manager of Yellowknife Transportation Company Ltd., recalled one time when his cat train crew arrived in Yellowknife after a long trip in the bush.

"When we were hauling the wood in for the Consolidated Mining and Smelting, and were coming into Yellowknife, we came up a road that went past a little cabin, which had been taken over by a madam and her troupe. The sleighs would go right past that and on up to where they dumped the load and came back to the encampment where

the outgoing materials for the mine would be loaded. This time they came back in and somebody had a bottle and they got drunk. Then they decided that they wanted to visit the gals, so they went down there. When they got there the gals wouldn't let them in. They were entertaining the boys from Consolidated Mining and Smelting.

"Our boys thought that was rank discrimination. So they went back and got the cats and chains, and they threw chains around the cabin, hooked the cats on, and started moving the cabin into Yellowknife Bay. One of them – I forgot who it was – came and got me up. By the time I got there they had worn down a little.

"Now, the gals' cabin had heavy shutters on the windows. The madam was holding the shutter up and talking to George, and she reached out and took a swing at him with a hammer. At the same time he shut the window from the outside. And of course her arm went through the window and [she] cut her arm. So the next day she went down to the RCMP and charged him with assault. The charges were later dropped."[15]

Yellowknife was not the only town in the North that had its "Glamour Gals." Back in the 30s, along the Grimshaw Road to Battle River Prairie, there was a stopping place that a few old-time truckers might remember. It was run by three women. Truckers had to be very careful when ordering a chicken dinner. If they ordered roast chicken with all the trimmings, they'd better mean it, as they could end up being escorted upstairs by one of the women.

Code of the Road

Whether a trucker owns one truck or 100, drives on a paved highway or on logging roads in the northern bush, he is more than likely expected to adhere to certain rules, sometimes called the code of the road.

The Canadian North tests the trucker like no other part of North America; it makes stringent demands not only on a trucker's driving skills but also his knowledge and ability to survive in the bush. Unwritten rules of the road have evolved to ensure the safety of both a driver and his truck and the safety of fellow drivers.

Truckers who started as young men on the Mackenzie Highway quickly learned that there were certain things you did and didn't do. Most had begun driving as young boys with grain trucks and graduated to bigger trucks. But having the technical know-how was just a small part of being a trucker in the North. He had to learn the code of the road. He would either abide by this code or the word would get around among other truckers, and one of them would set him straight. Many of these rules deal with survival in the north, and other rules are just plain courtesy and common sense.

Don't pass anyone by who may need help.

If a driver of a car or truck had a breakdown or accident on an isolated northern highway, it could be hours or days before help arrived. Along the lonely stretches of road between Hay River and High Level, Jerry Eyford of Hay River Truck Lines recalled

Norm Mercier's overturned tanker truck. Note the tires have been removed from the rims. Ed Leguerrier collection.

several times that he came across people sitting in their cars, almost frozen to death. They had had a break-down or were out of gas. In wintertime in the North when it is 30 below [-34°C], passing someone who was in trouble might result in that person's death. It just wasn't done. Part of a truck driver's code of the road was to never pass by someone who might need help.

Les Stranahan, retired trucker and former bus driver for Canadian Coachways, explained the code in his article "Driving Coachways Bus on the Mackenzie Highway":[16]

> *"At that time people travelling on the Mackenzie Highway helped each other. A sort of code prevailed: You stopped if you found someone in trouble. This code just expanded when the buses started to run, and included us. We helped or were helped. There was a feeling that it was important that buses with their mail and passengers get to their destinations."*

Communication was not the same as it is today. It was mostly by word of mouth. If a trucker broke down, he would send word with the guy coming the other way, if he needed parts or help with repairs that could not be improvised on the road.

Les Stranahan tells a story about the time he was driving a Coachways bus between Meander River and High Level.

"It was a very hot evening, around 4 a.m.... the bus blew a front tire and we ended up in the ditch. Quite a few passengers were wakened in a hurry. I got out and sized up the situation, got the jack and tire wrench out, with some help from one or two of the men travelling with us. A car came by and we sent word to High Level that we were in the ditch with tire trouble. After a great deal of hard work and trouble I had the blown tire off and a very poor spare tire on. Fred Lorenzen and Lyle (Happy) Owens had brought a truck from High Level to help. They took some passengers in the back of the truck and I drove the bus into High Level. We found that there was no spare or rim available in High Level. Fred said, 'My truck tire will fit, take it.' So we took off one of his tires and used it to replace the poor spare. Fred said that he needed some sleep anyway, so he'd just wait there until the bus came back from Peace River the next morning. At 3 a.m. the next morning he had his tire back, we replaced it on his truck and off he went North with his load of lumber."[17]

Mark a bad section of road to warn others.

If a trucker ran into trouble on a piece of road, he marked it so that others behind him would avoid having trouble on the same section. Calvin Courtoreille relates an incident he had while working for Menzies Fish Company of Faust, Alberta, in 1947. A group of men left Grimshaw to open commercial fishing on Great Slave Lake. While crossing a small lake, Calvin's truck broke through the ice, and he hit the windshield and broke his nose. While his brother Walter went off to get some help, the rest cut logs to get the truck out. The following evening Walter returned with a D8 Cat he borrowed from Dick Bond of Bond Construction.

"In those days it was not unusual to borrow a Cat or truck from a friend. We strung the cable out to the truck, hooked it on, and pulled the truck out of the lake. It took a long time and the men had to keep breaking the ice and feeding wood to the fire so we could keep from freezing. We finally pulled the truck to shore and parked it right close to the fire and started to drain it. After drying and draining, the truck started. We loaded up again and blocked the trail and marked the ice so no one else would fall through."[18]

Be prepared and plan ahead.

Back in the 1940s and 50s, trucks had poor heating or none at all. The cabs were frigid, so truckers dressed in layers to keep warm. They wore heavy underwear, wool shirts and sweaters, and lined jackets. On their feet they wore heavy wool socks, mukluks or fur-lined moccasins, and rubber boots. Some items might be purchased locally, but most of their gear and clothing was ordered from Eaton's or Simpson's catalogues. Almost all had sleeping bags or heavy blankets with them in winter and lots of bug spray in summer.

They carried well-stocked tool boxes that usually had a crescent wrench, a pair of pliers, and a roll of hay wire. Some had jumper cables. Most carried a big hammer so they could hit their tires to check the air pressure. Spare tires were a must, and they all carried tire chains for their wheels. What they didn't have in their tool boxes, they improvised from nature. Bernice Lorenzen recalls some truckers telling a story of replacing broken springs with a log they got out of the bush and wedged between the frame and axle to carry the load.[19]

Although most carried a bottle of aspirin with them, emergency medical kits as such were not common. "Things like Band-Aids that are common today – they didn't have them," said Bernice. "Fred said that if they cut themselves they just bled." If they carried "Hospital Brandy" or other liquor, it was more likely to be shared with another trucker they met on the road, than used for medicinal reasons.

Truckers normally tried to time their trips to get their meals at stopping places along the way; but in the early days of trucking on the Mackenzie Highway, there were no stopping places between Indian Cabins and Hay River. Truckers all carried grub boxes and tea pails. They stopped to light a fire, sometimes right in the middle of the road, and thawed out their meals from their grub boxes. In the grub box would be tea, coffee, flour, sugar, bacon, pork and beans, and cans of sardines. These foods would freeze and have to be thawed out before they could be eaten.

Fred Lorenzen recalls that one time he came upon some truckers who were broken down and were

"Grubbing up on the way to Mills Lake, February 1948." Left to right around the fire: Steve Keleman, Peter Keleman, Gordon Papp and Bruce Rome. Fred Lorenzen collection.

pretty hungry: "They had a shipment of meat for Blakley's stopping place. Half a pig. So they got it down, whacked some meat off and cooked it in a scoop shovel over the fire."

Take care of your truck and equipment.

Any self-respecting trucker had respect for his truck as well. It was his livelihood, so he was expected to take care of it. If he broke down on the road, he fixed his own truck. He also had to be prepared to change his own tires.

Les Stranaghan remembers the cumbersome job of changing and repairing a flat tire:

"There were no tire shops on these roads; flats were fixed on the spot. Tires were not of the quality of today's tires. You took the wheel off the truck, took the tire off its rim, pulled out the inner tube, patched it using rubber patches and a special glue which everyone carried, put the inner tube back into the tire, the tire onto the rim, the wheel back on the truck, and then – with hope in your heart – you pumped the tire full of air. This was done by unscrewing a spark plug and putting in its place a handy little tube 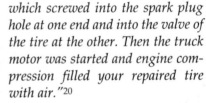 *which screwed into the spark plug hole at one end and into the valve of the tire at the other. Then the truck motor was started and engine compression filled your repaired tire with air."*[20]

A trucker might get some help from other drivers who came along the highway, but he couldn't count on someone showing up. He had to be prepared to be his own mechanic. Adele Boucher explains:

"It's almost farm mentality too. You'd be surprised, in this country, how many trucking companies have farmers as employees. Everybody who works for us in the winter season, they farm in the summer season. You get this upbringing on the farm, learning a little bit about machinery and the value of time. You do what has to be done, when the sun shines. And

Trucker changing a tire. Gordon Papp collection.

you just apply that to the job. They are the most loyal people in most trucking interests, in terms of looking after equipment. They know the value of a big piece of equipment by having owned a combine and a tractor."[21]

Some drivers became very attached to certain trucks, either their own or a truck belonging to the company they drove for. In *Denison's Ice Road*, Edith Iglauer wrote about the relationship drivers for Byers Transport formed with the trucks they drove:

"The man and his machine formed a close partnership of mutual dependency that evoked strong emotions: grief when the truck broke down; intense jealousy when another driver took the wheel; pride if the truck performed well and brought them both smoothly through a bad trip. The driver knew his truck inside and out. He must. He had to be able to diagnose correctly any erratic behavior and repair breakdowns."[22]

Abide by the right-of-way

Abiding by the right-of-way was a carry-over from days when people travelled in horse-drawn wagons on narrow trails. If two wagons met on a trail, the empty wagon would pull over into the bush to let the loaded one pass. The driver of the loaded wagon would then help pull the empty wagon back on the trail.

The original Mackenzie Highway was narrow and, usually in winter, there was only room for one truck to get by when the only snowplow between Peace River and the Northwest Territories had plowed one side of the highway. The code of the road was that the heavier vehicle had the right-of-way. Les Stranahan explains:

"It took several days for the round trip, so often the road was very deep with snow between plowings. When you met somebody, the heavier vehicles stayed on the road, and the lighter ones pulled off. The heavier unit then drove past and returned to pull the lighter one back on the road and made sure all was well before going on."[23]

Look out for other drivers' safety

During the Second World War, when the American army widened the winter road, trucks travelled in convoys for safety reasons. Later, after the Mackenzie Highway was completed, travelling in groups was not always practical or feasible.

Bernice Lorenzen explains:

"A lot of times if a load came in on the freight train to Grimshaw, it might require four or five trucks to haul it on up north. The trucks would come in, and when they got loaded up, they'd take off. But as far as guys waiting for each other, and going in convoys of four and five, I don't think they did that. Sometimes a couple of them used to "buddy up" and travel together and wait for each other. But they all kind of looked out for each other too, you know. Like, if they knew a guy was on the road and hadn't shown up, they would be sending messages back."[24]

Drivers who hauled dangerous goods, fuel haulers, and haulers of dynamite and explosives had to be especially skillful and alert. Their lives were often at risk on northern roads. Hal Tipper, a retired trucker who hauled fuel in the Peace River Country, related an incident that happened to him on Alberta Highway No. 2 in 1952. It typifies the special fraternity of truckers who watched out for each other, even if the other trucker was a stranger.

The trucker's code of the road is not dead. It still exists in the Canadian North, even though most of the Mackenzie highway and most of NWT highway No. 3 to

---

Hal Tipper's Story

One June night, tired but just a few miles from High Prairie and bed, I was navigating the last few corners east of Enilda. The road was powder dry and dust, held in suspension by the still night air, seriously reduced the range of my headlights. Coming towards me was another truck, a big one judging by its display of clearance lights. As I edged my vehicle closer to my side of the road, I kept my eyes on the ridge where gravel gave way to weeds and soft dirt...

Seconds before our meeting, the oncoming truck's headlights blinked out, eliminating glare and allowing me to raise my eyes from the ditch. I did, then madly jammed on brakes when my dimmed headlights picked up a flash of red. As my truck slowed and the oncoming one rumbled past, lights again shining brightly, I rolled toward the source of the red flash. My unknown truck-driving benefactor had spotted the hazard and guessed that I might not. A pole trailer is a basic attachment used to transport oil well casing. It consists of a long heavy pole or pipe with an axle and trailer wheels near its rear end. The pole projects behind the axle for several feet. That night some careless oilfield trucker had abandoned his pole trailer on my side of the road, and, contrary both to law and common sense, he'd set out no warning lights or flares. The trailer's hitch rested on the ground, elevating its tail end to the height of the windshield of my truck. Hanging beneath that tail was one rather muddy red reflector.

His alert dousing of lights enabled me to pick up the red reflection and come to a stop only a few feet short of the pole's deadly projection. Lacking that brief glimpse I would have driven straight into it. It would have smashed through my windshield, possibly impaling me and certainly penetrating the fuel tank behind me. Since my tank carried 1700 gallons of automotive gasoline, I have no doubt his courtesy saved my life.

Just a random act of kindness.[25]

Yellowknife are now paved. Truckers will generally stop to help, or to call on their cell phones or radio telephones to report an emergency. The following article from High Level's newspaper, *The Echo*, exemplifies truckers who go far beyond what is expected.

TRUCKER SAVES THREE LIVES

High Level RCMP attended a single vehicle accident, 8 kilometres south of Paddle Prairie on Highway #35 at 12:10 am on July 16, 1994. The vehicle hit the ditch at approximately 85 kilometres an hour [53 mph], travelled 50 feet [15m], went over an intersecting highway, travelled another couple of hundred feet before catapulting across the highway.

It then went into a creek and became totally submerged. A trucker behind the vehicle pulled an 83-year-old male from the front passenger seat and the 48-year-old female driver. He determined another person was submerged and went into the creek, found an arm and pulled a 15-year-old boy from the vehicle.

The High Level ground ambulance responded. Three of the four passengers were taken to High Level Hospital where they were treated for various injuries. The 83-year-old male was medevacked to Edmonton where he passed away on July 19, 1994.

David White is credited with saving these lives, and the driver is charged with [driving without] undue care and attention. Seat belts were worn, and there was no alcohol involved.

David White works with the trucking company Northwest Transport out of Edmonton. He lives in Sherwood Park, and company officials say that he drives through the High Level area three times a week.

A postscript to this story is that David White was awarded the Firestone National Award for heroism by truckers for 1994.[26]

I have had my own experience in needing roadside assistance. Back in the winter of 1995-96, I was working in the Peace River Country on a research project. I was driving on an icy back road southeast of Fairview, photographing the historic church at

A gathering of truckers near the Northwest Territories border. Cliff Canning collection.

Friedenstal. I pulled over onto the shoulder of the road to park my Le Baron and discovered that there wasn't any shoulder, just three feet of snow. The right side of the car sunk like a stone. It was 35 below [-37°C] and the nearest farmhouse was about a half a mile away. I got out and started walking toward it, but only got a few yards down the road when a youth of about 16 driving a four-wheel-drive pickup came by and stopped.

He asked, "You need any help, lady?"

"I sure do," I said and explained what happened.

He replied, "Give me 10 minutes or so and I'll be back with a chain to pull you out." So I went back to the car and waited. Sure enough, in 10 minutes he was back with a chain and pulled me out. He waited long enough to see that I got the car started, then he drove off. I never had the chance to find out who he was or to thank him properly. I have been grateful ever since to that young man, and glad to know that the Code of the Road is still alive and well and is being passed on to the next generation.

Fuelling up from barrels. Fred Lorenzen collection.

Notes

1 Interview with Adele Boucher, Peace River, August 18, 1997.

2 Ibid.

[3] Edith Iglauer, *Denison's Ice Road*, Madeira Park, B.C., Harbour Publishing, p. 208.

[4] Interview with Adele Boucher, Peace River, August 18, 1997.

[5] Ibid.

[6] In Bruce Hills' story, from *Tales of the Mackenzie Highway*.

[7] Interview with John King, August 19, 1997.

[8] Ted Nagle and Jordan Zinovich, *The Prospector North of Sixty*, Edmonton, Lone Pine Publishing Ltd., 1989, p. 40.

[9] Gladys McCurdy Gould, editor, *Jock McMeekan's Yellowknife Blade*, Duncan, B.C.: Lambrecht Publications, 1984, pp. 93-94.

[10] Ken Coates, *North to Alaska: Fifty Years on the World's Most Remarkable Highway*, Fairbanks: University of Alaska, 1992, p. 100.

[11] Svein Sigfusson, *Sigfusson's Roads*, Winnipeg: Watson & Dwyer Publishing Ltd., 1994, p. 137.

[12] Ibid.

[13] Interview with Jock Shannon, Didsbury, October 28, 1998.

[14] *Jock McMeekan's Yellowknife Blade*, pp. 95-96.

[15] Interview with Earle Harcourt, July 15, 1998.

[16] In *Tales of the Mackenzie Highway*, pp. 24.

[17] Ibid.

[18] Calvin Courtoreille, "A Memorable Trucking Experience," *Tales of the Mackenzie Highway*, p. 26.

[19] Interview with Bernice Lorenzen, October 13, 1999.

[20] From Les Stranaghan's recollections of driving on the Mackenzie Highway for Gordon Papp, Edmonton-Yellowknife Trucklines, March 5, 2000.

[21] Interview with Adele Boucher.

[22] Edith Iglauer, *Denison's Ice Road*, p. 16.

[23] Op. Cit., p. 25.

[24] Interview with Bernice Lorenzen, October 13, 1999.

[25] Hal Tipper's article appeared in the Edmonton *Journal*, September 10, 1996.

[26] Thanks to Katrina Wilson, High Level, for sending the article to the author.

Chapter 8 – Road to Riches

The Mackenzie Highway was built as a postwar project by the Alberta and Federal governments for better overland transportation in the North. During the 30s the Northwest Territories had become a mecca for prospectors and mining engineers. Trapping and fur trading were still a very important part of the economy in the North among Native and non-native trappers. The water transportation hub of the North was still at Fort Smith, but once the Mackenzie Highway was completed, Hay River became an important terminal for transshipment of freight from truck to barge.

When the gold mines began operation around Yellowknife in the mid-30s, they generated a building boom. Small timber and sawmill outfits, like the Sheck Brothers Mill, sprung up around Great Slave Lake to provide much-needed lumber for construction of buildings in Yellowknife.

Fishing before 1945 had been pretty much a localized industry, although some fish was transported by airplane to eastern markets. After 1945, several commercial fishing companies set up operations around the lake. The Mackenzie Highway would shift much of the transportation activity to the western end of the lake. The highway, and the trucks that hauled on the highway, made commercial fishing on a large scale a viable enterprise. As Hay River was the terminus of the highway, it became the centre for the transport of large quantities of fish south by trucks to the railhead at Grimshaw.

Commercial Fishing on Great Slave Lake

Fishing on Great Slave Lake before the 1920s was mostly a local activity done by Native groups that supplied fish to the fur trade posts and missions. The first commercial fishing on Great Slave Lake developed as early as the late 20s and early 30s. E.R. Demelt of Hay River supplied the RCMP, the HBC, and the Anglican mission with freshly-caught fish. After the Second World War, fishing became more than just a local industry. David A. Harrison wrote: "Wartime shortages of protein and oils increased the demand for fish products."[1] In 1945 the Federal Government instituted studies of the fishing resources on the lake in order to set quotas. That same year the government began to issue licenses to commercial fishing outfits, which hired many local Natives.

The first large-scale commercial fishing operation on Great Slave Lake was McInnis Products Corporation of Edmonton, in July 1945. This company, which had started commercial fishing in 1916 on Lesser Slave Lake and Lake Athabasca, shifted its operations to Gros Cap, on the northwest end of Great Slave Lake. Whitefish and lake trout were processed at Gros Cap and shipped by the company's own refrigerator barges and

Although this photo was taken in the early 1980s, the fishing techniques were those used by commercial fishermen in the late 40s. The man on the left is holding a needle bar, and centre, another man is inserting a jigger into the hole in the ice. Paul Rubak collection.

through the water transportation system to Waterways, where the fish were then transported by railway to Edmonton and to eastern markets.

In the winter the fish were transported by trucks on backhauls from Hay River. Harrison states that "The Gros Cap fishery continued its successful operation virtually without competition until the summer of 1949 because of the transport system controlled by McInnis Products and the lack of overland transport via Hay River during the summer months."[2]

Although no records of the number of fish were kept the first two years, by the summer of 1947 the company had air-freighted 250 000 pounds [113 400 kg] of whitefish and lake trout. By 1949, there were seven companies operating on Great Slave Lake. In the summer of 1949, there were 63 boats in operation and a total of 611 fishing licenses issued.[3]

In August 1948, the W.R. Menzies Fishing Company, based in Faust, Alberta (Lesser Slave Lake), began fishing on Great Slave Lake once the Mackenzie Highway was nearly completed. "Within a period of three weeks, this company caught approximately 87 000 kg [193 000 lbs.] of white fish and lake trout in close proximity to Hay River."

Whereas it took the refrigerated barges of McInnes Products about 120 hours to transport the fish to Waterways, it took only about 20 hours [depending upon road conditions] to transport the fish by truck to the railhead at Grimshaw. This allowed reasonably fresh fish to get to markets much cheaper and faster. In the winter, when the highway's surface was harder, the travel time was about 15 hours.

By 1949, the seven commercial fishing companies on the lake employed about 300 fishermen, and the headquarters for the transshipping of fish was based in Hay River. By 1950 there were 10 commercial fishing companies on the lake. Al Hamilton, Grimshaw Trucking and Distributing, got his start hauling general freight north, and fish south on backhauls. Terry's Trucking also got its start hauling fish. In the early 50s, John Richard of Grimshaw hauled fish when he drove trucks for Bert Bulmer, and later for Herman Carter of Hay River. He hauled the fish from the packing plants in Hay River to the railroad stations at Grimshaw and Peace River. At this time, however, the production of fish on the Great Slave began to decline slowly and the number of fish operations decreased to five.

Hay River, NWT – Transportation Hub of the North

During this time, Northern Transportation Company (NTCL), a crown corporation, Yellowknife Transportation Company (YTCL), and McInnis Products all had barge service between Yellowknife and Hay River.

One of the largest boats on the lake was owned by YTCL. Always an innovator in transportation, manager Earle Harcourt bought a Second World War U.S. landing craft. He had it refurbished for domestic use in Vancouver, transported it north around Alaska to the mouth of the Mackenzie River and upstream to Yellowknife.[4] Harrison wrote: "A converted landing craft, the *Yellowknife Expeditor*, could handle approximately 250 tons of cargo, 40 tons of refrigerated products and 50 passengers."[5] The *Expeditor* operated twice weekly between Yellowknife and Hay River.

Although much of the freight continued to be hauled by boats and barges, freighting by truck over the Mackenzie Highway continued to increase in the early 50s.

About the time that commercial fishing was cooling down, the Cold War was heating up. By the mid-50s a new type of cargo began to be shipped by truck from Grimshaw to Hay River and the Far North. The DEW line (Distance Early Warning) was being constructed in several locations in the Arctic, along the northern coasts of Alaska and Canada. Truckers were soon freighting construction materials and equipment on the Mackenzie Highway for transshipment to the Arctic.

The Cold War and the DEW Line

Fears of an invasion of North America by the USSR following the Second World War brought about defensive measures by both Canada and the United States. By the late 40s it was believed by many that if Russia did launch an invasion, it would be over the North Pole and down the Mackenzie Valley. With our 20-20 hindsight following the collapse of the Soviet Union in 1989, some may dismiss the whole buildup of armaments during this period as an unnecessary waste of money and resources. But the fear of Soviet invasion of North America was widely held. In Leslie Roberts' book, *The Mackenzie*, he articulates the fears of the time.

> *"If and when the North American continent should be attacked by a Pacific power again, that attack will be launched through the Mackenzie Valley, or the country that surrounds it if it should come through the air in the form of guided missiles...It has not been easy to set such things down on paper in the spring of 1948, when the North American world was in a state bordering on frenzy in respect to its relations with the people living on the other side of the polar highways. What is said here is not written to fit these special circumstances, however, but to make the point: First, that if at any time in the future the North American nations should go to war...the Far North is this continent's soft underbelly.*[6]

> *"...any attack launched into the underbelly, though it was to go either through or over Canada, would have as its objective the great industrial output of the United States...Hence the first line of defense of the Republic against attack upon itself is on the soil of another, but friendly, power."*[7]

The construction of the DEW Line was a direct result of this defensive war between the USSR and North America. As a first line of defense, a series of radar stations were installed along northern Alaska and across northern continental Canada. Many tons of supplies to construct the DEW Line were hauled by truck over the Mackenzie Highway to Hay River, transshipped by NCTL barges and air freighted to the Far North.

In the mid-50s, Grimshaw Trucking & Distributing had a contract to haul truckloads of cargo from Edmonton to Hay River. Most of the cargo was sealed in boxes and crates, and the drivers didn't have a clue what they were hauling. The freight could have been anything from food stuffs to highly sophisticated radar equipment or explosives.

Pitchblende, with its uranium and radium concentrates, continued to be an important backhaul for truckers during the Cold War period, as the United States stepped up its testing of atomic bombs. Also more money and research was being done on domestic use of atomic energy. Port Radium on Great Bear Lake was shipping these concentrates. The pitchblende was packaged in 120 lb. [54 kg] bags and shipped in the back of trucks. Gold and silver concentrates from the mines around Yellowknife continued to be an important backhaul.

Agriculture

Trucks became the main mode of transportation, not only for hauling crops and livestock to the railheads at Grimshaw and Peace River, but farm machinery and goods ordered and shipped by truck from Edmonton and other large centres. The 1950 railroad strike had resulted in a new era in trucking. Trucks were becoming primary movers of freight, not just between the railhead and the customer, but across Canada. It would be safe to say that without truck transportation, agriculture would have remained a fairly small, localized industry in northern Alberta.

Northern Alberta has had a long history of agriculture. Early fur traders and missionaries had planted small gardens to supply the posts and missions along the Peace River with potatoes, onions, turnips, and other foods. Reverend J.G. Brick had success with growing wheat and barley at Shaftesbury in 1885. In 1886, the Lawrence brothers farmed at Fort Vermilion, growing a Ladoga variety of wheat. Sheridan Lawrence probably did more to promote the agricultural richness of the lower Peace region than anyone. By 1897 large quantities of wheat were being ground into flour and supplied to HBC posts and further north.

The Fort Vermilion Experimental Farm, established in 1908, had a large impact upon local agriculture, with its experiments in new varieties of crops suitable for northern latitudes. The long summer days compensated for the short growing season, which was about 90 days.

Prior to the construction of a gravel road between High Level and Fort Vermilion in the early 50s, it was uneconomical for farmers in the area to ship their grain. It was fed to hogs and cattle that were shipped upriver by boat to Peace River town and loaded onto railway box cars for shipment to the slaughter houses in Edmonton.

The area around Keg River Post was surveyed in 1916 and following the First World War, new lands were opened for homesteading. Frank Jackson arrived in the early 20s, and saw the potential of the Keg River area for agriculture.[8] He combined mixed farming with fur trading. The real influx of settlers that came to homestead in this district occurred in the late 20s and early 30s. Agricultural land further south was already heavily settled and too expensive for many farmers to buy.

Rocky Lane, about 50 km [31 mi.] east of High Level, was settled in the 1930s by many experienced Ukrainian-Canadian farmers who had moved north after "drying out" on the prairies. Between 1931 and 1934, Mennonite families from Manitoba began settling, first in the area around Carcajou. After the disastrous flood in the spring of 1934, several who had settled on the flats moved to higher lands around Buffalo Head Prairie. By the end of the 30s, Mennonite families from Chihuahua, Mexico, immigrated to Canada and settled in the area.

In 1938, the Alberta government passed the Metis Betterment Act, and set aside land around Paddle Prairie for a colony that would provide a permanent land base for Metis. In 1939 several Metis families moved onto the settlement. Many of them grew hay for their horses and cattle and in the winter did trapping. The area was rich in fur-bearing animals: fisher, marten, wolverine, weasel, mink, wolves, bear, beaver, lynx, fox, otter, muskrat, and squirrel.

After the completion of the Mackenzie Highway in 1948 and the construction of an all-weather gravel road between High Level and Fort Vermilion in 1952, more land for homesteading became available. Wheat, barley, flax, legumes, and rapeseed (Canola) thrived in this northern latitude. Because of the better access to the railhead at Grimshaw, it was now possible for farmers to haul their grain by truck, instead of having to feed most of it to livestock and shipping the livestock by boat up the Peace River.

After the Great Slave Railway was completed in the mid-60s, farmers in the La Crete area could haul their grain to the new elevators at Manning. Keg River had a United Grain Growers elevator by 1964. At High Level, the first elevator opened November 3, 1964.[9] By 1970 the town had three elevators. The farm land between High Level and Fort Vermilion comprises the most northerly agricultural district in the world.

A Dying Highway

By the mid-50s, the Mackenzie Highway had deteriorated to a muddy mess from the pounding of more and more trucks. It had been poorly built in the first place, but following the spring of 1957, the road was in terrible shape. Trucks and cars were mired axle-deep in the mud. Complaints from local people seemed to do little more than elicit Band-Aid measures from the Alberta government, which would send out a grader to patch up the road.

This photo shows the kind of road conditions truckers had to deal with on the Mackenzie Highway by the mid-fifties. Upper Hay River Coffee Shop, owned by the Lizotte family, 1954. The truck belonged to Hank Karst, who was hauling to Hay River. Ed Leguerrier collection.

Valle Gray at the Blue Top Lodge in High Level got sick and tired of the terrible condition of the road. On a trip to Edmonton with one of her daughters, she took a camera and a roll of film and documented several places where trucks were bogged down in the mud. It took a lot of courage for her to take the roll of film to the Edmonton *Journal*.

"I went to the Edmonton Journal with a roll of film I'd taken. And I was scared. They asked me questions…they phoned these different companies and told me to come back tomorrow. So I went back the next morning and they gave me a couple of papers. Two of my pictures [were published] out of that roll." [10]

The newspaper used her photos to illustrate their story titled "Taylor Says Crews Ordered to Restore Mackenzie Road" in July of 1957. The article embarrassed the Department of Highways, but no permanent solutions to the problem came about until financial assistance from the federal government to the province made it possible for a complete reconstruction of the Mackenzie Highway.

Roads to Resources Program

John Diefenbaker became Prime Minister when the Conservatives swept the Liberals out of power in 1958. Diefenbaker came through with one of his campaign promises to revive natural resources development, which included improving the transportation infrastructure of the provincial norths and the Northwest Territories.

This photograph gives new meaning to the term "piggybacking." Henry Dillman of Manning was contracted by CN to haul the 46-ton locomotive from Meander River to Pine Point Junction in January 1964. Travelling an average of 15 mph [24 kph], the 143-mile [230 km] transport of the locomotive took 11 hours. The locomotive was used in constructing a branch line of the Great Slave Lake Railroad to the mines at Pine Point. Henry Dillman collection.

Diefenbaker launched the federal government's "Roads to Resources" Program. The program featured widespread surveys of natural resources and financial assistance in the form of equal sharing between the provinces and the federal government to develop better roads in the North. The program lasted from 1959 to 1970 and aided in the construction of 4000 miles [6400 km] of new roads, mostly in the provincial norths.[11] The Roads to Resources Program aided in the reconstruction of the Mackenzie Highway and other improved gravel all-weather roads in the Northwest Territories, including the Great Slave Lake Highway (NWT No. 3) that extended around the west side of the lake to Yellowknife, and a highway to Fort Smith (NWT No. 5) and the beginning of the construction of Dempster Highway between Dawson City, Yukon, and Inuvik on the Mackenzie Delta; the all-weather gravel highway was completed in 1979. The federal government assisted, separately, the Canadian National Railway in constructing the Great Slave Railway from Roma Junction, near Peace River, north to reach the lead-zinc mines at Pine Point, NWT, by 1965. Improved transportation opened other areas of the North and Far North to new explorations of mineral and petroleum resources.

Reconstruction of the Mackenzie Highway

In 1951 the Alberta legislature had passed the Transportation and Highways Act, and Gordon Taylor became the first Minister of the new Department of Highways. He was to remain Minister of Highways throughout the period that the Mackenzie Highway was reconstructed. More stringent requirements were put in place under his administration. In a speech given at the Alberta/Northwest Territories boundary during the 50th anniversary celebrations of the highway, Gordon Taylor talked about the early years when he was Minister of Highways.

"I found things very awkward. Before that, the highways department was part of the Department of Public Works. Public Works were wonderful at building buildings, but they fell far short when it came to building highways."[12]

During Gordon Taylor's tenure as Minister of Highways, from 1951 to 1970, he oversaw the construction and reconstruction of many highways in Alberta. The Mackenzie Highway was one of several highways in Alberta that were built or improved. Taylor ensured that road construction companies built these roads according to the new specifications.

"I wasn't the minister for more than two days when the MLA from Peace River phoned me and said, 'Mannix is here building the road the old way.' ...I was astounded. I immediately phoned Mannix, told them to stop the work immediately and to also meet me in Peace River next morning....I met the Mannix people in the restaurant in Peace River and told them why I was cancelling the program. The manager of the group got up and said, 'Thank you for cancelling the program. There will be no penalty, because we hate building roads that won't stand up.' "

After Gordon Taylor had the work go to tender, Mannix was again the low bidder and reconstructed the highway according to modern specifications. Gordon Taylor articulated the Department of Highways' policy. "We built from the bottom up. Not from the top down. Consequently we were building on a solid foundation."

The reconstruction of the Mackenzie Highway from 1958 to 1961 was based on this policy. The road was scraped, widened, straightened. Many of the problem hills, like 280 Hill, were bypassed or graded.

Constructing the open-topped Meikle River bridge, July 1960. George Predy collection.

Surveyors like Chuck Shaul helped to survey the reconstructed highway, and Ed Zack, who worked on the original survey, was now District Manager for the Department of Highways, out of Peace River. Bill Mueller and Bill Beattie also worked on the original and reconstructed highway.

The highway crews had slightly better accommodations in camps and more modern equipment. However, communication was still a problem. Chuck Shaul remembers:

"We had no communication. No telephones in this country in those days. We had no radio system either. We used to use the Forestry tower to send messages back and forth. The nearest telephone was down in Manning."[13]

It had far more gravel spread on its surface, a good 20 inches [50 cm] compared to the 6 or 8 inches [15-20 cm] of the original highway. Gravel was a key element in building a better road. At first, however, there was a problem finding enough gravel. Ben Casson and Jim Supernault came to the rescue.

"We...Found...GRAVEL!"

by Esther Supernault[14]

In the 1950s, Northern Alberta still had terrible roads. They were composed of what local residents called, "that damn Peace River Gumbo." A mixture of sediment silt, white alkali, and clay, this soil was the stuff of nightmares. Like a bad dream, where people want to run away in horror, this gumbo bogged feet down to a miserable, slow motion crawl. Rain or spring thaw turned the dirt to gooey globs that clamped to shoes, building four or five inches of new soles with every step. Walking became a step...kick off the mud...thud motion, combined with a prayer that a boot wouldn't fly off too. Sometimes the prayer worked. Thick, heavy muck wrapped vehicle tires in long rolling slabs. Eventually fenders became totally clogged, grinding laboring vehicles to a standstill. Hapless drivers then had the wonderful task of unplugging wheel wells using sticks, tire irons and curses. If it continued to rain, the gumbo switched to a slimy, greasy, slippery mess. With no traction at all, cars and trucks and buses zigzagged down the roads in dizzying switchbacks, often ending up crosswise, blocking everything from moving in any direction. Heavy transport trucks sank to their axles in the middle of the road! Tow trucks, when and if they came, often shared the same fate as those they set out to help.

In 1957, Prime Minister Diefenbaker wanted good roads developed through to Yellowknife, to access mines in the Northwest Territories. In order to build these roads, the Department of Highways needed gravel, lots of it, nearby and accessible. Immediately!

Ben Casson, a wiry young university student, had worked for the Department for five years in the Gravel Research division. He was told, "Go up north and find gravel. Your contact is a man with a horse in Paddle Prairie. His name is Jim Supernault." Armed with aerial maps of the area marked with possible sites, Ben bought a new brown Ford at Healy Motors in Edmonton and set out. He soon discovered that the major highway to High Level was nothing but a dusty dirt road. On dry days, the fine silt trailed dust clouds for half a mile behind travelling vehicles. On quiet evenings, dust hung in the air, thick as fog, for hours. From Grimshaw to Manning, Ben found the road passable. From there northward, when it rained, everyone got stuck.

Paddle Prairie was a small Metis settlement just 80 miles [129 km] north of Manning. Ben found out where Jim lived and was welcomed into his house. After confirming that he indeed had a horse and that he'd help Ben, they talked salary. Jim agreed to the going wage of the day for himself and his horse: $1.25 per hour, for 10 hours a day. He was a tall, rawboned man, about 33 years old at the time, part Cree and part French. People remember Jim as an easy going, cheerful person who usually had a story to tell. He made a point of having time for anyone who needed help.

Jim kept his dark bay horse, Lady, in their camp, but clouds of vicious horseflies drove her crazy. They bit her so hard in the folds of her skin, she bled. The men bought

"Off" by the case and constantly sprayed her, but it didn't help. Every night Lady would break her rope and run home to her barn in Paddle Prairie. And every morning, Jim would get into the power wagon and bring her back. In desperation, Jim mixed up a thick paste of creoline, a nauseous-smelling disinfectant, and used oil. He took a rag and plastered Lady head to hooves with the smelly goop. It worked! And a somewhat sticky Lady stayed in camp.

The two acquired an ugly orange power wagon with a 300 foot [91m] cable on the front to winch themselves out of the wet spots. And they found lots of them! The Department sent them a catskinner, Jim Willens from nearby Keg River, on a Dillman D-7 Caterpillar and backhoe, once Jim started finding gravel on horseback. The small cat was far more maneuverable in the dense undergrowth than the bigger D-8s or D-9s. The three men spent the late summer and early fall living in the bush. Ben had a small camper but Jim and the driver preferred Jim's big white-wall tent with its high ridge-pole and four foot walls.

Ben didn't have to know Jim long to realize what a special person he was. Ben remembers him as "just a pleasant person to be with, always upbeat. No matter how tough things got, Jim would handle it with a grin." The man had a built-in compass. Regardless of the density of the bush or how deep they travelled into it, Jim always knew where they were and how to get back. He'd walk along snapping small twigs right and left to mark their path. The only time Jim became upset with himself was the day they sank the D-7 cat into a muskeg. They had to walk out to get help. When they returned with a big D-8 it was already getting dark and Jim could not find the sunken cat. Finally the crew was forced to make an unexpected overnight camp, with no gear, no tent, and no food. They made a fire to keep from shivering in their T-shirts and light jackets. Jim strode into the bush with his slingshot and soon returned with two fat prairie chickens. Ben claimed, "Jim was not one to waste stones." That night four hungry men sat around the fire and feasted on juicy roast chicken. Afterwards they spent a long night curled up close to the blazing fire. They would roll over, cook on one side, freeze on the other, then roll over again. Next morning Jim found the sunken cat, no more than a stone's throw away from their campfire.

Ben recalls Jim coming into camp one night, grinning ear to ear, thinking he had found the Mother Lode. But it was just a small gravel area, nowhere near the massive amounts needed for the Mackenzie Highway. Jim, Ben, and the catskinner searched the banks of the Peace River, digging further and further south and west of the Paddle Prairie Settlement, towards Manning. They used a big cat to punch out bush trails as they went. Roads were needed anyway, once they found the gravel.

Ben wound up with an abscessed tooth and had to travel to the town of Peace River for aid. Three days later he came back and found his trailer crawling with mice. The entire country was full of mice that year. When Ben and Jim dug trenches looking for gravel, the mice fell in by the hundreds. There were so many, they were cannibalistic. But the next morning, only the bigger mice, now huge and bloated from gorging themselves, remained in the trenches. Jim hung a couple of grouse on a tree near his tent, thinking they would be safe from the mice. In the morning, to his disgust, all that remained were four fleshless leg bones! He kept no food in his tent so the mice stayed away. Ben's trailer, on the other hand, was a horror scene. Mice moved in furry hordes from his bedding, through his clothes, and into his cupboards. Everything edible was gone, including all the paper wrappers off his canned food. Bits of half eaten mice and blood covered window screens, counters and floors. Ben used a scoop shovel to push masses of them towards the door. Jim hooked them with another shovel and threw them out. But as fast as they shovelled, the crazed mice ran and jumped and squeaked their way back in. Finally the men found the hole in the floor where the mice were squeezing in between sewer pipes and the underfloor.

North of High Level they found another pit close to the Steen River. Unfortunately, it was all big, rough boulders that needed a gigantic Bull Crusher to break them down to a size the ordinary gravel crushers could handle. A huge D-9 cat with gigantic teeth ripped up the stones so the loaders could haul it to the crusher. One of these teeth accidentally came off and went through the crusher. The instant shutdown lasted for over a week while the contractor, Standard Gravel, frantically hauled parts and mechanics in from Calgary to fix it. Standard was responsible for hauling, stock piling, and crushing the gravel.

In the meantime, Jim and Ben continued to hunt for bigger and better gravel pits. They turned back south towards High Level, fanning further and further away from the Peace River. One night Jim walked into camp and quietly announced, "Ben, we...found...GRAVEL!" A scant 13 miles [20 km] off the highway, just south of High Level, they found "The Mother Patch!" Twelve to 15 feet deep [4-5m] and an area of 20 acres [8 ha]! Beautiful, small-stoned, clean gravel! 'Clean' meant it contained none of the red iron of the more southern pits. The rusty stuff turned gravel red, coated everything with dust, and clogged motors in heavy equipment. With very little overburden of boulders, dirt or trees, the pit was easily accessible. The only drawback: a gigantic muskeg between the pit and the highway. Department of Highways couldn't afford a long road around the massive swamp. Gravel trucks were paid by the mile. So Jim helped build a winter road straight over the thick bog of peat moss, ice, and large clumps of slough grass. All that winter, 250 trucks hauled day and night.

Ben recalls, "Those truckers spent a lot of money on repairs because the road was so lumpy and rough. Yet they kept the pace until spring thaw. Then the whole area started to move with the trucks. Wheels sank to the axles and beyond." By then, they had enough gravel, enough to cover the newly-widened roadbed of the present Mackenzie Highway, a solid, accessible link with the north's industry.

Road Construction (Jock Shannon's story)

The contracts went out for the construction work in the fall of 1959. Jock Shannon, of Shannon Construction (Alberta) Ltd. of Didsbury, and his partner Reg Francis went up to look over the job. Although Jock had been in the North during the Canol Project working for Imperial Oil, he had never been over the Mackenzie Highway.[15]

> *"We met this engineer and his crew coming out of the bush like a wild man. 'What are you fellows doing up here?' I said, 'We're looking at this job.' 'Oh,' he said. It was Roy McFinnick, the resident engineer. He was stationed at Keg River. So we looked over the job, came back to Edmonton and we bid the job. Fortunately – or unfortunately – we got it."*

They brought in the brush-cutting outfit, cleared the right-of-way, and piled the brush before freeze-up.

> *"There was a lot of heavy timber. They took a 150-foot [46m] right-of-way all the way through and we had to clear it all. They also established areas to excavate. They called them 'borrow pits' and [they] were to be fashioned as water reservoirs because of the fact that there is a shortage of water up there. When they had the runoff in the spring, if they could catch it they pooled the water in case of fire. That's what they planned all the way along, which was a good idea. They tried to obscure the borrow pits, keep trees between them and the right-of-way so you wouldn't see them going along the road."*

In the spring of 1960 Shannon Construction moved up, along with Stettler Construction, owned by Gerald Stettler and brothers.

> *"It was sort of a joint contract; we took them in and they did the portions of the north of Keg River Cabins. And we did the portions from Kemp Creek...They wanted us to start from Kemp Creek....We got the job pretty well finished up but there was 11 miles [18 km] in the north and three miles [5 km] in the south of us that weren't completed. We had a subcontractor come in the fall. He was an engineer from New Zealand. Well, it didn't work out too satisfactorily. We had to go back the following year and clean up what we'd done and do the 11 miles to the north. Then in the spring of 1961 I wasn't satisfied with the 11 miles. It was spongy. Of course the engineers said, 'Oh, just scarify that.' I said it would never work. So we took the whole centre of the road out and re-compacted it and put it back in."*

The crew stayed at Keg River Cabins, owned and operated at the time by the Tardiffs. "Mrs. Tardiff was a very fine woman. She was from Fort Vermilion." She interceded for a local Native, who was there at the Cabins, looking for work. She asked Jock if Shannon Construction hired local people. Jock asked, "Who do you have in mind?" "This young Indian fellow," she replied. Jock thought the short, good-looking Native was about 14 or 15 years old. "He's too young," Jock said. But then she told him that the young man was 22 years old. "Of course we hired him," said Jock. "And he was one of the best men we ever had. He worked with us right up to the end of the job. He was a Beaver Indian from around Fort Vermilion. George Alook was his name."

Other people worked for him, including a character named Charlie Freeman, who worked as a blacksmith. "He grew up in Drumheller. His father was a blacksmith and worked in the mine. So Charlie followed in his father's footsteps. He worked in the mines as a blacksmith as well and when welding became an everyday thing, he became a welder." Charlie could fix just about anything. When Poole Construction needed a blacksmith to fix one of their big Euclids, they borrowed Charlie to do the job.

Jock didn't have as much luck with some of the crew he brought from the south. "The ones we took from here [Didsbury-Calgary area] boy, they just disappeared [off the work site]. That was a big problem." Mosquitoes were part of the problem, and the crews from the south were not used to them or the 'no-see-ums'. "The worst was the 'bulldogs', or horseflies, that weren't satisfied with just taking a little blood, but wanted a piece out of you."

The following spring of 1961, Shannon Construction worked on a piece of the highway north of Paddle Prairie. They had a problem with one of the locals who brought in a crew to clear the brush and clean up. They made the mistake of paying him the crew's wages, thinking that he in turn would pay the members of his crew. That didn't happen, however. When the overseer of Paddle Prairie came into camp one day, he asked, "When are you going to pay these men?" Jock's partner, Reg Francis, showed the overseer that the time had been kept progressively for each member of the crew and the payments had been made to the crew's foreman. But the guy had been absconding with the money of his own crew members. "We got out of that one," said Jock. "We had done our part."

In 1961, living conditions for the construction crews were better than those of the original crews that worked on the first Mackenzie Highway in 1947 and 1948. Shannon Construction had its own camp of trailers and a cookhouse, and set up the camp when they worked on the Paddle Prairie stretch of road. There were still no telephones in the north, and the radio reception was not always reliable.

> "We had our own power plant generating electricity, and we had our own communication – short-wave radio. We set up our tower when we were at Keg River. We happened to be sitting in a very good communication area at Keg River, where our tower was. It was just pure luck, because another 10 miles [16 km] away you couldn't communicate at all. They used to come down from other places to use our communications."

On the original road, machinery parts had to be brought in by aircraft or water transportation, and the delays during a breakdown could be days or weeks. By the 1960s, during the reconstruction period, there was daily bus service, provided by Canadian Coachways. Grimshaw Trucking also brought in parts too large to handle on the buses. "They were good, reliable as could be. We had some of the best service for spare parts we ever had, at this site. We'd phone in before midnight the night before to the suppliers in Edmonton, and we could have the parts up there the afternoon the following day. They'd load those in the back of the bus and bring up the parts. It was the best service we ever had...The north people are that way. If you didn't get the parts, nothing happened."

"The gravel was hauled from the Peace River and stockpiled. They had a tremendous pile of gravel there. The trucks hauled all winter, because they couldn't haul in the summer. Trying to get up from the river, the roads were too soft. So they stockpiled the gravel and crushed it right there, and they rejected the boulders out of it. That was ideal for us, as we stockpiled the boulders for riprap rock."

Jock talked about the condition of the old road at the time. "It was just a bare trail. They were getting through with trucks, but barely at times. We'd have them come onto our work, and they had trouble."

When the reconstruction work on the Mackenzie Highway was completed at the end of the 1961 season, a high standard all-weather road was the result. The discovery of oil in the Rainbow Lake area came a few years later. The reconstructed highway became a conduit for oil and gas exploration, and trucks pounded up and down the highway, hauling derricks, oilfield equipment, and camps. The upgraded road paved the way for the increased development of the forest industry in the North Peace.

Petroleum Exploration and Development

The early exploration for oil and gas in the Peace River Country revealed rich reserves of petroleum resources. The potential of the oil sands in the Peace-Athabasca district had long been recognized. Although the development of the oil sands is centred around Fort McMurray, the oil sands and heavy oil reserves extend well into the lower Peace region.

Early Discovery Wells

Some early oil and gas wells were drilled near the town of Peace River and within 30 miles [48 km] up and down the river by the Tar Island Oil Company and the Peace River Oil Company in 1914 and 1915 respectively. The wells went down about 500 to 1500 feet [150-457m]. They discovered oil, but when they drilled deeper they struck a heavy flow of water. Near Fort Norman, in the Northwest Territories, oil was discovered in 1920.

In the Peace River Bloc of British Columbia, the first discovery well was drilled in 1940 at Commotion Creek. The petroleum industry in the Peace River Bloc did not really take off until after the Second World War. The first oil well of promise was drilled in 1951 by Pacific Petroleum near Fort St. John, the first successful producer in British Columbia. Five years later, Pacific Petroleum built a refinery at Taylor Flats, and in 1957, the Westcoast Transmission pipeline from Taylor to the U.S. border was completed.

In the late 1940s, Amerada Petroleum did seismic testing and "slim-holed" shallow wells between DeBolt and Valleyview. The first discovery well in the South Peace was drilled at Sturgeon Lake in 1953 by Amerada. The North Sturgeon and South Sturgeon fields soon proved to be good producers. The oil was shipped first by truck to the railhead at High Prairie and was loaded into tanker cars to be railed to the Edmonton refineries. After the cut-off road between Whitecourt and Valleyview was completed in 1954, the oil was shipped to Edmonton by truck until the first pipeline was built by Peace River Oil Pipeline Ltd. In December 1954, construction began on a 5-million-dollar pipeline from the Sturgeon field to the pumping station at Iosegun Lake in the Swan Hills.[16]

Oil Exploration in the North Peace

Oil exploration continued north in the 1950s. South of Manning, seismic work was started in 1950. At that time natural gas had few markets, and finding conventional oil was the main object. When the first drilling rigs began drilling in the Manning area, many of the wells were gas wells. There were no pipelines to transport the gas, so the wells were capped or abandoned.[17]

Oil rig, late 1940s. Ed Dillman collection.

In 1965 the Rainbow Lake field was a centre of exploratory activity. The Peace River *Record Gazette* announced:

"The Banff-Aquitane Socony group has chalked up quite a score to date this year. Six oil wells in four separate pools, four dry wells and six wells are presently drilling. All this in a 15-mile [24 km] radius. The newest well was brought in half a mile north of the discovery well in Keg River reef for Imperial Oil."[18]

Exploratory wells were drilled between the Manning and the Chinchaga River. It wasn't until the discoveries of oil and gas in the Rainbow Lake area in the 1960s that a 20-inch [50 cm] pipeline was put in west of Manning in 1967 and another pipeline designed and built by Rainbow Pipe Line Company Ltd. from Rainbow Lake to Nipisi oilfield near Slave Lake. The pipelines provided a means of transporting northern Alberta gas and making the gas a marketable commodity.

At first the access to the oil and gas fields around Rainbow Lake and Zama was in the winter, because much of the terrain was low muskeg country. A forestry road ran between Manning and Chinchaga, and there was a winter road between Keg River and Rainbow Lake. Many local farmers found winter employment with the exploration and drilling companies.

Other residents developed transportation or construction businesses servicing the oil rigs or constructing roads or hauling camps to the oilfields. Dirk Vos Transport of Keg River operated a warehouse and hauled drilling supplies to the rigs.[19] Hank Thompson, John King, Gordon Papp, and Fred Lorenzen all expanded their transportation businesses during the 1960s and 1970s oil boom in northern Alberta. Hank Thompson and John King combined road construction and oilfield hauling services in the Rainbow Lake area. Later John King of King's Construction would spend many years hauling freight and construction materials into the Far North and constructing roads and oilfield leases. Gordon Papp, owner of Papp's Truck Service Ltd. based in Peace River, became a specialized hauler of large drilling rigs in the north, after signing a two-year contract with Shell Oil for moving an 800-ton drilling rig in 1970. Starting in 1950, Kaps Transport, based in Edmonton and managed by Reinhold Kapchinsky, became specialists in off-road hauling in northern Alberta, British Columbia, and the Northwest Territories, using "Foremosts," large tracked carriers, in the late 60s. The Lorenzen family of Manning, Lorenzen's Gravel and Water, became specialists in hauling water to oilfield camps.

Advertisement for a Foremost off-road tracked vehicle. Alberta Business Journal, *1970s. These tracked vehicles were built by Foremost Industries Ltd. of Calgary.*

Forest Industry

Most of northern Alberta is boreal forest. White and black spruce, jack pine, balsam poplar, aspen, and birch are the primary types of trees found in the northern forests, and all were put to use. The use of logs for construction was a local industry for hundreds of years. Natives used logs to build teepee-like structures and lean-tos and used birch bark and spruce roots to build their canoes. The first permanent buildings the North-West Company and Hudson's Bay Company fur traders built in the late 1700s and early 1800s were of squared off logs, hewn by hand-axe. York boats and later paddle wheel boats that plied the northern rivers were built of local timber using two-handled pit saws. The Anglican and Roman Catholic missions in the North all had an arsenal of hand tools, and some had small steam-powered sawmills.

To homesteaders, the vast boreal forest was a barrier to clearing enough farmland for proving up their land. Most of the timber was cut down and burned as slash. Not until small towns were built in the North was there enough of a market for sawmills, and every hamlet between Grimshaw and Hay River, at one time or another, had a small sawmill. In the late 30s, the mines of Yellowknife required timbering, and the construction of the town itself created a market for small sawmills to blossom on the south end of Great Slave Lake. The sawn lumber was shipped across the lake by barge. Sheck Brothers had a sawmill near Fort Resolution, and used their own tugboat and barges to haul forest products to Yellowknife.

The construction of the Mackenzie Highway provided a short-term need for timber for use in building culverts and bridges. The Blakleys hauled logs to the government sawmill that was situated on their property at Mile 230 and hauled the sawn timber to locations along the highway. Ambrose Parenteau of Paddle Prairie hauled lumber from Williamson's mill, between Manning and Keg River, with the first truck he bought in 1945, a used KS5 International. When the new town of Manning began to be built following the Second World War, Terry Baxter started hauling lumber from Battle River Lumber Company to Manning.

The Mackenzie Highway had less of an impact upon the forest industry than CNR's Great Slave Railway, completed in the 60s. With the arrival of the railway to High Level in 1963, the town became an important centre for the forest industry. High Level Lumber Sawmill and Planer Company had their operations going in 1963. Leo Arsenault incorporated North Peace Logging and Sawmill in 1964. The Manford Nelson planer mill was built in 1965, and the Boucher family had a sawmill at Footner Lake in 1967. A new division of the Alberta Forest Service had a building constructed at Footner Lake, north of High Level. While most of the forest products destined for distant markets were shipped by rail, the logs had to be shipped to the mills by trucks, and the Mackenzie Highway became a conduit for the log trucks to the mills.

In the 1980s many small family-owned sawmills disappeared in the North when the Alberta government began to favor the construction of larger sawmills and pulp mills.

Mag Boucher loading logs at Black Gold Truck Rodeo, Grimshaw, August 1999. Mag founded a trucking business doing salvage logging. Fred Lorenzen collection.

More and more timber was set aside for the use of larger timber corporations, such as CANFOR (which bought out Swanson Lumber Company) and Daishawa-Marubeni International Ltd., the pulp mill at Peace River. Many of the logging trucks hauling on the Mackenzie Highway today are destined for these larger mills.

Mag Boucher of Peace River developed a successful trucking business, Mag Boucher Trucking, logging and hauling salvage timber from oilfield activity and other rights of way.

Road to Riches Today

The Road to Riches continues to reflect the "boom and bust" cycle that has always been part of the North. Now the "riches" are diamonds. In 1998, truck traffic on the highway was very sparse. But during the winter of 1999 and 2000, a steady stream of

George Predy's Story, Hotchkiss, Alberta

In the spring of 1946, my brother Neil and I came to the Battle River district in search of farmland. We settled in Hotchkiss along the old highway. While looking for land we met Everett Clark and Charlie Daigle, who directed us to the construction site of the first bridge across the Meikle River. The grade approaching the bridge cut through my homestead. For years truckers stopped at the farm for coffee and a rest. Some became good friends, especially Sam Houston, a fish hauler.

During the winter of 1947 I worked with Jack Landry, under Fred Guest's supervision, hauling bridge timbers from stock piles situated at Meikle River and Paddle Prairie to specific sites along the waterways from Meikle to Steen River.

My Dad and I owned a sawmill from 1948 to 1952. We were contracted to saw and deliver timbers for culverts along the highway between Peace River and Keg River. I also spent several years trucking grain to Grimshaw and livestock and lumber to Edmonton.

By 1960 traffic became heavier and loads were bigger, so it was decided to reconstruct the Meikle River bridge to accommodate high loads. An open bridge was built by Pool Construction in 1960. In July, under the supervision of Stan Radzik, I worked using my W6 IHC tractor and front end loader, to supply the cement mixer with sand and gravel. In August the job was completed.

Now, 50 years later, the highway bypasses our farm. However, our memories of the old road and of those who travelled it remain with us.

trucks began to haul north, pulling goods and materials for the construction of diamond mines north of Yellowknife. Each boom and bust has changed the pattern of development, settlement, and transportation in the North. It has also changed the Mackenzie Highway. The Alberta government has begun construction to twin the highway, making it four lanes instead of two.

Sir Alexander MacKenzie, who called the Mackenzie River the "River of Disappointment," would be amazed at the changes in the North at first, but would soon feel very much at home. After all, he was at heart an entrepreneur and adventurer, and there are still plenty of entrepreneurs and adventurers in the North today.

Notes

[1] The major source of the information about commercial fishing in this chapter is from David A. Harrison's Ph.D. thesis, *Hay River, NWT. 1800-1950: A Geographical Study of Site and Situation*, Department of Geography, University of Alberta, 1984.

[2] Op. Cit., p. 210.

[3] Op. Cit., p. 211.

[4] Interview with Earle Harcourt, July 15, 1998.

[5] Harrison, p. 219.

[6] Leslie Roberts, *The Mackenzie*, New York: Rinehart & Company Inc., 1949, pp. 244-245.

[7] Op. Cit., p. 247.

[8] In 1953, the Jackson family won the prestigious Master Farm Family award, which is given to farm families that encourage young people to go into agriculture, and demonstrate the ideals of successful farming and good family and community life.

[9] Gordon Reid, *High Level, Alberta: The Little Town That Couldn't – but Did! 1963-1983.* High Level, Alberta: Lower Peace Publishing Co. Ltd., 1983, p. 33.

[10] Interview with Valle Gray, August 18. 1997.

[11] Zaslow, p. 253.

[12] From a speech taped during the "Grand Opening of the Mackenzie Highway" at the NWT border visitor's centre, August 20, 1998.

[13] From a slide show and talk given by Chuck Shaul, High Level, August 19, 1998.

[14] The author wishes to thank Esther Supernault for permission to include her engaging and entertaining story in its entirety.

[15] Interview with Jock Shannon, Didsbury, October 28, 1998.

[16] Roberta Hursey, *A Sense of the Peace: A Historical Overview and Study of Communities and Museums in the Peace River Country*, Peace River, Spirit of the Peace Museums Network, 1996, pp. 111-113.

[17] *Saga of Battle River, We Came – We Stayed*, p. 728.

[18] Peace River *Record Gazette*, September 29, 1965.

[19] *Way Out Here: History of Carcajou, Chinchaga, Keg River, Paddle Prairie, Twin Lakes*, p. 66.

Chapter 9 – Trucking Companies After 1948

The Mackenzie Highway ushered in a new era of trucking in the North. After 1948, when the highway was completed to Hay River, several family-owned trucking companies operating one or two trucks began freighting over the highway. Some of these companies remained basically owner-operators over the years, but a few expanded into much larger operations. Trucks also got bigger and heavier, especially after the reconstruction of the highway beginning in the late 50s. More and more tandem and semi trailers were put to work as well. Trucking companies also became more specialized. Some continued to haul general freight, but others specialized in oilfield hauling or logging. Many trucking companies continued to combine freight hauling with road construction.

This chapter is about trucking companies that started operating on the Mackenzie Highway after highway construction was completed.

Albert Hamilton, Hamilton Brothers, and Grimshaw Trucking & Distributing

Albert Hamilton is one of the most respected pioneers in northern transportation. His achievements are not only in trucking, but in building winter roads. A man of vision and not afraid to take risks, Albert guided the small, family-owned trucking company that became Grimshaw Trucking & Distributing (GT&D), the largest trucking company hauling general freight to the North during the 1950s and 1960s. A large number of truck drivers in the North either drove for GT&D at one time or another or subcontracted to the company.

Albert Hamilton was born in 1916 and raised in Lloydminster, a town on the Alberta/Saskatchewan border. In 1943 he started trucking for E.J. Spinney, a large trucking company that had a contract with the American army to haul freight along the Alaska Highway, between Dawson Creek and Johnson's Crossing, Yukon. At that time he was hauling barrels of diesel fuel. When activity slowed down on the Alaska Highway, E.J. Spinney got a contract to haul freight out of Grimshaw, by cat train, into Yellowknife. Albert also moved to Grimshaw about the same time. When the fishing industry was beginning to become a major industry on Great Slave Lake, Albert was one of the earliest to haul fish on the backhauls.

"I landed in Grimshaw in the winter of 1945-1946. I was hauling freight [into the North] and fish back… I had what they'd call a first right. It was a pretty good deal for me because I was doing something for myself. I moved over to Grimshaw when E.J. Spinney had a contract out of Grimshaw with a cat train, and was taking the cat train

into Yellowknife from Grimshaw. I used to go in there with a load of freight and I'd buy a load of fish. I was peddling fish to the Peace River Country. ...I had done a lot of this kind of work in Lloydminster with my dad, when I was a young chap."[1]

In the summer of 1946 Albert started hauling gravel for Scanlin Gravel, a Calgary-based company, during the construction of the Mackenzie Highway.

"I graveled for three summers while the Mackenzie Highway was being built and then I decided to start freighting when the highway was completed. This was how I got started in the freight business. I bought a great big truck. I hauled freight in and fish back out. By then I was no longer buying fish and selling, I was hauling fish."

By 1949 he was hauling about two truckloads a week, mostly perishable goods and small shipments for stores. He also had a mail contract for about a year and a half, between Peace River to Hay River. "I didn't make a very good bid on it. I bid higher the next time and I never got the contract. I was glad I was rid of it."

Hamilton Brothers Trucking

In 1951, Albert was joined by his brother Frank Hamilton and they worked together under the name of Hamilton Brothers Trucking. Fritz Schmidt was hired as bookkeeper. The Hamilton brothers had four trucks operating out of Edmonton. "Buck McFadden looked after Grimshaw and my brother looked after Edmonton. I looked after everything else. I was a travelling salesman in the North and that was where I was getting my business." Hamilton Brothers also acquired a gas tanker and hauled fuel from Edmonton to the bulk fuel agent at Grimshaw.

In August 1953 Hamilton Brothers bought out the highway operating rights from Northern Freightways to run between Grimshaw and Hay River. At this time the company was hauling general freight for local businesses and mines in the North – perishables, dry goods, mining equipment, lumber, and other goods. On the backhauls there would be lots of fish. The following year the brothers incorporated under a new name, Grimshaw Trucking and Distributing (GT&D), on January 9, 1954. The company had about 10 International trucks at the time.

Much of the freight GT&D hauled was perishable. In the winter they used propane heaters in the trailers to keep the food from freezing and in the summer perishables had to be packed in ice. But once the company purchased refrigerated vans, which became widely available in the mid-50s, it was possible to control the interior temperature of the trailers year round.

"They came out with what was called Thermo King reefers. There was also Arctic, but I liked the Thermo King. I had four or five of them. In the winter you could set that thing at 40 degrees [4°C] and that was what your van was reading inside. They had sensors to control the motor. It would kick in the motor when it needed cooling or heating, then when the temperature was right, they'd just go back to idling. They were expen-

sive. There were others that just cooled. We'd use those for things we just had to keep cold."

Grimshaw Trucking's Edmonton office was essential to the whole operation. Frank Hamilton managed the Edmonton office. Within a year, he hired Ted Gosché to set up the billing system.

"We made out manifests and trip tickets, numbers and things like that. Same as computers only everything was manual. Everything had to be written down. Like, the trip ticket would have the driver's name, truck number, trailer number, type of load, whether it was perishable or dry."[2]

Communication with the drivers was infrequent when they were on the road.

"They used to check in at Grimshaw. When we started there were no telephones in the Northwest Territories. We used to have to use radio telephones. We actually had our own. Grimshaw Trucking had its own radio system. But if the northern lights were playing games, we couldn't get through."

Grimshaw Trucking also had teletype connections with the different branches. "They used to be pretty busy all the time. Communications is a big thing in the trucking industry," said Ted. By the early 1960s Grimshaw Trucking had branches in Grimshaw, Peace River, Fairview, High Level, Hay River, Fort Smith, and Yellowknife.

Around this time, the construction of the DEW Line was taking place in the North, and GT&D were hauling freight for the installation. But exactly what they were hauling was a mystery. Ted recalls:

"Everything was crated. There was a lot of secrecy. We used to send it [a truck] over to their loading area and leave it there. They'd load it up. It would all be in wooden crates. There were no regulations at the time. For all we knew, we didn't know what was on it."[3]

Ted recalled one problem they had with a backhaul of fish that needed to be taken to the railway in Edmonton.

"I remember one time we had a load of fish in. The fish always came in on the weekends because the fishermen were out all week fishing. They'd get them into the dock on Fridays and we'd have to deal with it on the weekend. We had one load that had to go to a boxcar downtown, for this fish company. I was on duty that weekend. I sent a truck down and they wouldn't let them in the yard. What were we to do with that load of fish that was supposed to go? The Queen was in town. We were down in there and security was all over the downtown. I had to do an awful lot of finagling to get that load in there."

Ted remembers one of the more unusual loads Grimshaw Trucking took on. A huge tunnel called a Penstock that was to be used in the building of the Taltson River Dam near Fort Smith had to be transported.

This truck, belonging to Grimshaw Trucking & Distributing, was transporting a Penstock for the Taltson River Dam near Fort Smith. The Trailer was pulled through the Penstock, which was then braced to the flatbed. Grimshaw Trucking Ltd. collection.

"It was too big for our trailer. So, what we did, we had them pull the trailer inside the tunnel, the trailer was long enough. So they lifted this tunnel up and braced it to keep it up... so the Penstock was around the whole trailer. They hooked it on and away they went."

Hamilton's Winter Roads

Albert Hamilton got into building winter roads in 1957/58, constructing and maintaining a winter road and hauling 2000 tons of freight into Rayrock Mines. In 1959/60, GT&D constructed and maintained a winter road into the Snare Falls Hydro Project. In 1959, Hamilton saw a need for a winter road for trucks between Hay River and Yellowknife. At that time, freight was hauled up to Hay River in the summer time, loaded onto barges operated by Yellowknife Transportation Company or Northern Transportation Co., and hauled either across the Great Slave Lake or down the Mackenzie River. But after freeze-up much of the freight that came over the Mackenzie Highway had to be stockpiled at Hay River until break-up or hauled by cat trains or air transport. Transportation costs were a lot higher in winter than in summer and air freight was especially expensive.

Albert knew that he could do it much cheaper by trucks. To see if his idea of building the winter road for trucks was feasible, he approached a number of businessmen in Yellowknife and convinced them that he could haul freight in by truck for much less than by air transport. His plans were to build a winter road between Enterprise and Yellowknife. Bond Construction had attempted to build a winter road previously but had problems with it. The road had been abandoned for a couple of years.

Hamilton had a harder time convincing the federal government to give him exclusive rights to build and operate the winter road. He went to Ottawa, where he was told that if he built the road other trucking companies had to be allowed to use it. He finally struck an agreement that he would build a winter road at his own expense and have exclusive toll rights for five years. The rates were set at $10 a ton.

Albert contracted Beecher Linton to brush out a road with cats.

"I brought in a Bombardier for Linton Construction in Yellowknife, took the contractor out of Yellowknife to see what we could do with this road. I asked, 'Can you do anything with this road?' and he said, 'No problem.' We made a deal and he charged me $32 000 to build that road. So I gave him the job to go ahead and put me a road in, and I never got in to Yellowknife until the fourth of March....I was late in getting in there and people wondered, when the first attempt had failed, if I was going to fail too."

But Albert Hamilton and Beecher Linton didn't fail. The road was completed and GT&D had the first overland truck into Yellowknife. Between March 4th and April 11th, 1959, some 250 tons of freight moved north by truck convoys. Grimshaw Trucking opened and maintained this winter road (approximately 338 km or 210 miles long) for five years until the Federal government built an all-weather road between Fort Providence and Yellowknife. During this time, GT&D provided the first scheduled freight service by truck into Yellowknife. His wife Virginia explained:

"At the time only the planes came in on a scheduled basis. But Albert changed all that when he got his trucks freighting on a scheduled basis and kept it up. This brought down the prices that planes could charge.[4]

"The end result of the forethought of Albert Hamilton to build and maintain winter roads to Yellowknife, Fort Smith, Fort Simpson, Pine Point, and Fort Resolution resulted in the development of all-weather roads to these points, with the Town of Grimshaw as Mile 0 on the Mackenzie Highway."[5]

There was a lot to learn about building ice and snow roads, especially on lakes and ice bridges. There was no textbook on how to build and maintain winter roads. One learned from experience.[6]

"I took the big drags behind my cats and I just leveled that snow right down, then packed her down so it was just like being on ice. I could run over rocks on the highway, but there was so much snow over them that you didn't know what was under there. I had a nice road and I wasn't having breakdowns. The only trouble I was having was when a fresh snow would come, about six or eight inches, that would draw the frost

out of your road. You had to get that off of there as quickly as possible because it would soften up the road. It didn't take long either. ...If you left snow on there, and your road would be full of big holes so fast you wouldn't believe it. I had big trucks going in...I didn't even have a grader on them; I'd just put the drags on behind the trucks and they would pack that snow right down."[7]

One also had to learn by experience about driving over ice roads. Albert learned that lake and river ice behaves differently at different temperatures.

"I learned a lot about how to do things. Guys don't believe me but I was on that ice. At 40 below, stay off that ice because she is brittle as can be and it can break up right in front of you. But as soon as it warmed up and you had about eight inches [20 cm] of ice you could go in there. You needed to work on the roads, so there was more ice forming every day. After a good cold spell...you had six or eight inches more of ice on your road. I was taking tests all the time, but I never could figure out why all this stuff was going on. It was just based on experience. The ice was always better when it was mild rather than when it was really cold. The ice had more flexibility. When it was really cold we had to be really careful running on the ice."

Driving trucks over ice was tricky in the best of conditions, but when it was very cold it was extremely dangerous.

"I had one of my trucks go through the ice, at 40 below. We'd been crossing it for two weeks. It got down around 40 below and he wanted to go. He went into the drink, into the Mackenzie River. It was only about 30 feet [9m] of water, and he was pretty lucky. He jumped out of that truck, and he had to walk about 10 miles [16 km] to where he was staying. He was travelling so fast and the water was coming up behind him fast, so he had to get out."

Another time they were taking loads into Rayrock Mines, about 150 miles [240 km] northwest of Yellowknife, where uranium was being extracted. Albert had a close encounter with disaster on a pressure ridge.

"On that ice my last truck was running in six inches [15 cm] of water. I was pretty nervous. I didn't know what to do. I was on there and couldn't turn back. There wasn't one truck loaded under 15 tons. I was in the Bombardier, and I was with the last truck. My driver was nervous and so was I, but we got through. Then the next day two of us were in there when there was six more inches of ice on top of the road. I was about 200 yards from a pressure ridge, about half way from the pressure ridge to the truck. The driver was sleeping in the truck, and I was walking over the pressure ridge when it exploded from the pressure. He thought it was an earthquake, and it damned near knocked me down. He jumped up and pretty soon I heard the motor revving, and he's coming after me."

Fishy-backing on Barges

Trucking into Yellowknife in the summer was a whole different matter. There was no summer road, and everything had to go in by barge or by airplane. In 1956, Grimshaw Trucking initiated a "fishy-back" service from Hay River to Yellowknife. Albert approached Earle Harcourt, manager of Yellowknife Transportation Company Ltd. (YTCL) and worked a deal to have GT&D's trailers hauled by barge between Hay River and Yellowknife. "That went on for two or three years…It worked out pretty well with the barge operation," said Hamilton. Hauling by barge in the fall before freeze-up was very risky, as storms could come up suddenly on Great Slave Lake.

"Fishy-backing" was introduced by Albert Hamilton. Grimshaw Trucking's trailers were hauled across Great Slave Lake on YTCL's barges. Earle Harcourt collection.

> *"In the fall I had about six great big trailers sitting there, loaded for Yellowknife. He [Earle] called and said, 'Albert, come on down, I've got to talk with you.' So I went on down, and he said, 'Albert, I can't take those trailers because bad weather is coming and I'd never be able to control those barges out there with the wind. I don't think you should take those trailers on there. I'm just warning you, I'll put them on, but let's not get into big trouble.' So I said, 'Well, you're the boss. If you don't think you can handle them, we'll just have to wait and move them when the roads tighten up.'"*

It was a very wise decision, as it turned out. Yellowknife Transportation had a beautiful tug boat, the *Sandy Jane*. Named after his daughter, the steel tug was Earle

Harcourt's favorite. Albert remembers the incident vividly, as do many other northerners.

> *"That trip they ran into a storm and the* Sandy Jane *went down. Sunk. The last two barges took off and ended up on the east arm of the lake, on a pile of rocks. They had the other boat come out, and they took the men off the* Sandy Jane *just about two minutes before it went down. It was the* Richard E. *that came out and saved the lives of all those men. They had a hard time getting up close to the barges to take them off. So, I was sure lucky I didn't put my trailers on that day....Earle was very smart in telling me he didn't want those trailers."*

Grimshaw Trucking & Distributing – the Later Years

In 1963, Albert Hamilton purchased 25 Mack trucks to add to his large fleet of International trucks.

> *"When I bought those 25 Macks, it was a $500 000 deal. They were $20 000 apiece, and today they're worth $100 000 to get the same thing. I thought I was really getting into business when I got 25 new trucks, but I just got 25 headaches; they weren't working. I still say Mack is the best truck in the business today, but those were trouble. I couldn't get them as far as the corner without blowing a piston. They slowed my business down terribly. I had 20 trucks in Grimshaw and five in Edmonton broken down. There was 25 trucks and 10 of them were broken down all the time, so I was hiring trucks I didn't plan to hire....It set my business back a lot."*

In the late 1960s, GT&D had about 32 trucks on the highway as well as a number of city trucks and trailers. The company had about 150 employees on its payroll. Many men in the North drove for Grimshaw Trucking in the 50s and 60s. Perhaps the longest-time employee was Buck McFadden of Grimshaw, who started with Hamilton Brothers in 1949. Buck had worked on the first YTCL cat train to Yellowknife. In January 1949 he went to work driving one of Albert Hamilton's trucks and worked for Hamilton for 24 more years. He stayed on with Grimshaw Trucking for another 10 years after Hamilton sold the company to Northern Transportation in 1972. Another long-time employee of GT&D was Jim Glen, who was employed for 21 years. Rose Hess worked for Albert Hamilton a number of years as secretary.

> *"She was working for a service station doing the books and things where I filled up my trucks. She comes hurrying out and says, 'Albert, when are you going to pay your gas bill? I said, 'I've got no money right now, I've got to do some collecting.' Then I asked, 'How'd you like to come and work for me?' About three days later she was working for me. What a smart cookie she was!"*[8]

Later Rose Hess became head of all the weigh scales in the north Peace River Country.

In 1972 Albert Hamilton sold out to Northern Transportation Ltd. (NTCL), a government-owned crown corporation. He tried retirement for two or three years, but then decided to go back to trucking. He moved to Grande Cache and worked for McIntyre Mines driving a coal truck. In 1998 he had two trucks operating in Grande Cache. "I'm still trucking. I was still driving up until a few years ago. I'd like to quit, but I don't know whether I should or not."

Under the ownership of NTCL, the company continued to operate under Grimshaw Trucking Ltd. It wasn't easy for the employees that stayed on afterwards to have to learn to work under some of the federal government's red tape. "We had to contend with some of the political stuff, government ways of doing things," said Ted Gosché. "We used to get into heated battles with some of the other trucking companies because, 'Aw, you're owned by the government. You're financed by the government.' This was not true. We made our own way. We were never owned by the government; we were owned by Northern Transportation, a crown corporation."

In 1995, Northern Transportation sold Grimshaw Trucking & Distributing to Mullen Transportation Inc. Grimshaw Trucking Ltd. continues to operate under its own name. Joseph Bogach, a long-time employee of GT&D, is the President. Most of Grimshaw Trucking's business today is running LTLs throughout Alberta and the Northwest Territories. And most days, along the Mackenzie Highway, you can see the familiar trademark of Grimshaw Trucking, the company that Albert Hamilton built.

Gordon Papp, Papp's Truck Service Ltd.

Gordon Papp was a pioneer trucker who began hauling freight during the Canol Project. The freight came to Peace River or Grimshaw by rail and was bound for Norman Wells, NWT. His personal story rightly belongs in Chapter 5 "Pioneer Truckers," but it has been included in this chapter because Papp's Truck Service Ltd., the company Gordon founded in the 1950s, continued on for another 20 years after his death in 1960. Les Stranaghan, who drove for Gordon Papp for a few years beginning in 1946, wrote the following:[9]

> "Gordon was 16 when he got his first truck, a 2-ton GMC, in 1942, and started hauling freight for the U.S. Army, which had a base in Peace River from where freight was being sent north to Norman Wells, NWT. Andy [Gordon's father] often accompanied his son on these first trips. Soon a second truck was acquired, a Dodge 3-ton."

Les Stranaghan began driving for Gordon in 1946, hauling gravel with a new Diamond T truck. The gravel was hauled from the crusher, located about 10 miles [16 km] east of Mile 150, and stockpiled along the Mackenzie Highway, which was under construction. The men lived in tents until December when the stockpiling was completed. Les recalls:

> "Papp's Truck Service put trucks on a haul that was moving freight from the railhead at Grimshaw into Mills Lake, where in the summer, barges would carry the freight north to Norman Wells. Carloads and carloads of empty barrels were part of this freight. All of them had to be loaded by hand onto the trucks. One had to make sure

the load was no higher than the girders on the bridges that lay ahead. Meals along the cold bush trails were mostly a tin of something thawed over a campfire that was built in the middle of the road. Lots of pranks were played, dangers narrowly avoided, and strong bonds developed between the truckers who helped each other.

"Chef" Gordon Papp, founder of Papp's Trucking Service Ltd. 1946. Les Stranaghan collection.

"In 1947, Bruce Rome became partners with Gordon Papp. They named their business Edmonton-Yellowknife Trucklines. Two years later, D & S Trucking [owned by John Denison and Bob Seddon] amalgamated with Edmonton-Yellowknife Trucklines. This grouping of truck lines lasted a couple of years until 1950. After some buyouts, Edmonton-Yellowknife Trucklines combined with Northern Freightways, based in Dawson Creek. Papp's Truck Service Ltd. emerged again in 1950, with Gordon once more the sole owner.

"Gordon saw opportunities in the burgeoning oil-field-related work that started in the North in the early 1950s. From then on, Papp's Truck Service Ltd. worked in the oil patch, and moving rigs was its specialty."

Off-road heavy hauling for an oil company could take truckers anywhere, and some of the terrain in northern Alberta that Papp's truckers had to drive through was unbelievably rough. An article called "Muskeg, Mosquitoes, Mud, and Men" appeared in Union Oil Company of California's magazine in September 1957, and it describes some of the terrible conditions Papp's Truck Service encountered near Union Oil's Red Earth discovery well, north of Lesser Slave Lake:[10]

"The bulldozers and graders began pushing a road through the deep forests, skirting the more dangerous muskeg areas....By July the road was ready. A good dry weather road. But it was more nearly a wide dirt path, for not a shovelful of sand or gravel could be found anywhere.

"On a bright sunshiny Sunday morning, 18 trucks with diesel engines, pipe, mast sections, and other essential equipment for Union's tenth Red Earth well began moving over the road. At mid-afternoon a shower began. By nightfall it had become a downpour which was to last intermittently upwards of three weeks.

Papp's trucks moving equipment for an oil rig, 1958. Mae Papp collection.

"A few of the trucks managed to struggle through to the location campsite where drilling crews and their families had already been installed in trailers. The balance of the fleet, as it fought the ever-deepening mud, slid off into the engulfing muskeg, broke four axles, wrecked three universal joints, ruined five transmissions, and had 20 flat tires caused by bits of grader blades churned up in the quagmire. After nearly 80 miles [128 km] of this they could go no further – both men and machines were exhausted.

"Trucks were abandoned where they were. After a few hours' rest, truckers piled into a 4-wheel drive 'power wagon' and began retracing their route. Many times the men towed their vehicle by chains and sheer manpower, using small tree trunks as 'collars,' as the Volga boatmen did. They later estimated they were forced to winch out their power wagon 40 times. On the fourth day of their struggle one trucker developed the mumps. Halfway back they ran short of food, but a mile further on found a cook trailer mired down. On the sixth day, with supplies running short, food was dropped to them from a Halliburton plane. The pilot's aim was too good. A big sack of bread made a direct hit on the shack, crashed through the roof and let in the downpour. On the evening of the 10th day after starting their back-breaking trek the truckers reached the end of the 'bush,' having traversed a route which ordinarily would have required about 8 hours.

"'I've been working up here for 16 years and this is the toughest thing we've ever encountered,' says rugged Gordon Papp, trucking contractor."

The families, however, were still marooned in the bush, with one driller's wife pregnant and another one ill. Finally Don Hamilton of Pacific Western Airways was able to land a small plane and take out the women and two children. The story related some of the problems with beavers damming up culverts and small bridges. As one road contractor commented: "Beavers and rain made this the worst mess I've been in, in over 30 years of earthmoving in Alaska and around the world." The rains continued. Gordon Papp said, "We never measured it – it was just too damned much." After three weeks of rain, Gordon Papp was able to send in crews to tow the trucks out with heavy Cats.

After Gordon's untimely death in the spring of 1960, Ray Sampert was hired as manager of Papp's Truck Service, and he continued in this position for eight years. Now retired and living in Bruderheim, Alberta, Ray recalls some of the high points of his years with Papp's.

"In the fall of 1960, when I arrived in Peace River, the firm's office was a very small old building which had once been a service station, about 200 feet square. Our shop was a one-bay affair, impossible to heat. When we put the Kenworth inside, the shop door couldn't be shut! There were, I think, 8 big trucks then and a pickup or two. I arranged to move our base across to the west side of the river, into the vacated Hudson's Bay Gas and Oil building.

"In April of 1963, three of Papp's trucks were part of a group of Byers Transport trucks that went to Port Radium on Great Bear Lake to bring out generating equipment belonging to Canadian Utilities, for delivery to various points in Alberta. This was the first 'ice road' venture there, and the subject of a book, Denison's Ice Road, *by Edith Iglauer some years ago.*

"In 1964 Papp's set up a satellite camp, office, washroom, and bunkhouse at Kinuso, Alberta, to accommodate our crews who were working rig moves at House Mountain and Deer Mountain, in the northern part of Swan Hills, and the Lesser Slave Lake area. In December of 1964 Papp's was the first company to shut down rig moving for Christmas Day. We were threatened, we were told we would be run out of the 'patch', but the following year everyone shut down!

"In April 1965, at spring break-up, Papp's left three trucks in Rainbow Lake area for the Mobil Oil Banff discovery. They'd been driving in on winter roads, but there were no bridges for summer access. So the trucks had to stay if they were going to move any rigs during the summer. We flew the drivers in and out as required."

Papp's Truck Service also hauled the bridge timbers and steel spans for the construction of Great Slave Lake Railway bridges at various river crossings in the 1960s.

"In October of 1966, the work had shifted to Rainbow and High Level, so the satellite camp moved to High Level. That fall of 1966 we had ground work done for a new building on land near the airport west of Peace River. We moved into our new quarters in early summer of 1967. The winter of 1967-68 we had a total of 66 company and leased trucks working. By the time I resigned in 1969, Gordon's sons Rick and Dennis had also become part of the team."

In an article that appeared in the *Alberta Business Journal* in 1968, Papp's Truck Service Ltd. was praised for its reliable service:

> *"The Papp's operation is a far cry from the undependable, breakdown-prone, shirt-tail operations common to the oilfield trucking industry of the past. Although still a tough, rough, and ready outfit, Papp's has brought the sophistication of the modern business world into oilfield hauling."*[11]

Good communication with all the job sites was vitally important. The company had the availability of a Cessna 172 owned by Ray Sampert, and it was used to fly into remote job sites. If a truck broke down, the plane was used to deliver the needed parts that could be dropped into remote sites if necessary. Ray Sampert also used the plane to scout road conditions. The new building had a room called "the attack centre," where maps mounted on the walls had colored tags showing drilling operations and potential well sites. Mike Karpa, the operations manager who kept the maps up to date, was able to make estimates of the cost of moving a rig, and to determine the type of terrain involved, the distance, and road conditions.

In the late 60s Papp's Truck Service Ltd. had about 30 trucks, two truck-mounted five-ton hydraulic cranes and off-road equipment that included bulldozers and tracked vehicles. Some 70 men were on the payroll and about 30 owner-operated units were added during the busy winter season.

Other managers took over the operation of Papp's following Ray Sampert's departure. Then Papp's Truck Service was sold in 1981 to Peace Trailer Industries. This company kept the lighter highway trucks to move their camp buildings and sold off the heavy trucks and allied equipment. Peace Trailer Industries built on two additional bays to the shop to service their camp buildings. The property is still used today to store many of their camp buildings.

One of Papp's trucks stuck on a muddy road, June 1964. Mae Papp collection.

Jim Chapman, Byers Transport

In 1919, at the age of 14, Jim Chapman quit school and went to work on the farm with his dad. As a teenager, he got involved in highway construction of local roads and railway construction. His first trip north happened when he was 17 years old. He went to Lesser Slave Lake and worked for a fish company. He then worked for six fishing seasons at Buffalo Lake, Saskatchewan. The company freighted fish by team to Fort McMurray, where it was sent by train to the Chicago market. It took four days by team, over 100 miles [160 km] of road. The work was hard but it paid better than other labor jobs. In 1934 Jim bought his first truck, a 2-ton Ford.[12]

In 1943 Jim Chapman went north to work on the Alaska Highway, and worked for Gordon Wilson Trucking Company, subcontracting. Jim was paid by the ton and hauled construction steel. One time he had a load of ketchup and pickles because he had a rig he could tarp tightly. He had to keep moving, driving for two days so the ketchup and pickles wouldn't freeze.

Jim started Chapman's Trucking Service and hauled mostly heavy material, bridge decking, telephone poles, and general merchandise, using a pole trailer. Later he went in with Gordon Trenchy and they decided to build a truck terminal in Edmonton, at 102 Street and Kingsway, across from the Royal Alexandra Hospital.

Morris Byers had bought out Blue Line Transfer at Wainwright, which operated the route between Wainwright and Edmonton three days a week. In 1948 Byers invited Jim Chapman to become his partner in Byers Transport. He wanted Jim to put in some money and take over the books. Jim bought a half interest for $25 000. At that time, in 1949, one could buy a good tractor unit for $4500 and a second hand trailer for $1200.

Chapman family buys Byers Transport

In January 1951, Morris Byers died from carbon monoxide poisoning and Jim ran the line for a year. Then he bought out Byers Transport from the Byers estate and Jim Chapman took his son, Jim Jr., into partnership. The company had a number of pickups and 15 to 18 trucks at the time. In 1954, the Chapmans moved the terminal from Kingsway to North Edmonton, onto four acres of land he bought for $26 000. Byers Transport hauled general merchandise and insulation, which was cheap and bulky, for HBC. Jim Chapman drove his last semi trailer in 1955.

In the late 50s and early 60s, Byers Transport faced a new challenge of freighting in northern Alberta and the Northwest Territories. John Denison, one of the partners of Northern Freightways, came on board with Byers Transport. Branches were opened in Hay River and Yellowknife. The company also established a terminal on NWT No. 3, which was in jest called "Fort Byers." It became the launching point to service the building of its ice roads to Great Bear Lake. With John Denison in charge of the construction, Byers Transport built the first ice road to Port Radium on Great Bear Lake, in 1960. It was an expensive endeavor at first. Jim Chapman stated that the company lost $30 000 that first winter, as the company developed new techniques in building ice and snow roads with trucks.[13]

> *"Mile by mile, Byers faced the obstacles of trucking across an unforgiving land. To defeat the unique problems facing them, they created innovative solutions such as laying down ice roads across frozen rivers, lakes, and muskeg and attaching snow plows to the front of the trucks so they could clear paths through the snow as they travelled."*[14]

Building ice roads in the North

Asked about Byers Transport's involvement in building ice roads, Jim Chapman explained:

> *"We were operating into Hay River and Yellowknife and we conceived the idea of going on our own ice and snow roads into Discovery Mines, which was 60 miles [96 km] out of Yellowknife. It was quite an active mine at the time. They were opening a new mine ... about 200 miles [321 km] north of Yellowknife. There was a lot of building material, fuel tanks for fuel storage – all had to be taken in there. Between John Denison and two of the Natives up there at Yellowknife, they came up with the idea of building this ice road. Instead of using the cat trains, which were a slow, ponderous idea, when we got our road in good shape we were into the mine up at Tundra and back in Yellowknife in 24 hours. This would be 1963-64, about four or five years before we became involved with PWA [Pacific Western Airlines]."*[15]

Like Albert Hamilton of Grimshaw Trucking & Distributing, Jim Chapman, his son Jim, and John Denison learned the hard way about the unpredictability of ice and the dangers and difficulties of driving cats and trucks over ice roads when they lost three trucks and trailers.

> *"They were pretty daring, those fellows. Some of the drivers would drive on ice with the door open and stand on the running board and steer with one hand while the ice is bending underneath them. Very, very fortunate, as I said before, we never lost any men. We did have, I guess, three complete units that went down to the bottom of Hottah Lake. We were never able to recover them. The bottom of those lakes are silty muck, about two feet deep. And as soon as you touch anything it just riles up and you can't see a thing."*

Jim also learned about how ice behaves in different temperatures:

> *"It was strange too that the ice conditions at the time we lost those units were never bad. The ice was four feet thick, but it was so cracking cold. The ice was just as brittle as can be. Without warning a crack can open up the ice and just run. The colder the temperature, the brittler the ice gets...I've stood on the edge of a lake and watched a crack and listened to it. They come in the distance just like thunder and you can hear it go ripping across the lake. Pretty soon you see a crack two to four feet wide. And then when the weather turns warm and the ice starts to swell, the crack closes*

right up again. When it continues to get warm, the ice begins to pile. This is what you call an ice ridge. You are either building bridges to take you across the cracks or chopping down huge mountains of ice to get through. Some of the ice ridges could be 25 feet [8m]. The power of lake ice is just as powerful as tides in the ocean."

Airlifting Freight to the Arctic Islands

By the 1960s, Byers Transport had gotten involved in all types of transportation. It interlinked with barge transportation that continued down the Mackenzie River. The company also got involved with Pacific Western Airlines in air-lifting freight to the Arctic Islands.

"It was kind of a strange thing how we got involved with them too. We had just completed an airlift and used all of their equipment to haul all of our freight out of Yellowknife. The airport out there was practically covered with our freight. We had 40 plane-loads stacked up there at one time, and they didn't start moving it until the first of May. We were afraid our ice landing would be going out on us. They came in there and really started moving the stuff out in a hurry. I wound up owing them a half million dollars and I didn't have any money to pay them with. When their accountant came over to see me, I said, 'Think nothing of it. It's just like money in the bank.' He said, 'Why don't you write me a cheque?' I said, 'I will when the Roman Catholic Church pays me, the HBC pays me, and the federal government. When I get their money, you're all paid.' Well, PWA got the idea that this trucking was really a lucrative deal. Together with the airlift we could put together something really good. This was when they started talking about taking over Byers Transport."

Years of Expansion

After PWA bought Byers Transport in 1971, the company expanded once again. It bought out Monarch Transport, a smaller company that had been one of its competitors. (Years later it would revive the Monarch name to handle truckload traffic.) Byers opened terminals in Peace River, High Level, and Fort McMurray. Then in 1974 the Alberta government bought Pacific Western Airlines, but the government decided to sell off the trucking division. Byers Transport became an employee-owned company when a group of 120 employees pooled their resources and bought Byers. The company expanded its operations in northern Alberta to include Grande Cache, Hinton, and Jasper. In 1979, Byers bought Oldhams Transport, expanding its operations into southern Alberta and southeastern British Columbia. Today Byers Transport Ltd. is owned by Herb Assman.

Black Friday

In its 50-year-long history, one of the worst setbacks happened on July 31, 1987, at 3:30 p.m., the day that Edmontonians have since called "Black Friday." At the new Byers facility which had been built in east Edmonton in 1980, the devastating tornado struck down the terminal, its offices, and most of its trucks and equipment that were parked in the yard were a total loss. Within a few days, however, Byers Transport rallied and was back in business, rebuilding the facility within a year.

Jerry Eyford, Hay River Truck Lines

Jerry Eyford moved to Hay River in 1949, where he founded Hay River Truck Lines, a general freight company. During the 22 years he owned the company, he pioneered winter bush roads into Fort Resolution, Fort Simpson, and Fort Smith.[16]

Before moving to Hay River in 1949, Jerry fished and hauled fish for Alaska Fisheries and Menzies Fisheries. Both companies were fishing out of Great Slave Lake at the time. In 1947, Jerry bought his first truck, a 1946 Ford three-ton, which he had driven for a year before he purchased it from the company he was driving for. "It cost a lot of money in those days," Jerry said. "Eighteen hundred dollars, not including the spare tire, and gas was 25 cents a gallon."

In Hay River, Jerry founded Hay River Truck Lines in 1949. His wife May kept the books for the company. Most of the hauls he made were on the Mackenzie Highway. "I hauled anything and everything." During the fishing season, he hauled fish from Great Slave Lake to Peace River. One of the early hauls he made was for Jimmy Jones, who was from Athabasca, Alberta, as well. Jimmy built the first hotel in High Level with the materials hauled by Hay River Truck Lines in the early 50s. Jerry recalls: "There was nothing but bush. In fact, I didn't know where High Level was. It didn't have a name yet. We called it the Fort Vermilion turnoff."

Another early haul was to Montana, with a load of fish. During the railroad strike of 1950, there was no way to load the fish on the train at Peace River. Bill Menzies told Jerry to drive the load to Montana. Jerry drove one load of fish and Charlie Demarrier drove one of Menzies' own trucks. The trucks had to be iced down at Hay River and again at Peace River. Jerry remembered the road from Peace River south as being fairly good. He crossed the border into the States to get it on the train. "I wouldn't want to eat the fish when they got where they were going."

During the first three years, Hay River Truck Lines' main hauls were mostly between Peace River and Hay River. After that, the company freighted out of Edmonton and Hay River. Jerry and May were the agents for Orange Crush in Peace River, and for Robin Hood Flour and Canadian Propane.

"We had a warehouse in Edmonton – Hangar 16 on the north side of the [Municipal] airport. We dealt with everybody: Gainers, Palm Dairies, Horne and Pitfield. Everybody had a different supplier."

In the days before refrigerated vans, all perishable goods had to be iced down. Jerry remembers one summer trip back in 1951 or '52, when he was hauling ice cream and it started to melt. He was stuck in the mud south of Keg River. The highway was out and the water came over the highway. He was about 30 hours in the mud when he decided to give away the ice cream, bananas, bread, lettuce, and other perishable foods from the back of the van. "There's some of the boys still here in town who remember. One of them said, 'You made us all sick. We had so much ice cream we got sick from it.'"

By the early 1950s there were several other trucking companies hauling general freight into the NWT over the Mackenzie Highway. A small company like Hay River Truck Lines needed to maintain its business and find new opportunities as well. Jerry Eyford developed overland winter roads into places that had never had roads other than ice roads. Al Hamilton had built an ice road into Fort Resolution and nearly went through the ice. In 1962, Jerry Eyford put in the first overland winter road into Fort Resolution from Pine Point. He and a friend of his took a cat and headed across to Fort Resolution, following the winter trail that was used by dog teams. Jerry said, "The government was some excited over that. We knocked a lot of willows down."

Hay River Truck Lines put in an overland winter road into Fort Simpson.

"We crossed the Mackenzie River at Providence and headed for Fort Simpson. We took the truck and headed in there, got down to Simpson and got on the other side of the river. I looked down and I could see cat tracks. So I said, 'Just keep going.' So we went across."

Jerry's brother Emil was working there for the government at the time and living in Simpson.

"When I got to my brother's house, he said, 'What are you doing with that truck? Did you bring that across?' I said, 'Yeah.' And he said, 'Well, there's only 10 or 11 inches [25-27 cm] *of ice there in some places.' So we went there and looked, and the river was water from shore to shore. Water running over the ice. But it froze by the next day, and we had a good winter road until spring."*

Another time Jerry was hauling in the wintertime to Fort Providence. John Goodall and his wife had a general store there. He said, 'You know, Jerry, we have a lot of trouble getting our freight in the summer time. If I put a boat in the river, would you haul freight and fresh produce down here to Providence?' I said, 'Yeah, we're already going there.' It was a pretty good deal. We had summer and winter freight business except at break-up and freeze-up."

The following year Captain "Ed" Lindberg built a boat in Edmonton, which Hay River Trucklines hauled by truck to Fort Providence. At the ferry landing, they backed the boat into the water and realized, when the boat began to fill with water, that Captain Ed had forgotten to put the drain plug in at the back. They ran the boat upstream to flush the water back out of the boat and put in the plug.

Hay River Truck Lines hauled everything from school books and boats, to meat and fresh produce into Fort Simpson. After the government opened the winter road into Norman Wells, Hay River Truck Lines took the first truckload of perishable goods into Norman Wells in the winter of 1971-72.

General freight hauling was not the only business for Jerry Eyford. Around 1953, he homesteaded some land and founded a stopping place, where Enterprise is today. It was the first building and the beginning of Enterprise. His family moved from their home in Hay River to Enterprise, where they lived for two years. "The population was four: the wife and I and two kids." His wife, May, ran the café as well as the bunkhouse and gas pumps, and kept the books for the trucking business.

Delivering materials from a dismantled U.S. Army camp at Fort Smith to Enterprise, for Jerry Eyford's stopping place, 1959. Left to right: Bill Rowe, Jerry Eyford, Ed Leguerrier, and probably "Shorty" Dersh. Ed Leguerrier collection.

The work was very hard for the Eyfords, trying to run a stopping place and a trucking company as well. "We never worked harder in our lives. We sold out after about two years. I never realized there were so many thieves on the road. You couldn't leave nothing outside; they'd just go and take it." After selling the stopping place to Pacific 66 Petroleum, the Eyfords moved back to their home in Hay River.

Jerry and May Eyford owned the Hay River Truck Lines for 22 years. Then Jerry sold the company in 1971, to Peter Graham and Joe Loree. He continued on to manage the company for another 10 years, until 1981, when Graham and Loree sold out to Pathfinder Trucking. Pathfinder lasted for six months, until one of its oversized trucks collided with an underpass in the States. The damage costs drove the company into bankruptcy.

Jerry Eyford had purchased many different makes of tractor units for Hay River Truck Lines over the years. "I started out with a Ford. I tried everything – Internationals, Kenworths, Macks. The Macks were the only ones we ever owned that were easy on fuel and needed very few repairs."

Asked if he retired after he was no longer with the company in 1981, Jerry said, "Oh, no. I kept on truckin'." He continued trucking until 1996, when several hip operations forced him into retirement. He looks back on his days of trucking with a feeling of satisfaction. "It was a good life. I loved every part of it, and I never thought I'd get tired sitting on my rear end. That's how I made my living all my life."

Dick Robinson, RTL Robinson Enterprises Ltd.

Based in Yellowknife, NWT, Robinson Trucking Ltd. is one of the largest and most successful trucking companies in western Canada. The founder, Richard "Dick" Robinson, has been active in northern transportation and construction since the early 1950s. He started driving a truck when he was 16 years old and has never looked back. He has that rare combination of risk-taking and caution that has guided RTL through thick and thin for over 30 years.

Dick Robinson left school in grade seven to go to work for his father. "Dad had a KB-5 International…He was trucking then and that seemed like what I wanted to do. I learned to drive a KB-5, then I went into gravel hauling for him." Dick started working for Byers Transport Ltd. in 1953.[17]

> *"My job was mainly loading freight in Edmonton and then I started running to Wainwright. Then I came north in the winter of '55 with Byers, with a load to Hay River for the DEW Line. I was 19 years old when I made that first trip."*

He pounded along the highways between Edmonton and Hay River for a number of years until 1958, when he made his first trip into Yellowknife. About this time John Denison joined the Byers group, having been with Northern Freightways. Dick went to work with John Denison, who was in charge of Byers' northern operations in Yellowknife. Dick hauled on the first ice road that John Denison put in for Byers to Discovery Mines and then to Tundra Mines on MacKay Lake in 1959. These were the first wheeled vehicles that ever went north of Discovery mines into the Barren Lands.

> *"I was going to work with John, and I was up on the winter roads another time. I don't know why I took a love to that, leaving my wife and kids at home all winter, for $400 a month. It really paid off because it's something I still like. It's a challenge; it's risky though. You gamble and you have to be careful. You put in 8 inches* [20 cm] *of ice and you think you should have a pack of 18 or 20 inches* [45-50 cm]*."*[18]

Dick Robinson had 10 years' experience driving in the North on the Byers' ice roads when he decided it was time to begin his own business.

Robinson bought a couple of gravel trucks, a loader, and a portable gravel crusher, which were heavily financed. He took these, and his wife Esther and four children, and moved to Yellowknife in 1969. "I was actually broke and too stupid to lay down and die. I took $40 000 worth of debt with me and the family. I'm sure the parents all thought I was crazier than hell, but it worked out."

Above: Dick Robinson started in crushing and hauling gravel for road construction. RTL Enterprises Ltd. collection.

Below: Building and maintaining ice roads is an important part of RTL's business. RTL collection.

It was kind of a rags-to-riches story. Dick and Esther had their first office in a 52-foot-long [16m] house trailer, which they lived in as well. Later they built a porch onto it for a bedroom and an office. Esther, who owned 49% of Robinson Trucking Ltd. (RTL), was in charge of the office operations, while raising the children – Marvin, Karen, Rickie, and Donnie. "She did all the books. And then we built a garage out on the airport road and had the office there. So she's been part of it right from day one." The company first concentrated on road construction. Dick had taken the first portable gravel crusher into Yellowknife and started gravel trucking and crushing in the summers. In 1972 he got involved in building winter ice roads out of Yellowknife.

In 1979 the company put in a winter road to Contwoyto Lake, in the Barrens, 600 km northeast of Yellowknife. "That was the first wheeled vehicle that was ever into that part of the country."

Around the mid-80s, RTL got involved with hauling scheduled freight between Edmonton and Yellowknife and the northern mines. Today freight hauling is the larger part of the business, but at that time building, and freighting over, winter roads was their bread and butter.

> *"We were always on winter roads with freight. But we didn't have the extra-provincial operating authority to run across the line. So I bought Reinhart Transport authorities from Mullens Transport. Then we started hauling scheduled freight out of Edmonton."*

In 1985, the company bought out Superior Equipment Haulers and its facility at Winterburn, west of Edmonton. This became Robinson's Edmonton terminal.

The four children became involved in RTL's operations at an early age and they learned it "from the ground up." Marvin, the oldest, recalls:

> *"I always found myself, even in Edmonton, going over to the shop after school and on weekends with my Dad. I began greasing the trucks and washing them, driving them around a little bit, in and out of the wash bays. When we moved to Yellowknife, we were virtually broke, and found that every aspect we could help in was appreciated because we didn't have the money to pay other people."*[19]

Daughter Karen also helped out. "It was fun. It was a way for us to be together as a family, and we made it fun." Son Rickie recalls his first job when he was 11 years old. "I got kicked off my first construction job at the age of 11. I was driving a 988 loader. They called up Dad, told him I was too young. Two days later, they called and asked for me back. Dad said no."

Today the Robinson children own the company. Marvin took over as president of RTL in 1989 and took over the daily operations of the company when Dick and Esther decided to retire. Donnie is the vice president of northern operations, and Rickie is vice president of the southern operations. Karen was a shareholder until recently, and worked in RTL's accounting department.

RTL's helicopter using a fork cradle designed by RTL. Freight is shuttled across the Mackenzie River by helicopter during spring break-up and fall freeze-up. RTL collection.

Today RTL has around 400 people employed at peak times and hires about 200 lease-operators in the winter. It owns about 175 trucks, three complete crushing spreads, and a road building spread that includes 50-ton trucks. They also have 80-ton trucks and several tractors and loaders. They operate about 10 plow trucks in winter, making ice roads.

Building ice roads is different today than it was when Dick started with Byers. They use GPS to locate their position. "Today with all the electronic measuring devices, it sure cuts down some of the risk. It's still risky when you run into a pocket of thin ice. But once you get your road established, it's pretty well a known thing and safer than running on the highway." The company tries to make sure that the trucks running on the ice roads go in pairs or three or four trucks. "It depends what the traffic is," explained Dick. "If you had the kind of traffic that travels over the roads today to the mines, it was two every half hour, 24 hours a day. Somebody asked me once, 'Aren't you scared of breaking down out there?' And I said, 'No, I feel a lot safer there than I do on Whitemud Freeway [in Edmonton]. Because if I broke down on Whitemud Freeway, somebody would try to run over me. Out there [on the winter roads] at least they'd stop and help me.'"

Other Trucking Companies

Kapchinsky brothers – Kaps Transport Ltd.

When the oil industry began putting in discovery wells in northern Alberta, the trucking industry became more specialized, and companies became closely associated with the movement of oil camps and drilling equipment. Kaps Transport based its operation on providing services to oil companies. The Kapchinsky brothers, Reinhold Kapchinsky (known as Ron Kap) and Gerhard and Helmut Kapchinsky, started a trucking company that moved rigs for oil companies. They sold this company in 1957, but bought it back in 1961, when oilfield activity began heating up in the North. Kaps Transport began specializing in off-road transport and servicing the oil industry.

Kaps Transport, headed by Ron Kap, designed several tracked vehicles suitable for off-road hauling of fuel and heavy equipment. Perhaps the most notable were built by Foremost Development and Flextrac-Nodwell, both of Calgary. In 1967, Kaps' operations included not only the Rainbow Lake-Zama Lake areas, but also northern British Columbia, in the Fort St. John-Fort Nelson area. Foremost built for Kaps Transport the largest off-road tracked vehicle at the time, at 30-ton capacity. The Foremost was designed to haul over muskeg, ice, and the roughest sort of terrain. In 1971, Flextrac-Nodwell built a rubber-tired tracked vehicle to Kaps' design, which was equipped with 32 tires, 16 dual wheels, and eight axles driving.

Kaps Transport expanded its operations to include river transportation on the Mackenzie River, when oilfield activity began in the Arctic, giving Northern Transportation Company Ltd., which had a virtual monopoly, some competition. Kaps obtained a license in January 1970 to operate tugs and barges on the Mackenzie River system, including the Liard River. The largest tug owned by Kaps was the *Beaufort Sea Explorer*. This large tug was described in the *Alberta Business Journal*:

> *"Pride of the Kaps fleet is the Beaufort Sea Explorer, a $1.2 million tug, designed for work in the Beaufort Sea and launched in June [1971] of this year. The 2500 hp tug is capable of carrying 200 tons of petroleum supplies on deck and can haul four 1200-ton barges fully loaded."*[20]

Kaps also expanded into air transport. One of its subsidiaries was Mackenzie Air Ltd.

Clifford Lizotte, C. Lizotte Trucking, Fort Vermilion

Clifford Napoleon Lizotte started his trucking company, C. Lizotte Trucking, when he bought out Jimmy Ward's Trucking, in Fort Vermilion. He had three trucks, two Internationals and one Ford. He hauled grain and livestock from Fort Vermilion to Peace River and on the backhauls would bring back supplies and freight for stores and restaurants. He also hauled to North Habay, Little Red River, High Level, and Rocky Lane and was one of the first truckers to serve these communities. He had to hire someone each year to lay gravel and prepare the road into Little Red River. To get over the river, he had a custom boat built to ferry his trucks in the summer and drove over an ice bridge in the winter. In 1959, he sold out to Tony Tretick, who owned Tony's Truck Service.

Jim Klone, Klone Transport Company, Hay River, NWT

Jim Klone's company, Klone Transport Company, was one of the largest carriers based in Hay River. From 1961 to 1978 he operated his freighting company. By 1963, Hay River was the end-of-steel for the Great Slave Railway. He started with two semi-trailer trucks and expanded his fleet to more than 35 trucks. At the time the company was considered to be the largest private business venture north of Peace River, Alberta. Some of the work he pioneered in the North included building an ice road to link the communities of Fort Franklin and Fort Norman; delivering critical supplies to communities that had never been served previously by truck; and assisting Lutheran Church ministers that flew into remote communities in the North. In 1998, Jim Klone was working as a consultant for Byers Transport Systems of Edmonton and raising llamas as a hobby on his acreage near Wetaskiwin.

Monarch Transport Ltd.

One thing about the North – the beer had to get through, or there would be a lot of angry, thirsty people. Monarch Transport, an Edmonton-based trucking company, was formed in 1956 to haul for three Alberta breweries. When the railroads took over the lion's share of hauls between larger cities, Gordon Frisby, president and general manager of Monarch Transport, started looking to the North for other freighting opportunities. Bib Bibaud was hired as operations manager.[21]

In the winter of 1957, Monarch Transport started offering scheduled service once a week into Fort Smith via the Mackenzie Highway to Hay River and over winter roads. Merchants in Fort Smith, who were previously serviced by air transport, found that freight rates by truck were much cheaper. The trip was a distance of 1394 km [866 mi.] from Edmonton and took 45 hours. In some places the trucks could only go 20 miles [32 km] an hour. Later Monarch Transport increased its scheduled service into Fort Smith to two days a week, using three single-axle Kenworths.

Monarch Transport, like other trucking companies that hauled in the North, travelled extensively on winter roads and crossed ice bridges. Some of these roads and ice bridges the company built. Said Frisby, "To cross a river we'd build the ice up by pumping water on it; sometimes we'd lace the ice with logs."[22]

Travelling on winter roads and crossing ice bridges was always risky. In 1958, Elmer Lemare joined Monarch Transport, and later became its operations manager and troubleshooter. Each winter he went north in December and stayed there until break-up. He had started trucking in 1946 for T & V Van Lines into the Peace River Country via Highway 2. "My whole life has been the north," he stated. "I thrive on cold weather. I enjoy it. I remember the day a Cat went through the Buffalo River. All I could see was a hand. I pulled him out. It was 45 degrees below zero."

In 1959, Monarch Transport began hauling freight and general merchandise to Fort Simpson, and put in a winter road for trucks between Fort Providence and Fort Simpson. Each truck was equipped with a steel drag on the back, to keep the road level. In 1962, the company tried to build its own winter road from High Level to Peace Point (on the lower Peace River in Wood Buffalo Park). The road was 293 km [182 mi.] long and would cut 644 km [400 mi.] off the trip between Edmonton and Fort Smith. The winter road was only used the winter of 1962. Monarch ran out of funds and "...the road, because of geographical problems that had to be overcome, proved to be unworkable."[23]

In 1964 Monarch Transport had scheduled service into Fort McMurray, and the following winter to Rainbow Lake over the oil companies' toll roads. In 1968, the company began hauling from Fort Chipewyan into Uranium City, Saskatchewan, on the northeast end of Lake Athabasca. This meant driving trucks for 171 km [106 mi.] across lake ice. In 1969, Monarch lost three trucks that broke through the lake ice; one truck took two and a half months to recover. However, no lives were lost, and the cargo was recovered.

In 1970, Monarch had a total of 36 units. In the summers the trucks were hauled on barges between Hay River and Yellowknife, and Fort McMurray to Fort Smith. In 1971, Byers Transport acquired Monarch Transport, and the two companies were merged under the name of Pacific Western Trucking, a division of Pacific Western Airlines.

Notes

[1] Personal interview with Al Hamilton, April 24, 1996.

[2] Personal interview with Ted Gosché, April 3, 1998.

[3] Ted Gosché worked for Grimshaw Trucking & Distributing longer than any other employee, for almost 50 years. He started in 1955, continued with the company when Northern Transportation bought out Grimshaw Trucking in 1972, and when it was in turn bought out by Mullen Transport in 1997. As of 1998 when this interview took place, he was Traffic Manager for GT&D. He has been a valuable source of information about the history of the company.

[4] Personal interview with Virginia Hamilton, April 24, 1996.

[5] *Land of Hope and Dreams*, p. 289.

[6] One of the earliest pioneers to build ice roads was Svein Sigfusson and family of Manitoba. Beginning in 1945 the Sigfussons built and maintained winter roads with cats in northern Saskatchewan, Manitoba, and Ontario. Their first winter road was to Reindeer Lake, Sask., to support their fishing operations. The company pioneered equipment and techniques in ice road development that revolutionized the way northern roads were built. See Svein Sigfusson, *Sigfusson's Roads*, Winnipeg: Watson & Dwyer Publishing Ltd., 1992. This is the most detailed information I have found on how to build winter roads and the use of cat trains for freighting in the north.

[7] Personal interview with Al Hamilton, April 24, 1996.

[8] Ibid.

[9] A special thanks to Les Stranaghan and Ray Sampert for their recollections of Gordon Papp, and to Mae Papp for providing the photographs.

[10] "Muskeg, Mosquitoes, Mud, and Men," *Seventy Six*, published by Union Oil Company of California, September 1957, pp. 4-6.

[11] "Heavy Hauling in a Hurry," *Alberta Business Journal*, July-August, 1968, pp. 79 and 81.

[12] Information about Jim Chapman and Byers Transport came from two sources. The first is a taped interview with Jim Chapman on October 30, 1981, by June Drinnan on behalf of the Alberta Trucking Association. These tapes are on file at Glenbow Archives. The second source is from a pamphlet produced by Byers Transport Ltd. titled "A History of Byers Transport," published c1989.

[13] ATA interview with Jim Chapman, 1981.

[14] "A History of Byers Transport."

[15] ATA interview with Jim Chapman, 1981.

[16] Telephone interviews with Jerry Eyford, September 28, 1999, and January 11, 2000.

[17] Information about Dick Robinson and Robinson Transport Ltd. is primarily from Paul Rubak's taped interview with Dick Robinson and John Denison at Hay River, August 1998, and a brochure titled "A Leader in the North: Robinson Enterprises Ltd.", which appeared as a supplement to *Alberta Report* in 1996.

[18] Interview with Dick Robinson, by Paul Rubak, August 1998.

[19] "A Leader in the North," p. 3.

[20] "Kaps is a Mover," *Alberta Business Journal*, July-August 1971, p. 66.

[21] Information for this section is from Jim Vincent, "Monarch and the Long, Lonely Road," *Alberta Business Journal*, December-January, 1970-71, pp. 36-38.

[22] "Monarch and the Long, Lonely Road," p. 37.

[23] Ibid., p. 38.

⬛ Chapter 10 – Passenger Service ⬛

Passenger service in the North Peace was fairly casual in the 1930s and 1940s. If someone needed to go to town, he or she would hitch a ride with a relative or neighbor. Perhaps the first regular passenger service was school bus service, by horse-drawn wagons and cabooses. School buses were introduced when roads got better and older children needed to go beyond the schooling offered in their community's one room school. John Richard went to a small country school called Wilcox School near Grimshaw in the early 40s. "Walked two miles [3 km] to school until I had to go to school in the Town of Grimshaw," he wrote. "My father Nestor Richard then became the school bus driver for seven years. When the bus couldn't make it he used a sleigh and a team of horses."[1]

Clarry Doherty and his school van, pulled by Dandy and Peggy. He drove this school van from north of Dixonville to Dixonville School beginning in the late 1930s to early 1950s, on the Battle River Trail. Clarry Doherty collection.

Trucks provided passenger service on the Mackenzie Highway long before there was scheduled bus service. Truckers usually did not charge for this service, as having a passenger along relieved some of the tedium and loneliness of the long drive. George Frith of North Star, who had a mail route, provided a more regular service between

Grimshaw and North Star; for a dollar a passenger could get a ride. If the passenger had no money, George would give him or her a ride anyway. The arrangements were fairly casual. Tony's Truck Service also carried passengers. Les Stranahan wrote:

> *"Very seldom we went up the roads or came back alone. Almost always someone needed a ride. Nurses, policemen, priests, nuns were often passengers out of Assumption. Two nuns in the cab with a floor shift, you often wondered how to change gears politely."*[2]

Otto Krause of Notikewin offered the first scheduled bus service on the Mackenzie Highway, between the Battle River area and Peace River. He had moved to Notikewin in 1945 to provide this needed passenger service. Krause acquired a franchise and ran a bus three times a week between Hotchkiss and Peace River.[3]

Canadian Coachways Ltd.

Canadian Coachways of Edmonton expanded its operations into the Peace River Country in 1946. The company acquired a license to operate a bus service between Edmonton and Dawson Creek via High Prairie and Lesser Slave Lake. In order to offer this service, the company purchased two smaller bus companies – Morrison & Sargeant Lines (Grande Prairie-Crooked Creek) and Anderson Bus Service (Grande Prairie-Dawson Creek). The following year, Coachways bought Peace River Bus Lines (Peace River to Fairview) and began offering regular service. Then in 1950, Coachways expanded its service on the Mackenzie Highway by purchasing the rights from Gateway to Yellowknife Bus Lines.[4]

Passengers destined for Yellowknife had to travel by other means. Once they arrived by bus in Hay River, they could transfer to NTCL's or McInnis's boats, or in winter, catch a flight across the lake with Canadian Pacific Airways. CPA had an office in Hay River and provided a regular weekly service between Hay River, Yellowknife, and Peace River.[5] In the summer of 1950, Coachways and YTCL struck an agreement to provide direct passenger service from Edmonton to Yellowknife twice a week via Coachways bus and YTCL's *Yellowknife Expeditor*.

First Coachways Bus Driver on the Mackenzie Highway

When Canadian Coachways began its scheduled bus service on the Mackenzie Highway, its first bus driver was Les Stranaghan, who had the route between Peace River and Hay River. His story is told in full in *Tales of the Mackenzie Highway*. The following are some excerpts from this highly entertaining and informative article:

> *"My first trip on the Mackenzie Highway was made in 1945, driving a truck for Palace Transfer (a Peace River business owned by Tony Tretick)....By the time I started driving a Canadian Coachways bus, I had been trucking on the Highway for five years.*

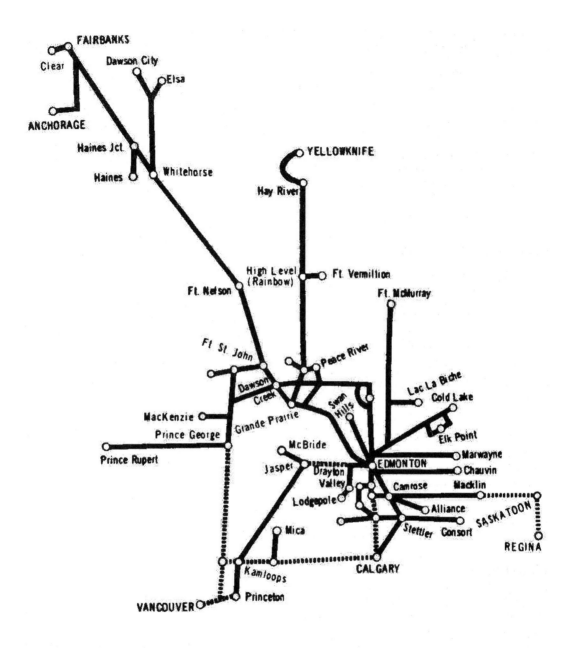

Canadian Coachways bus routes in 1962.

The Yellowknife Expeditor

The Yellowknife Expeditor was launched on August, 14, 1949, from Victoria, with Captain F.A. Coe in command. The Vancouver *Daily Province* offered the following article, dated August 6, 1949:[6]

EXPEDITER BOUND FOR THE ARCTIC – DESTINATION GREAT SLAVE LAKE

The 160-foot Expediter [sic] leaves in about a week from Victoria Machinery Depot on its 4000 mile [6500 km] voyage. She will touch at Dutch Harbor, Bering Straight, Nome, Point Barrow and across to the Mackenzie Bay. Then her 12-man crew will take her 1200 miles [1900 km] up the river to Great Slave Lake, where she will operate between Hay River and Yellowknife.

For the North Vancouver captain the trip down the Mackenzie River [actually upriver] will be a "first." Yellowknife Expediter will round Alaska just ahead of the Arctic icepack a month before freeze-up on Great Slave Lake. She has two 600 horsepower diesel engines which will give her a speed of 13 knots.[7]

After an eventful voyage, the *Yellowknife Expeditor* arrived in Yellowknife on September 21, after a brief stop at Hay River. The Edmonton *Journal* proclaimed it "the first time in transportation history a boat has completed a voyage from the Pacific coast, through Arctic waters, and up the Mackenzie River to tie up at Yellowknife."

The first scheduled run between Hay River and Yellowknife had to wait for several months while the Board of Transport Commissioners decided to give YTCL a license to operate. Two other companies, Northern Transportation Company and McInnis Fisheries, were already providing similar service. At a public hearing held at the Ingraham Hotel in Yellowknife, J.H. Wilson, general manager of YTCL, stated his case that YTCL could provide a cheaper service and it would avoid a Crown monopoly. Despite its doubts, the Board finally allowed YTCL an operating license, and the first scheduled service from Hay River to Yellowknife took place on June 29, 1950. The passenger service offered connections with Canadian Coachways and other freight operators. The passenger fare via Canadian Coachways and the *Expeditor* was $42.50 from Edmonton to Yellowknife. "A passenger could leave Edmonton at 8:00 a.m. either Saturday or Thursday, and arrive in Yellowknife at 10:00 p.m. Sunday or Wednesday [sic]."[8] The service only lasted two years, ending after a series of mechanical and electrical problems and a misadventure with a sand bar. The following season the problems continued. The *Expeditor* grounded on a reef at the mouth of Yellowknife Bay on July 6, 1951, damaging the rudder, shaft, and propeller. Further delays were due to needed repairs. Ferry service was suspended altogether on October 7th. The ship was remodelled to push barges on the Mackenzie River. It was used in 1963 to haul equipment off the DEW Line.[9]

When NTCL bought out the YTCL's fleet in 1965, the *Expeditor* continued to ply the Arctic coast, where it suffered further damage. The "Queen Mary of Great Slave Lake" was finally cut up and sold for scrap in 1969.

The Yellowknife Expeditor, *owned by Yellowknife Transportation Company Ltd., shuttled Canadian Coachways passengers across Great Slave Lake, between Hay River and Yellowknife. Earle Harcourt collection.*

"I became a Bus Driver in a way that would be impossible to imagine in today's world of hiring practices. Canadian Coachways was a small growing company. The company sent two of its drivers (Bill and Vic) from Edmonton to inaugurate this new run to Hay River, and to find a driver to run this new route. I met them, we chatted, they found out that I not only had experience in driving a truck but experience on the right Highway.

"'Would you like a job?'

"'No, bus driving is not for me!'

219

"'Well, just come with us to Manning. We have to go there today. Come for the ride.'

"Going to Manning they slyly urged me, 'Just take the wheel, see how it handles. We'll look after the tickets and freight.'

"I think we overnighted in Manning, then came back to Peace River the next morning. That afternoon, Bill and Vic, along with a group of us, attended a Donkey Baseball Game that was being held in Peace River. Bill and Vic participated whole-heartedly in the foolishness of trying to run bases while riding on a Donkey, and since no one can do this sort of thing without a little something to make the ride smoother, it was obvious by early afternoon that Bill and Vic would not be able to drive the bus scheduled to go to Hay River that evening. I was approached in late afternoon by Earl Boyd, the bus agent. "Would you please go home and get some sleep, so you can drive the bus tonight?' I did that, expecting that Bill and Vic would at least ride with me. But no, they did come down to see me off, though, leaning on each other and shouting cheerful advice to me as I pulled out of the depot that night.

"What a strange trip. The only thing I was sure of was that I wasn't going to get lost on the road. The agents helped with tickets, the passengers helped with luggage, and we did get to Hay River and back. Arriving in Peace River I found that Bill and Vic had gone back to the city, and had already assured the owner of Coachways that things were all looked after as far as the new Hay River run was concerned. They had a driver – me."

Les Stranaghan drove the Coachways bus for 10 years, four years on the Hay River run and then three on the Fort Vermilion run, beginning in 1954. He also drove bus to High Prairie and to Hines Creek for a few years. One time he came upon a car stopped in the road, halfway between Hay River and High Level, at 4:00 a.m. Two men got out and asked Les if he could spare any gas. Neither Les nor the two men had any gas containers, but the problem was solved when one of the men "pulled off his cowboy boot and said he reckoned about 5 bootfuls would get him to High Level. That was Jack Perkins and he stood in his socks as I filled his boots. As each one was filled, his partner carried it to the car and carefully poured the gas into the empty tank. Jack put his boots back on and they drove away."

Les carried the mail in those days, and at Keg River Cabins the mail was left there, as the bus didn't go into Keg River.

"Harry Bowe was the postmaster, and he would drive out to Keg River Cabins to meet us. People would gather from all around the area, and when we arrived, Harry would take the First Class mail bags, unlock them, and dump the mail into the back of his pickup. People would dig through for their own mail. Anything left over would go back with Harry to the Keg River Post Office."

One of his regular passengers was a heavy lady who had trouble getting on the bus. After the first trip, she carried a little stool with a six-foot rope attached. "She'd put the stool down, step onto the bus, then reel the stool up by the rope."

Les Stranaghan faced many of the same problems that truckers did with a deteriorating highway. When it rained or snowed, the roadbed was as slick as grease. One trip in the spring, Les ran into problems with tires that were smooth and he couldn't get any traction. Steve Kowal came by with his team and sleigh with bags of grain, and Les got him to unhitch the team from the sleigh and hook them up to the front of the bus. Trying to guide the horses, Kowal would lose his footing and Les was afraid the bus would run over him. "So he got in the bus, I took the reins through the side window and drove the horses and the bus for a quarter of a mile until we were out of the slippery, drifted area."

When the Coachways bus got bogged down in ice and snow. Steve Kowal came along with his two horses to pull the bus out of trouble. 1954, Les Stranaghan collection.

Les Stranaghan remembers many of the bus drivers, some from the 1950s when he drove, and others that came after him and drove before Coachways was bought by

Greyhound Bus Lines. Two drivers, Oscar Sodequist and Harold Soderquist, became managers of bus depots:[10]

> *"Oscar Soderquist drove for some years, then he took over the bus depot in Grande Prairie. Later he moved to Dawson Creek and ran the depot there until his retirement. Harold Soderquist, after driving for some years, ran the Fort St. John depot until his death."*

Northern Bus Driver – Never a Dull Moment

Clyde Berryman of Peace River became one of the bus drivers for Coachways when he was 29. Six times a month he made the 400-mile [644 km] journey from Peace River to Hay River. Clyde and another driver, Don McKay, would take turns in making the 782-mile [1258 km] round trip. The run was nearly always an adventure. In an article written by Ron Hayter, a former staff writer for the Edmonton *Journal*, Clyde said, "After a few months most runs get monotonous, but not this one. This is a run with personality. No two trips are the same; you never know what's going to happen next."[11]

Ron Hayter accompanied Clyde on one of his trips during the summer of 1960. He described Clyde as more than just a bus driver:

> *"He is the mailman who distributes about 30 bags of mail per trip among communities north of Hotchkiss; he is the man who brings them their daily newspapers and delivers parts for a disabled tractor needed on a construction project, and the man who agrees to pick up a birthday card for a woman living at a lonely wayside point. Above all, he is their friend."*

Clyde told Hayter: "You can't beat the people along the highway....They're absolutely wonderful. They make you feel right at home. You can never get tired of their friendliness."

Clyde Berryman was especially appreciative of truckers he encountered along the Mackenzie Highway. In the winter of 1958 the water pump had to be repaired on a desolate stretch of the Mackenzie Highway, miles from the nearest community.

> *"In those days we just used water in the radiator, so I had to drain it to prevent it from freezing up while I tried to fix the pump. When I got the water pump back in working condition, I found myself without any water for the radiator. Just then a truck, going in the opposite direction, stopped and the driver asked what was wrong. I told him and he said: 'Don't worry, we'll get you to some water.' He turned his vehicle around, hooked onto the bus and towed it 12 miles [19 km] to where I could get water."*

On another trip, he stopped at Indian Cabins to check his tires when he heard someone groaning at the back of the bus.

> *"I looked inside and saw it was a woman who had boarded the bus at Steen River. I asked her what was the matter and she replied: 'I'm going to have my baby.' Man,*

you could have knocked me over with a feather right then. I rushed into the café, bellowed 'Let's go!' to the rest of the passengers and I got the bus rolling in no time flat. That was one of the fastest 90 miles [144 km] I've ever made with a bus. I pulled up in front of the nursing station [at Hay River] and got the woman inside. Ten minutes later, she was the mother of a bouncing baby boy."

Clyde remembered the terrible muddy conditions of the Mackenzie Highway in the summer of 1957:

"The Mackenzie Highway was a ribbon of mud....It got so bad we had to use two drivers on each bus, with each taking his turn at the wheel. On some trips, we left Peace River at 9 a.m. and didn't arrive in Hay River until the following day after 10 a.m., the scheduled returning time...Near High Level we didn't move a wheel for 15 hours. There must have been 25 trucks lined up. The passengers were hungry, but there wasn't an eating place for miles. However, I managed to get some bread, marmalade, and canned meat from a trucker who was hauling a load of groceries to the North, so we all ate in style."

The Bruck

The northern routes that Les Stranaghan and Clyde Berryman drove demanded a coach that would withstand the extremes of weather and road conditions, and provide a versatile passenger and freight service. In 1956, the owner of Canadian Coachways, M.R. "Mickey" Collins, ordered a new type of bus from Western Flyer of Winnipeg. It was christened the Bruck, as it was both a bus and a truck. He sent some well-used Western Flyer Standard buses to the factory in Winnipeg and had the new Bruck built around the old frame and shell.[12]

The first Bruck was converted from a 1944 Flyer Standard. It had 16 seats and 400 cu. ft. [11 cu. m] of express area. Because the Bruck proved to be an invaluable addition to the Coachways fleet, Collins ordered three more Standards to be modified and put into service. Later models accommodated 20 passengers and had 600 cu. ft. [17 cu. m] of space. The heated load compartment of the Bruck had access from the back of the bus. Between 1956 and 1964, Coachways used about a dozen Brucks for scheduled service from Edmonton to Hay River and other locations in the Peace Country.

The Coachways Bruck carried some unique loads in its time. The largest single item was a Cummins diesel engine weighing 2200 pounds [997 kg]. Its passengers included prospectors, miners, and drilling crews with their baggage and equipment, destined for remote areas of the North.

The Bruck was a true work horse of the North. But after 1966, Coachways started phasing them out, replacing them with Western Flyer Canucks, and later, Cargos. By 1966, only two Brucks were in use on the Ft. Vermilion to High Level run.

In 1969, Greyhound Canada purchased Canadian Coachways and began to take over the former company's operations. Greyhound had a preference for Motor Coach

Here the Coachways Bruck arrives at North Star, 1958. The Bruck, half bus and half truck, was a true workhorse of the North Peace. It was built by Western Flyer of Winnipeg for Canadian Coachways. Brian Sullivan collection.

Industries (MCI) products, so the Cargos were replaced with MCI buses. Today, Greyhound Canada is owned by Laidlaw Transit, but still operates under the Greyhound name. In the Peace Country there is still a need for more cargo space than passenger seating on Greyhound's runs in the North. Today Greyhound buses pull a trailer in the back.

Notes

[1] John Richard, "John Richard," *Tales of the Mackenzie Highway*, p. 29.

[2] Les Stranaghan, "Tony's Truck Service," *Tales of the Mackenzie Highway*, p. 35.

[3] *Saga of the Battle River – We Came, We Stayed*, p. 324.

[4] Information on Canadian Coachways history is from Brian E. Sullivan, "Coachways Equipment History," *Bus Review*, published by the Bus History Association, Minneapolis, Minnesota, March 1969. A special thanks to Brian Sullivan, for permission to use his photographs of the Bruck, taken while on a run between Edmonton and Yellowknife in 1967.

[5] David Harrison, *Hay River, NWT 1800-1950: A Geographical Study of Site and Situation*, p. 224.

[6] Vancouver *Daily Province*, August 6, 1949.

[7] Ibid.

[8] David Harrison, "Queen Mary of Great Slave Lake," *Up Here*, March/April/May, 1991, p. 40.

[9] See Chapter 5, "Bruce Rome – Entrepreneur in Northern Transportation."

[10] Correspondence from Les Stranaghan to the author, February 7, 2000.

[11] Ron Hayter, "There's Never a Dull Moment for Driver of Northern Bus," Edmonton *Journal*, July 12, 1960.

[12] Roberta Hursey and Brian Grams, "The Bruck – Canadian Coachways' Work Horse of the North," published in the July/August 1998 Alberta Chapter ATHS newsletter.

Chapter 11 – The "Mac 50" Cavalcade

The Mackenzie Highway, which was completed in late summer of 1948, was never officially opened, either by the federal or Alberta governments.[1] In the time-honored fashion of northerners, several local communities, on and off the Mackenzie Highway in northern Alberta and the Northwest Territories, decided to take the matter into their own hands. They planned an official opening of the highway themselves.

After 50 years, on August 20, 1998, at 2:00 p.m., the official opening of the Mackenzie Highway finally took place beside the Visitor's Centre on the Alberta/Northwest Territories boundary at the 60th Parallel. About 300 people were on hand to take part in the events. Sweltering in suits and ties, politicians from both sides of the boundary were on hand to help in the celebrations with speeches – mercifully short as the day was a hot one.[2]

In the crowd was Stanley Longname, a northern pioneer trucker and long-time resident of High Level. Stanley's Polish surname was too long to paint on the door of his truck, so he has since then gone by "Longname." Harry Metacat and his wife Rose from Meander River Reserve were also there, in the heat, listening to lots of hot air. To Harry the ceremonies brought back many memories:

> "In 1945 to '47, we travelled by wagon and saddle horses from Meander River. We used to go by dog teams. It took three or four days to Fort Vermilion. High Level? It was nothing at that time. No more now. Yes, it has changed. You can't go back. It would be pretty hard to do that. All the Indians at Meander River have new homes now. I don't see anybody do without."

He says this with a laugh, pointing to his shiny, nearly new pickup truck.

Not a single representative from a major Canadian newspaper or television station (not even CBC!) was on hand to record the event. There were only a few reporters from local weeklies. Too bad. An opportunity missed by the media. Considering the importance of this vital lifeline to the North, the opening of the Mackenzie Highway deserved better coverage.

The week-long trek began early Monday morning, August 17th, at the Visitor's Caboose in Grimshaw, Mile 0. A ribbon cutting and release of hundreds of balloons launched the Mac 50 Cavalcade, which would travel in a leisurely fashion for the next few days to Hay River, Northwest Territories. Preliminary events had taken place over the weekend of August 15 and 16, in Grimshaw during the 4th Annual Truckers Reunion.

Some 130 people registered to take part in the cavalcade, but many hundreds more took part, joining the festivities at communities all along the highway.

Phyllis Stuart has lived on a farm by the highway since it was a wagon road in the 30s. She has "seen it all." Photo Roberta Hursey.

The Mac 50 Cavalcade was the culmination of months of planning by the members of the Mackenzie Highway 50th Anniversary Celebrations Committee: Bruce Hills, Bernice Lorenzen, and Leslie Peppler, Grimshaw; Joan Hitz, Dixonville; Mary and Mark Jaeger and Jack and Eleanor Landry, Manning; John and Anne Vos, Keg River Post; Emma Martineau, Paddle Prairie; Marvin and Helen Seward, Danielle Pawlik, and Lynn Le Corre-Dallaire, High Level; Marilee Toews, Fort Vermilion; and Ron "Badgie" Courtoreille and Eileen Collins, Hay River.

It was well organized, down to the smallest detail. The cavalcade was divided into groups of 10 or more and each group left Grimshaw spaced 15 minutes apart. The groups had their own Wagon Masters. These patient, capable men and several wives made the trip safe and free from complications and annoyances to other drivers on the road. Wagon Masters included Head Wagon Master Bruce Hills, Ambrose Parenteau, Mark Crawford, Roy Alm, Les Stranaghan, and Bill Mueller, all from Peace River; Marvin Seward, High Level; Bernie Richards, Edmonton; Wayne Hales, Lethbridge; George McKenzie, Brownvale; and Ed Carlson of Dawson Creek, B.C., who followed at the end of the cavalcade to help anyone out who might break down along the way.

This '48 Chevy came off the assembly line the same year the Mackenzie Highway was completed. Al Bendt of Peace River bought it at auction to drive on the Cavalcade. He brought his own "pit crew" to follow along behind him. Photo Roberta Hursey.

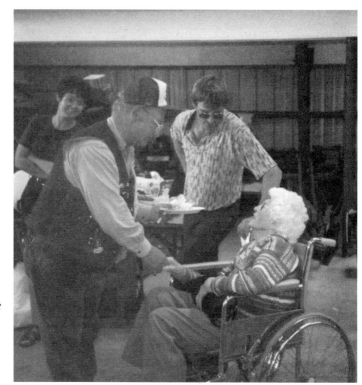

At Battle River Museum, Manning, Wagon Master Bruce Hills greets Dr. Mary Percy Jackson, pioneer doctor. Beside her is her grandson, Bob Jackson. Photo Roberta Hursey.

(Fortunately, the worst to happen were flat tires on a couple of RVs, and a water pump that had to be replaced on Al Bendt's antique 1948 Chevy.)

Bruce Hills gave the cavalcade a few simple "Rules of the Road." Each vehicle was to leave enough room between the one in front for other people on the road to pass easily. The top speed of the cavalcade was 80 km/hr. No alcohol was to be consumed while travelling on the highway.

Getting into their RVs, heavy trucks, pickups, vans, and antique trucks and automobiles, the cavalcade started to roll by 11:00 a.m. There were many pleasurable stops in communities along the way. First stop was Dixonville, where the cavalcade was treated to coffee and donuts at the Fire Hall. Lunch took place at the Battle River Museum at Manning. One of the highlights of this Manning stop was talking with Dr. Mary Percy Jackson, the pioneer doctor who was then in her 90s (she passed away in spring, 2000). There was a brief stop at Keg River for tea and delicious homemade desserts, and again at Paddle Prairie for coffee and musical entertainment. Later everyone gathered at the exhibition grounds at High Level to spend the night.

Bright and early on Tuesday, August 18, several members of the cavalcade boarded two tour buses and travelled along Highway 58 and Secondary road No. 697 to La Crete to visit the La Crete Pioneer Village, which interprets the history of this Mennonite community. There was a hearty lunch of borsht and home made rolls and live entertainment by a group of local teenagers. The village had many unique and historical artifacts and buildings, including a traditional Mennonite house and barn, and a historic flour mill once owned by Sheridan Lawrence.

Later, the buses travelled to Fort Vermilion, a town that shares the distinction, with Fort Chipewyan, as being the oldest continuously settled community in Alberta, founded in 1788. There the cavalcade was treated to a play interpreting the Fort's long and fascinating history, a tour of the community, and a visit to the Fort Vermilion Heritage

Historical buildings at Fort Vermilion provided the stage for a local theatrical group's presentation of a drama about Fort Vermilion's history. Photo Roberta Hursey.

Museum. There was further entertainment that followed a delicious and lavish banquet in the sports complex.

On Wednesday, August 19, most of the cavalcade took guided tours around High Level: visiting the Mackenzie Crossroads Museum, the Aeromedical Emergency Services, and the town of High Level. People from around the area came to visit old friends they hadn't seen for 30 or 40 years. The town put on a great barbecue and live entertainment for some very tired guests. A few men who had worked on the Mackenzie Highway got up and told their stories to the crowd.

Cavalcaders and locals gather at the border for the official opening of the Mackenzie Highway. Photo Roberta Hursey.

On Thursday, August 20, some 300 people gathered at the border for the official opening of the Mackenzie Highway. Speeches by politicians and other dignitaries took place on a "high boy," an appropriate choice of grand stand. After the border ceremonies, which included a ribbon cutting (the ribbon being a survey tape), the cavalcade continued on its own to Hay River, with stops along the way to see the scenic splendor of Alexandra and Louise falls. The local commercial fishing association in Hay River put on a fish fry that night.

Gordon Taylor, third from right, and other dignitaries cut a survey ribbon to officially open the Mackenzie Highway. Taylor was Minister of Highways for Alberta during the reconstruction of the highway in the late 50s. Photo by Chuck Shaul.

The following day marked the end of the festivities of the Mac 50 Cavalcade, with a pancake breakfast put on by the Royal Bank in Hay River. Afterwards some people drove on to Yellowknife or stayed for the weekend to take part in the Homecoming celebrations at Hay River.

One of the highlights of the cavalcade was the "travelling museum" that led the cavalcade and was set up at each community along the way. The Mac 50 Mobile Interpretive Centre was the brainstorm of Fred and Bernice Lorenzen, who bought the trailer and organized the installation of interpretive displays. It was pulled by a restored 1957 B61 Mack tractor owned by Northern Mack, and driven by Fred Lorenzen and John Richard of Grimshaw. It seems very fitting that a semi-trailer was used to interpret the history of the Mackenzie Highway. Called "From Cat Tracks to Black Top," the display inside the van was filled with stories and photographs of the pioneers of the highway. Displays of artifacts and models and a long map of the highway along one side of the van told the story of the events and people who played an important role in the 50-year history of the highway. At the forward end of the trailer was a media centre, where visitors could watch videos depicting the rich history of the North. The displays, inside and

Above: The Mac 50 Interpretive Van was one of the highlights of the Cavalcade.

Below: Stella Friedel, Bernice Lorenzen and Bob Lorenzen in the Interpretive Van. Photos Roberta Hursey.

out, were financed in part by advertisements of businesses in northern Alberta and the Northwest Territories, which were painted on the outside of the trailer, along with a large mural.

Legacy of the Mac 50 Cavalcade.

Why had so many people gathered together from all parts of Alberta and western Canada, and as far away as Ontario and the eastern seaboard of the United States, to participate the Mac 50 Cavalcade? What meaning did the Mackenzie Highway hold for them? The answers varied as much as the people themselves. Some of the older members of the cavalcade had hauled on the winter road or the Canol Road, or were involved in building the Mackenzie Highway. Others had run stopping places or other services along the route. Some had no real connection to the highway but had heard a lot about the Mac 50 Cavalcade and thought it was something interesting to do. But to some, the Mackenzie Highway was an integral part of their lives, so much so that it was inconceivable for them to miss going on this cavalcade, or to miss the opportunity to reunite with some of its pioneers, still living and telling their stories.

Ben Gordon, Bruce Rome, Vern Estabrook, John King, Vic Brandl, Don Claughton, and Wes Spencer. John King collection.

There were many stories worth listening to. Every pioneer trucker seemed to have a story about the highway, about mosquitoes and clouds of dust in the summer, and getting stuck in the mud. They talked about the special relationship of northerners, bound by a spirit of cooperation.

Don McCullough, a Foremost mechanic, and his wife Phyllis were travelling with the cavalcade. When one of the tour buses broke down in La Crete, he and Wayne Hale (an assistant Wagon Master) helped bus driver Angus Annapah repair a faulty electric starter. Hours later, while eating a bowl of borsht at La Crete Pioneer Village, Don told Angus a story that illustrates the northerner's attitude toward those who don't have the spirit of cooperation, who don't give assistance when they are needed.

"I had this young lineman they sent up from Edmonton Power years ago. And he didn't know nothing. Walking in the mud was taboo. He was raised in Edmonton where he had cement sidewalks. We had mud sidewalks. So, I took him way out in the bush, and I lost a track off my Foremost. It looked like we might have to camp overnight.

So, I said, 'Give me a hand working on this track.' He said, 'No dice. I don't know nothing about it. I'm not working on it.' So I said, 'Set up the tent then. We'll be here for the night.' He said, "Oh, no. I don't know nothing about putting up a tent.' All he wanted to do was eat. So, I worked till midnight and got the track on. Then I climbed up on the back and went to sleep. The next morning we got up and I threw everything on board. And he said, 'Well, we're getting ready to go, eh?' I said, 'Yeah, I am. But you're staying. You didn't help me. And I don't like you. Good bye.'

"We were 20 miles [32 km] *out in the bush. I left him and he watched me depart. I went down about three or four miles* [5-6 km] *and I pulled off on a cut line there. And shut it off. I waited and watched him run right by. I watched him till he ran just about out of sight. After that I went back ... and then picked him up."*

I wondered about the many people who had gathered, from all over Canada – and some from the United States. Why did they come? What feelings did they share with others about the Mackenzie Highway?

To Stella Friedel, who came from her home in interior B.C., the Mac 50 Cavalcade took on the aspect of a pilgrimage. She had lived so much of her life in northern Alberta. She had farmed there, got married there, had seven children, had run a stopping place at Indian Cabins, and taught school at Steen River, Meander River, High Level, Rocky Lane, Keg River, and Manning.

"I came back because I might never see these people again. It means more to enjoy people now than to spend trips just to your friend's funeral. When you get to be 60 or 70, you have a real imminent sense of your own mortality. If you have nothing better to do, why not? And there is also something encouraging and healing to see all of your friends still in reasonably good health. It's like a fraternity, really. We are all bonded by a background of pain and hardship and laughter."

Roll Call

The following are the names of people who registered for the Mac 50 Cavalcade. This list does not include the hundreds of people who had not registered but had gathered at communities along the way, to meet old friends and join in the festivities.

Gene Alm & Chris Kramer	Claude & Jeannine Dion
Roy & Paulette Alm	Lawrence & Edna Dillman
Russell & Dorothy Anderson	Ray & Mary Duperron
Len Anderson & Carmen Johnson	Marg & Bobby Dodds
Bill & Gwen Archibald	Marguerite Delancy
Paul & Jean Arseneault	Dez & Del DesLauriers
Howard Aikens	Carl Delany
Ralph & Vera Brown	Jim Delany
Jean Brease	Roland & Joan Desmarias
Alex Bentt	Mike Ewach
Dennis & Mineko Blakeman	Harry Ewach
Ken & Pearl Baker	Henry & Min Erickson
Pat Baird	Courtice Emes
R. Brooks	Vern Estabrook
Steve Brooks	Gary & Margaret Eldstrom
Terry & Bette Baxter	Clarence & Jean Eldstrom
William Beattie	Sandy Forrest
Paul Bernard	Ken Fischer
Vic Brandl	Lloyd Fischer
Ken & Shirley Braaten	Cecil Fishcher
Dan & Lilly Berreth	Curtis & Jean Fossum
Gene & Wanda Boucher	Stella & Carl Friedel
Norm & Pierette Boucher	Gary Friedel
Garnet & Jean Bulmer	Hugh Griffith
Harold & Lorraine Burroughs	Olga & Walter Gordey
Doris Christensen	Benny Gordon
Cliff & Ann Canning	Steve & Alice Hudema
Doris & Gordon Canning	Rose & Al Hammerschmidt
Les & Irene Campbell	Kay Hopkins
Ray Cowen	Wayne Hales
Mark Crawford	Bruce & Betty Hills
Barry & Eileen Claridge	Albert & Virginia Hamilton
Brian & Mildred Chrysler	Don & Evelyn Hamilton
Calvin & Louise Courtoreille	D. & M. Hart
Ed Carlson; Don Claughton	Dennis & Linda Holden
Matt & Matilda Chmielewski	Fred, Lund & Marie Harley
Harry Denison	Arlene & Pete Hodgson
Joe & Margaret Denison	Chris Haunholter
Andrew Denison	Roberta Hursey
John & Hanna Denison	Martin & Sue Iftody
Frank & Shirley Denison	Roy & Dorothy Jones

Harry & Connie Jones
Floyd & Marion Kostyk
Ryan Kunstleben
Jim Klone
John King
Evelyn Kurz
Herb & Mary Klassen
Gunnar & Heather Knauf
Dale & Mona Landry
Jack & Eleanor Landry
Trevor & Stella Lloyd
Bob & Lois Lyons
Dick & Marilyn Lebedynski
Robert Lowe
Beecher & Evelyn Linton
Gerald Logan
Bob Lorenzen
Susan Lorenzen
Bruce & Val Lorenzen
Fred & Bernice Lorenzen
Bill & Carol Mueller
Don & Phyllis McCullough
Louis & Mae Markling
Laurier & Irene Mercier
Evelyn Mercier
Miles & Marion Maney
Eric & Barbara-Joyce Madsen
George & Mary McKenzie
Jim McIntyre
Marie & Jim Monette
Gary Matheson
Gerald Martineau
Don & Betty McMullen
Douglas & Valerie Nixon
Steven & Vi Nording
Conrad & Shirley Nordstrom
Ron & Betty Novodorski
Mabel Omoth
Chester & Anne Olsen
Ken & Fern Paquette
Harold & Vi Peterson
J. Peterson
Andy Papp
Russ & Jean Popel
Ambrose & Elsie Parenteau
Ken & Inga Pederson
Allan & Hazel Rogers
Bernie Richardson

Orville & Sheri Raymond
Paul & June Rubak
Alice & Arnold Riedel
Byron Rutt
John & Marg Richard
Ike & Betty Richardson
Richard & Esther Robinson
Neil & Coby Roelveld
Bill & Rita Rowe
Bruce Rome
Gordon Reid
Marvin & Helen Seward
Albert & Lorraine Smith
Al Sides
Lori-Jean & Chris Schlenker
Harold Senft
Howard & Martha Simpson
Lawrence & Ruth Sloan
Carl & Betty Stitzenberger
Bob & Libby Sandercock
Sybil Sundby
A. & E. Storbakken
Ray & Marg Sampert
Pat Schantz
Pat Strang
Stan Sather
C.E. (Chuck) Shaul
Wes Spence
Les & Lois Stranaghan
Bud & Babs Tice
Merv & Marliss Townsend
Gordon E. Taylor
Gaston Talleur
Raymond & Marion Thomas
John Verdzak
Woody & Evelyn Van Natter
Harry Williams
Mary & Ron White
Fred & Marion White
Jim & Norma Walker
Jim & Elsie White
Len & Joyce Whitson
Glen & Ellen Wheaton
Gabe & Mary Jane Wald
W. Whittleton
R.E. Yamkowsky
Ed Zack

The Mackenzie Highway

By Susan Lorenzen

From Grimshaw to Hay River
    there's a winding stretch of road

That many truckers traveled
    laden down with heavy loads.

Many hardships were endured
    by these brave and fearless souls

And lots of trucks were lost
    on the road with many holes.

They forged ahead when others
    would have turned and headed back.

Thru summer, spring, fall, and winter
    on a winding, run-down track.

In '48 it was completed
    so the local histories say.

But it wasn't much to look at
    by the standards of the day.

It was named the Mackenzie Highway
    but was still a beaten trail.

It was the only way to travel North;
    it was long before the rail.

So thank God for all the truckers
    who never did look back.

They opened up the North for us
    on a winding broken path.

Today they laugh and joke around
    'bout "Times that weren't that bad."

So we should take the time to listen
    to the stories that they tell.

'Bout a winding narrow stretch of road
    that must have been "Pure Hell."

The Mackenzie Highway today. Photo Roberta Hursey.

Notes

[1] See Chapter 4, "The Mackenzie Highway."

[2] Speaking at the opening ceremonies were Ron Courtoreille, Master of Ceremonies; Don Moran, Premier of Northwest Territories; Charles Benson, Member of Parliament, Peace River; Minister of Transportation, Walter Pazenkowski, MLA Peace River South; Gordon Taylor, former Alberta Minister of Transportation from 1951-1970; Ron Williams, representing the NWT Minister of Transportation; Gary Friedel, MLA Peace River North, who joined the cavalcade at several stops along the way; Jane Gomay, MLA Hay River; Chief Pat Martell, Hay River Dene Reserve; Counsellor Les Nooski, Paddle Prairie; Gary Peterson, Mayor of High Level; John Woodburn, Mayor of Grimshaw; and Jack Rome, Mayor of Hay River.

Glossary of Terms

Bug, or Bombardier

An early snowmobile built by Bombardier of Montreal. Because a Bug was fairly light weight it was often used as an advance vehicle to scout out ice conditions on lakes and rivers, before heavier vehicles crossed. Also called a Bombardier (pronounced bomb-a-DEER). In *Denison's Ice Road*, John Denison explained to Edith Iglauer: "Couple of years ago I was driving a Bug – a Bombardier – of mine across Prosperous Lake, 12 miles [19 km] from Yellowknife, and I didn't see the ice crack. That stupid Bug went in, but it floated six or eight minutes, so I climbed out of my seat and jumped out the door. A Bug has a hull like a boat, except that it's full of holes, with windows and openings, and not watertight. A Cat, now that's something else again. It's solid iron and drops like a rock through water." [p. 31]

Catskinner

The term evokes a curious visual image. Purists say the term only applies to drivers of Caterpillar tractors, but it has become a generic term for all drivers of crawler tractors. The origin of the term "skinner" is a driver of draft animals, i.e., a teamster.

Cats

Purists would say that the term refers only to Caterpillar tractors, but it is a general term in the North for any make of tractor equipped with tracks.

Cat trains

A tractor train made up of one or more crawler tractors, each pulling one or more sleighs.

Caboose

The term "caboose" evokes the image of railway cabooses that once made up the end of a train. The term, however, also applies to the wooden trailers that were built on sleighs, pulled by horses and later by crawler tractors. On cat trains, the caboose, used as cookhouses or bunkhouses, made up the end of a swing.

COE

Cab-over-engine. Trucks and tractor units in which the cab is over the engine.

Cog Grinder

A trucker who remembers how to drive trucks with manual transmissions. Paul Rubak suggests it was "probably a euphonism first coined by Walter 'Cog' Harrington of Boston Bar in the Fraser Canyon in British Columbia. He had what he called the 'cog grinders club' and published a newsletter on rumors and other newsworthy items in the trucking industry. The 'cog grinders' were the pioneer truckers driving those trucks with the straight cut gears in the transmissions, which could lead to a lot of 'cog grinding' for those not adept at shifting gears."

Corn-binder

An International Harvester truck.

Crawler

A generic term for a tractor with tracks. Caterpillar operators used the term in a derogatory way for International tractors, which did not have the speed or power of a Caterpillar tractor. However, some operators of cat trains, such as Earle Harcourt of Yellowknife Transportation Company, preferred to use "crawlers" because they weighed less than Cats and were thought to be safer to use on ice roads.

Down North

In northern Alberta and NWT, the main rivers flow north and eventually join the Arctic Ocean. Thus the term "Down North" applies to travelling downstream. Conversely "Up South" meant to travel upstream.

Foremost

A large off-road tracked vehicle built by the Foremost Company of Calgary to haul over muskeg and muddy terrain.

Gin poles

Used in lifting heavy loads, gin poles consist of two steel poles attached one on each side at the rear of the deck on a flat bed truck. Paul Rubak explains: "When in use the poles are placed in an 'A' frame position with a pulley at the top in the centre of the 'A'. The poles are placed at a 95 to 100-degree angle from the deck of the truck with blocks and/or heavy chains to keep them at the preset angle. The cable from the truck's winch is run over the pulley at the top of the 'A' frame. "

Highboy

A generic term used by truckers to describe a "flat deck" semi trailer. Paul Rubak writes: "This includes a common flat deck trailer where the floor or deck is built on the frame of the trailer and is basically the same height from the ground, front and rear. A highboy in the general freight application is generally used to move machinery, pipe, building products, and freight not conducive to being loaded in a van. The term 'highboy' would also include the trailer known as an 'oil field float'. These trailers are built specifically for work in the oil patch. They are heavier framed, capable of carrying heavier loads and may include such equipment as a 'live roll' and 'pin pockets'. "

Ice Road

A road made of ice that crosses a frozen river or lake. Snow is kept plowed off the ice, which is at least 15 to 20 inches [38-50 cm] thick. In spring, an ice road is sometimes flooded at night to build it up in order to prolong its use. Thus, the road ice is thicker than the surrounding ice. It takes a great deal of experience to build and maintain an ice road and sometimes a good deal courage or foolhardiness to drive over one – especially when it may be covered with a foot or two of water.

Jimmie

A GMC truck.

Kicker

A small outboard engine used to power a boat or other watercraft.

Lowboy

Paul Rubak writes: "Truckers' slang for a low-bed trailer. Basically there are two varieties of this trailer which are dependent upon what is to be hauled on them. There is a single drop where the 'bed' or deck of the trailer is lowered by a step at the front of the trailer. The double drop has a steeper step at the front and has a step at the rear as well, just ahead of the rear wheels. These trailers are designed to carry extremely heavy loads. The lower beds or decks make loading of heavy machinery easier as well as allowing more overhead clearance for over-height loads."

Needle poles, or needle bars

A long chisel bar used to chop through ice. Used by ice fishermen before ice augers were readily available.

Orange gas

Because of the way gasoline is taxed, gasoline for general use is dyed orange and that for farm use is dyed purple. Paul Rubak explained: "The rates of taxes paid on gasoline is dependent upon its intended use. Gasoline for farm use is taxed at a somewhat lower rate than gasoline for all other uses. Farmers are permitted to use the purple gas on the farm to operate farm equipment and truck hauling his own goods to market. Use of purple gas in any other vehicle on Alberta highways is unlawful. All vehicles on the roads and highways must burn orange gas."

Pressure Ridge

Ted Nagle aptly defines a pressure ridge in his book, *Prospector North of 60*: "When two plates of ice come together, they heave, often lifting the edges in contact up, to become a pressure ridge. Pressure ridges can be 20 to 30 feet high [6-9m], and they sometimes separate at the tops. Beneath them, the cold dark waters of the lake open to swallow any man who drops into them." [176]

Refers or Reefers

Refrigerated vans, which became readily available in the North in the mid-1950s. Before refers, trucks had to keep perishable foods, such as milk or ice cream, iced down and wrapped in tarps. Trucks making backhauls of fish from Great Slave Lake over the Mackenzie Highway also had the fish packed in ice in the summer. It was imperative that there were no delays in trucking the fish to the railhead. When refers became widely available, it made life much easier for trucking companies.

Riprap

A road construction term meaning to fill in and provide support around culverts using boulders or sandbags.

Rough lock

Rough locks were a method of braking used by teamsters freighting goods by wagon. On steep down grades a chain was used to lock the rear wheels to the body or box of the wagon, thereby stopping the wheels from rolling. A make-shift type of rough lock was the use of a big log chained to the back of a wagon, to slow down the wagon going down steep hills. Early truckers used the same techniques to descend steep hills.

Sloop

A type of sled without runners, built like a flat-bottomed boat. Used for hauling wood, fish, and other freight over snow and ice. A stone boat.

Stopping place

Any house or building along a trail or road that offered meals and lodging for the traveller. Stopping places appeared beside a new road almost as soon as the road was built. The term is still used today extensively throughout northern Alberta and the NWT to refer to a truck stop, hotel, or motel.

Swing

A term Svein Sigfusson, in *Sigfusson's Roads*, uses to describe a single train made up of a tractor followed by one or more sleighs. A cat train is made up of one or more swings.

Tracking and poling

In early river transportation, tracking and poling were two means of advancing a canoe or scow upstream, when paddling was not possible. Poling was done to maneuver the boat upstream in shallow water; a man at the back of the boat planted a long pole into the stream bed and pushed the canoe forward. Tracking was done to get a boat over rapids. One or several tracking lines were attached to the main line that was attached to the boat. One or more men would walk on the riverbank and one or several men would pull the boat over the rapids. To keep the canoe parallel to the bank, a special bridle was made wherein one line was attached to the bow and looped back and attached again to the boat about a third of the way back. To this loop, the tracking line was then attached.

⬛ Selected Bibliography ⬛

Coates, Ken. *North to Alaska! Fifty Years on the World's Most Remarkable Highway*. Fairbanks: University of Alaska, 1992.

Coates, Ken and W.R. Morrison. *The Alaska Highway in World War II: The U.S. Army of Occupation in Canada's North West*. Norman, Oklahoma: University of Oklahoma Press, 1992.

Craig, Andy. *Trucking: A History of Trucking in British Columbia*. Saanich, B.C., Hancock House Publishers Ltd., 1977.

Finnie, Richard. *Canol: The Sub-Arctic Pipeline and Refinery Project Constructed by Betchtel-Price-Callahan for the Corps of Engineers, U.S. Army*. San Francisco, Betchtel-Price-Callahan, 1945.

Gould, Gladys McCurdy, ed. *Jock McMeekan's* <u>*Yellowknife Blade*</u>. Duncan, B.C.: Lambrecht Publications, 1984.

Hesketh, Bob, ed. *Three Northern Wartime Projects*. Occasional Publication Series No. 38. Edmonton: Canadian Circumpolar Institute, University of Alberta and Edmonton & district Historical Society, 1996.

Iglauer, Edith. *Denison's Ice Road*. Madeira Park, B.C.: Harbour Publishing, 1991.

Jackson, Mary Percy, as told to Cornelia Lehn. *The Homemade Brass Plate: The Story of a Pioneer Doctor in Northern Alberta*. Keg River, Alberta: Anne Vos, 1994.

Lorenzen, Bernice, ed. *Tales of the Mackenzie Highway*. Grimshaw, Alberta: privately published.

MacGregor, James G. *The Land of Twelve-Foot Davis: A History of the Peace River Country*. Edmonton: Applied Art Products Ltd., 1952.

McKay, Donald. *The People's Railway: A History of Canadian National*. Vancouver, B.C.: Douglas & McIntyre, 1992.

Nagle, Ted, and Jordan Zinovich. *The Prospector North of Sixty*. Edmonton: Lone Pine Publishing, 1989.

Ontario Trucking Association. *The Golden Years of Trucking: Commemorating Fifty Years of Service by the Ontario Trucking Association*. Rexdale, Ontario: Ontario Trucking Association, 1977.

Sigfusson, Svein. *Sigfusson's Roads*. Winnipeg: Watson & Dwyer Publishing Ltd., 1994.

Watt, Ted. *Yellowknife: How a City Grew*. Yellowknife, NWT: The Northern Publishers, 1990.

Zaslow, Morris. *The Northward Expansion of Canada 1914-1967*. Toronto: McClelland and Stewart, 1988.

Index

People

Communities

Lakes

Rivers

Boats

Companies

General